Unschooled:

THE WORLD TO COME

Rosi Thornton

Cefnpennar Press

WALES

Unschooled: The World To Come by Rosi Thornton, 1st ed.

ISBN 978-1-9164159-0-4 (paperback)

ISBN 978-1-9164159-1-1 (ebook)

Cover design by David Provolo https://www.instagram.com/david-provolo/

Book Layout ©2017 BookDesignTemplates.com

Published by Cefnpennar Press, Wales www.cefnpennarpress.com

For my daughter, Bryher Lily

Contents

Introduction

IN THE SCHEME OF history, home education is not the fad: school is the fad. School is an experiment. And as we all know, a good experiment should have a control group. For the experiment that is schooling, the control group should consist of children who have been never been to school. They are called 'home educated', 'home-schooled', or 'unschooled'.

There are a huge number of them. Why might numerous studies of schools never mention a control group? They may argue that they cannot find enough suitable students for a control group, but this doesn't really hold up given that even in countries like the UK, where the registration of home educators is not required, there are plenty of families who are known to the local authorities, vocal in promoting the cause of home education, and happy to cooperate with the media and participate in studies - as scientists who study home educators know. But while those few scientists who study home educated children regularly use data from school students for comparison, those primarily studying school students do not.[1] It is all too easy to come to the conclusion that people are afraid: the data shows, time and time again, that home educated students outperform school students, regardless of household income, parental education, social class, gender, or race.[2,3,4,5,6] Read that again. It is quite incredible.

When the two groups are compared, by all standards, schools are failing in comparison. So why are we continuing to tweak a system that is fundamentally flawed, while trying to restrict the freedoms of home educators? This book examines the consequences and potential of this, for society and for democracy.

Those of us in the 'democratised' cultures of the west are in reality enslaved to support a system imposed on us from above, and a major tool of that enslavement is schooling. Schools perpetuate inequality, power-based hierarchy, and uncritical obedience. By their very nature they must make failures of a large proportion of the population in order for the few to rise to the top. Despite all efforts to the contrary, we can still predict the future path of a child on the day they are born.[7,8] If we do not educate our children for freedom and independence from the start, they will struggle to achieve it as adults, as schools are designed to insure against this.

It is not individual teachers that are at fault; many of the most progressive and enlightened voices in the field of education are teachers themselves. But they are fighting within a system that is maintained despite increasing evidence to show that it is damaging and repressive. As one of the God-fathers of the home education movement, John Taylor Gatto, describes it, school is "the most ambitious piece of social engineering in modern history, and has been a brilliant success in reaching its goals. Of course, these are hardly the goals of ordinary citizens, of families, of religions, or of cultures, but they most certainly are the goals of management, whether of business, army, or government".[9] But there is another form of education that allows children to outperform their peers by all measures; an education that allows children to achieve beyond expectations, and comparably with each other, regardless of background. It bears repeating: time and time again, studies show that home educated students outperform school students in all areas, regardless of income level, parental education, race, gender or class.

Home education, and particularly that form of it known as unschooling, has strong parallels with traditional indigenous ways of educating - ways that have been tried, tested and refined for generation upon generation. Indigenous cultures tend to embody the consensus-based, true democracy that Westernised cultures have lost; a method of decision making that is often directly constructed to avoid one person gaining power at the expense of all others in the group, and one that contemporary activist groups are increasingly adopting (for example Anonymous, Idle No More, and the Occupy movement). Home educators too have organised themselves in this way for decades now. This is in direct opposition to the power structures we are used to in the West; structures that schools embody and perpetuate.

Simultaneously, governments around the world are trying to restrict and even ban home education, despite study after study showing that the freer the teaching environment, the more creative, motivated and successful are the children. The cutting edge of the education field advocates learning situations that increasingly imitate home education, yet governments are trying to dismantle the very situation that is producing the best results of all. One wonders if what is best for children is really the prime concern.

Humans have been referred to as the Teaching Species[10], having an innate need to teach others, just as we have an innate drive to learn. This has profound implications for a society where our lives are entirely compartmentalised by work and school, which is the natural result of our current economic set-up. Unschooling combats this by creating new social networks and revitalising our communities. The burgeoning unschooling movement is fuelled by a new generation of mothers (and often fathers) who are opting to raise their children at home, a role equal in importance and effort to any full time career.

In order to move from our current exploitative system to a more humanitarian and compassionate one, we must abolish schools as we currently know them. They nurture and maintain a distorted hierarchy, class distinctions, and competitive individualism. Our children may of course want to maintain this system (although current movements heavily suggest otherwise); at the very least we are polarised on the issue. What we do have the right to is a choice. This is being denied to generations raised to think and behave according to the values of consumerism, trained to fulfil a particular economic niche, constrained by a school system that is manipulated by unelected corporations in order to fill their own labour needs. Most educational theory and policies still focus on equipping the future workforce to fit the emerging economy, but do so through an education system based on an out-dated model.

Education is at the root of permanent social change. But does education have to mean school? We could even go so far as to say that 'school' by its own definition does not actually exist: in the same way that 'woman' and 'nature' are idealised constructs, surely 'school', as a social tool for raising up even the poorest, and educating all to their potential, is just as mythical? The ideal of universal schooling is yet another opium for the masses, convincing us that our children are being raised to be the best they possibly can be, while the adults fulfil their role as wage slaves, guilt-free.

The political ramifications of unschooling are not often enough discussed since Ivan Illich wrote *Deschooling Society*,[11] and Jonathan Kozol wrote his early, biting critiques of the school system.[12] There is a bandwagon of educators discussing the virtues of unschooling's potential for business and for future economies; there are many who write from an innate belief in freedom for children. But too few are considering the revolutionary potential for the whole of society. And as Illich wrote in *Deschooling Society*, "A political program which does not explicitly recognise the need for deschooling is not revolutionary; it is demagoguery calling for more of the same".[13]

Chapter 1, THE EXPERIMENT, looks at the origins of schooling, the benefits, the beginnings of doubt in the sixties as to the effects on children, problems with schooling, school as a commodity, and the way school affects society.

Chapter 2, THE CONTROL GROUP, describes the rise of home education in America and Britain, the impact and benefits of unschooling, how unschooling works, and what we need from education in the future.

Chapter 3, HOW SCHOOL HINDERS, asks if school is really improving society. Who benefits, citizen or state? Is it preparing us for the future, or keeping us in the past? How changing schooling can change society.

Chapter 4, FINNISH LESSONS, focuses on the successful Finnish education system. The parallels between the Finnish system and unschooling are discussed.

Chapter 5, LAND RIGHTS AND SCHOOLING, investigates the relationship between land and education, including enforced schooling; the impact of losing our connection with the land; sovereignty and self-determinism; and cross-cultural classrooms.

Chapter 6, LANGUAGE AND LEARNING, examines the use of schooling to impose Western worldviews on other cultures; how indigenous groups are controlled through language and schooling; and the implications of language loss for the way we think, communicate, and our ability to learn.

Chapter 7, CLASS AND CULTURE, discusses the myth of social mobility; how school maintains the status quo; the effect of class on our attitudes and the way we learn; how we define 'success'; the dangers of inequality; and why social class does not impact unschoolers.

Chapter 8, HERDING HUMANITY, looks at competition versus cooperation; attachment and separation; grading, failure and creativity; false authority; the myth of the lone genius; heroes and celebrities; and the cult of the individual.

Chapter 9, THE SOCIALISATION MYTH, asks what we mean by socialisation, and covers peer pressure; introverts; the issue of bullies; 'invisible children'; socialisation versus conformity; and increasing restrictions on home education.

Chapter 10, THE TEACHING SPECIES, highlights our innate drive to teach, including our need for meaning and responsibility; mentors and apprentices; indigenous and traditional ways of teaching; role models, authority figures, and elders.

Chapter 11, RECLAIMING MOTHERHOOD, focuses on unschooling from the point of view of mothers, including the role of women in the home; the benefits of attachment; identity and independence; reconciling work and home; grandmothers; and the flight to cities.

Chapter 12, TEACHING WITH TECH, investigates the knowledge economy; future skills; online academies; technology in the classroom; why games help us learn; unschooling in Silicon Valley; technology in an indigenous context; the cost of education; and the future of universities.

Chapter 13, THE CUTTING EDGE, highlights the parallels between online movements, hacker culture and unschooling.

It examines information overload; media and children; sur-veillance in schools; the Gaze of society; automation; and the potential of unschooling for the future.

Note on Terms Used

Home education is a term which legally defined means edu-cation other than at school. There are many ways of doing this, including using a curriculum and following a lesson plan. However, many unschoolers believe that this is merely repli-cating school in the home, and runs counter to the funda-mental idea of home education. To emphasise the difference between the various methods of home educating, many of us use the term 'unschooling' to describe what we do. We do not replicate the school setting, we do not follow a set cur-ricum as a rule, and we do not track or grade our children's progress. We use various resources which may include class-es and tutors as and when needed. Throughout this book I will use the word 'unschooling' for the most part, unless 'home education' is more suitable in a specific context.

The term 'public school' refers to fee paying schools in the UK, as opposed to state schooling which is funded by the government. When it is used in a quote referring to the American system, 'public school' means schooling provided free of charge by the government. Both uses are found throughout the book according to context.

Note on Research Papers and Studies

Whilst I have referenced source material wherever possible, so that readers can assess the evidence for themselves, sometimes this is not possible due to academic papers (often funded by the tax payer in the first place) being locked behind paywalls. Campaigns against this practice have been ongoing for some years now, including over 16,000 academics and others signing a petition to end the charging of access to knowledge. George Monbiot explains the problem: "I refer readers to peer-reviewed papers, on the principle that claims should be followed to their sources. The readers tell me that they can't afford to judge for themselves whether or not I have represented the research fairly. Independent researchers who try to inform themselves about important scientific issues have to fork out thousands. This is a tax on education, a stifling of the public mind. It appears to contravene the Universal Declaration of Human Rights, which says that "everyone has the right freely to ... share in scientific advancement and its benefits".[14]

CHAPTER 1

The Experiment: Schooling

For most men the right to learn is curtailed by the
obligation to attend school.

—IVAN ILLICH [15]

FOR MUCH OF HISTORY, people learned all that they needed to know by imitation. Children would learn by watching
and helping their family, or playing games which acted out
the routines of their community. As societies became more
complex however, it was necessary to teach certain things in
a more formal manner – mathematics, geometry or writing,
for example. The Mesopotamians, Chinese, Mayans, Egyp-
tians and Aztecs all established formal systems of education
as their societies became more complex. It was not unusual
for schooling to be available only to males of the wealthy
classes, who would be expected to follow a professional voca-
tion. But employing professional teachers, whether in the
home or a school, has been the luxury of the elite for most of

history. Until relatively recently, the vast majority of people were educated (if at all) by family members.

Schools as we know them today can be traced at least to medieval times in Britain, where we find the origins of our three-term year; divisions between primary, secondary and sixth form; and early French and Latin curricula. During the Protestant Reformation in the 16th century, Martin Luther advocated compulsory schooling so that all parishioners would be able to read the Bible for themselves, transferring power from the Church to the congregation. The first nationwide compulsory system of education developed in Scotland in 1616; by 1696 it was compulsory for every parish to provide a school, with fines and government enforcement where required. By the early 19th century, modern methods of public schooling - with tax-supported schools and compulsory attendance – had developed in Prussia and other German states.

In 1820s America, Democrats envisioned schools as an agency for eliminating all privilege and destroying all elites by giving all men the same good education. They believed in education supported by taxes as an instrument of democracy, according to some; others believe the movement was a way to protect the class advantage of the elite, by providing trained, compliant workers. Whilst there was much opposition to compulsory schooling, over the next 50 years the industrial revolution took men away from the home for long periods of the day; child rearing became the responsibility of mothers alone for the first time ever; and combined with the pressures of running a household, school became a welcome option.

It was a positive change for many poor children, who often worked long hours for low wages, in harsh conditions in industry and agriculture. George Monbiot has described children's lives as "characteristically wretched: farmed out to wet nurses, sometimes put to work in factories and mines, beaten, neglected, often abandoned as infants... Colin Heywood reports that 'the scale of abandonment in certain towns was simply staggering', reaching one third or a half of all the children born in some European cities. Street gangs of feral youths caused as much moral panic in late 19th-century England as they do today".[16] In countries today where education is not compulsory for children, child labour continues to this day. Carefree childhood may well be the invention of the bourgeoisie, as some suggest, but education has removed children from mines, factories and workhouses. However, removing children from situations of exploitation or toil by placing them in school, does not make schooling any less of a tool for cultural and economic brainwashing. Much as governmental organisations would like us to believe that school is the answer to all developing countries' ills, it may just be putting off the inevitable. The futurist Alvin Toffler writes that:

> *As work shifted out of the fields and the home, children had to be prepared for factory life. The early mine, mill, and factory owners of industrializing England discovered, as Andrew Ure wrote in 1835, that it was 'nearly impossible to convert persons past the age of puberty, whether drawn from rural or from handicraft occupations, into useful factory hands'. If young people could be prefitted to the industrial system, it would vastly ease the problems of industrial discipline later on. The result was another central structure of all Second Wave [industrialised] societies: mass education. Built on the factory model, mass education taught basic reading, writing, and arithmetic, a bit of history and other subjects. This was the 'overt curriculum'. But beneath*

it lay an invisible or 'covert curriculum' that was far more basic. It consisted, and still does in most industrial nations, of three courses: one in punctuality, one in obedience, and one in rote, repetitive work. Factory labor demanded workers who showed up on time, especially assembly-line hands. It demanded workers who would take orders from a management hierarchy without questioning. And it demanded men and women prepared to slave away at machines or in offices, performing brutally repetitious operations.[17]

The Effects of School

In 1964, the American teacher John Holt published a book, *How Children Fail*, based on a theory he had developed as a teacher: that the academic failure of schoolchildren was caused by pressure placed on them by adults. Holt believed that the primary reason children did not learn in schools was fear: fear of getting the wrong answers, fear of being ridiculed by teacher and classmates, fear of not being good enough. He maintained that this was made worse by children being forced to study things that they were not necessarily interested in.[18]

In the early 1970s, American educationalists Raymond and Dorothy Moore reviewed over 8,000 studies on early childhood education, and the physical and mental development of children. They found that formal schooling before the ages of eight to twelve not only lacked effectiveness, but was actually harmful to children. The Moores began to publish their findings that formal schooling was damaging young children academically, socially, mentally, and even physiologically. They presented evidence that childhood problems such as juvenile delinquency, nearsightedness, increased enrolment of students in special education classes, and behavioural problems were the result of increasingly earlier enrolment of students.[19] Their main premise was that the parental bonds and the emotional development made at home during the early years produced critical long-term benefits that were lost by enrolment in school, and could neither be replaced, nor afterward corrected, by an institutional setting. They maintained that the vast majority of children are far better off at home, even with mediocre parents, than with the most gifted and motivated teachers in a school setting.[20] As psychologist Howard Friedman says, "Most children under age six need lots of time to play, and to develop social skills, and to learn to control their impulses."[21] The effects continue today – a study published in 2009 by The Longevity Project found that an early school starting age was associated with worse academic performance in the long-term, midlife crises, and an increased mortality risk.[22]

At the beginning of the 1990s John Taylor Gatto was declared New York State Teacher of the Year, but resigned due to disillusionment with the system, and has been a vocal critic of it ever since. He believes that in removing children from the home to be educated, we are "prematurely breaking family and neighborhood learning". Children are in school all day, parents at work, siblings in separate classrooms and parents in separate offices. Entire communities are empty during ever longer working hours, and schools aim to promote citizenship, community and independence whilst subverting those very things: "Government schooling… kills the family by monopolizing the best times of childhood and by teaching disrespect for home and parents", Gatto wrote.[23]

Swedish academic Jonas Himmelstrand provides contemporary evidence of the damage caused by removing children from the family too early. 92% of Swedish children attend daycare full time from the age of 18 months. Himmelstrand writes, "Sweden has offered a comprehensive daycare system since 1975; since the early '90s, negative outcomes for children and adolescents are on the rise in areas of health and behaviour... Psychosomatic disorders and mild psychological problems are escalating among Swedish youth at a faster rate than in any of 11 comparable European countries. Such disorders have tripled among girls over the last 25 years. Education outcomes in Swedish schools have fallen from the top position 30 years ago, to merely average amongst OECD nations today. Behaviour problems in Swedish classrooms are among the worst in Europe".[24] Himmelstrand ties these problems directly to children being away from the family for so long, at such a young age. Baker, Gruber, & Milligan, in a 2008 study, found "the evidence suggests that children are worse off by measures ranging from aggression to motor and social skills to illness. We also uncover evidence that the new child care program led to more hostile, less consistent parenting, worse parental health, and lower-quality parental relationships".[25]

And still the criticisms flow in: Kyung Hee Kim, a Professor of Education in Virginia, examined the creativity of school children between kindergarten and twelfth grade. She found a massive decline in creativity as students progressed through the school system, with children becoming "less emotionally expressive, less energetic, less talkative and verbally expressive, less humorous, less imaginative, less unconventional, less lively and passionate, less perceptive, less apt to connect seemingly irrelevant things, less synthesizing, and less likely to see things from a different angle".[26] As Gatto asks "Where is documentary evidence to prove this assumption that trained and certified professionals [raise and educate children] better than people who know and love them can? There isn't any".[27] There is plenty of evidence however to show that home educating parents raise and educate children better than trained, certified professionals.

Gatto echoes many home educating parents when he says, "One thing you do know is how unlikely it will be for any teacher to understand the personality of your particular child or anything significant about your family, culture, religion, plans, hopes, dreams... even teachers so disposed don't have opportunity to know those things".[28] It would be impossible for even the most dedicated teacher to give a classroom of children the attention and time that their individual parents could – and in their formative years especially, time and attention makes all the difference. Experiments have shown that a teacher's expectations of a child can dramatically influence their performance, though this seems to be more pronounced the younger the child.[29] Conversely, children are hindered when little is expected of them.

This does not even take into account the disparity in maturity and age within any given year group. Children are compared with others in their class who are assumed to be of a similar developmental age, yet there can be up to a year's difference in terms of birth age, and even greater differences in terms of physiological development. Girls mature more quickly than boys, yet all pupils are expected to be achieving comparably, and are forced to compare their progress to each other. Tests are standardised across entire countries, so that pupils fight to develop a sense of self worth whilst being judged against students of varying age, physiological development, economic background and natural ability.

Malcolm Gladwell studied the lottery of success in his book *Outliers: The Story of Success*.[30] He noted that a disproportionate number of elite Canadian hockey players were born in the first few months of the year. The youth hockey leagues mean that children born on January 1st in a given year play in the same league as those born on December 31st. Children born earlier in the year tend to be larger and more physically mature, and so are often selected for extra coaching, and therefore have a higher likelihood of being selected for elite leagues. Gladwell calls this 'accumulative advantage'; others say "the rich get richer and the poor get poorer".

A Controlled Commodity

Some educationalists take their criticisms of schools a step further, arguing that schools have created a monopoly on learning. In the 1970s, the Austrian philosopher Ivan Illich wrote *Deschooling Society*. This book continues to influence educators worldwide. Illich described schooling as a monopoly, whereby it is almost impossible to imagine any meaningful learning occurring outside a classroom; we are taught to believe that all real learning requires an approved expert, compulsory attendance, a self-contained curriculum, a measurement of what has been learned, and a certificate of proof. Learning becomes a relationship of one person's authority over another's interests.[31]

Gatto describes it thus: "The whole blueprint of school procedure is Egyptian... It grows from the theological idea that human value is a scarce thing, represented symbolically by the narrow peak of a pyramid... It found its 'scientific' presentation in the bell curve, along which talent supposedly apportions itself by some Iron Law of Biology. It's a religious notion, School is its church. Socrates foresaw if teaching became a formal profession, something like this would happen. Professional interest is served by making what is easy to do seem hard; by subordinating the laity to the priesthood".[32] Where once education was a family affair, it has been removed entirely from the community and placed in the hands of 'experts', thereby denying anyone else the right to pass on any education of worth. Without an education channeled through, and certified by the system, one is effectively prohibited from entering the job market, supporting oneself, and taking part in modern life. School is the gatekeeper of society.

The French philosopher Jacques Ellul warned that prosperous children are more susceptible than others to the effects of schooling because they are promised more lifelong comfort and security for yielding wholly[33] – viz the 'old boys' networks of Eton and Oxbridge for example. Working class children meanwhile, have less expectations placed on them, and so have less to lose by not conforming fully. Gatto experienced that "Once the best children are broken to such a system, they disintegrate morally, becoming dependent on group approval... What kids dumbed down by schooling can't do is to think for themselves or ever be at rest for very long without feeling crazy; stupefied boys and girls reveal dependence in many ways easily exploitable by their knowledgeable elders".[34] Dorothy Sayers, in her essay *The Lost Tools of Learning*, describes one of the ways in which this dependence manifests: our susceptibility "to the influence of advertisements and mass propaganda to an extent hitherto unheard of and unimagined". She says of our children, "By teaching them all to read, we have left them at the mercy of the printed word. By the invention of the film and the radio, we have made certain that no aversion to reading shall secure them from the incessant battery of words, words, words... We who were scandalized in 1940 when men were sent to fight armored tanks with rifles, are not scandalized when young men and women are sent into the world to fight massed propaganda with a smattering of 'subjects'; and when whole classes and whole nations become hypnotized by the arts of the spell binder, we have the impudence to be astonished". An entirely different education, she writes, is needed "to produce a society of educated people, fitted to preserve their intellectual freedom amid the complex pressures of our modern society".[35]

This is another of Illich's criticisms of schooling – that it serves to perpetuate the myth of consumption and endless progress. School trains us to be consumers, to accept that our needs be fulfilled by others, to rely on others to provide what we need, and to be constantly looking for something new. Illich spent time working in Latin America, and highlighted how indigenous peasant culture, characterised by self-sufficiency, is undermined by Western culture which is based on the consumption of services, requiring people to be clients. He saw that schooling was used in developing nations to create new elites with a consumerist mentality, education being the way in which schools legitimise hierarchy, progress and consumption.

Schools themselves of course have fallen prey to the dictates of competition. Historian Keith Thomas, of the Council for the Defence of British Universities, wrote in 2012,

> *The very purpose of the university is grossly distorted by the attempt to create a market in higher education. Students are regarded as 'consumers' and encouraged to invest in the*

degree course they think most likely to enhance their earning prospects. Academics are seen as 'producers', whose research is expected to focus on topics of commercial value and whose 'output' is measured against a single scale and graded like sacks of wheat. The universities themselves are encouraged to teach and research not what they think is intrinsically worthwhile but what is likely to be financially most profitable. Instead of regarding each other as allies in a common enterprise, they are forced to become commercial competitors.[36]

The perception of education as a commodity is perpetuated at a personal level. Illich warned that "People who submit to the standards of others for the measure of their own personal growth soon apply the same ruler to themselves. They no longer have to be put in their place, but put themselves into their assigned slots, squeeze themselves into the niche which they have been taught to seek, and, in the very process, put their fellows into their places, too, until everybody and everything fits".[37] They continue to promote social hierarchy from within.

School's Hidden Agenda

During the 1970s, prominent thinkers began to criticise schooling from a more radical perspective, seeing schools as a tool of oppression employed by the ruling class to ensure their dominance. Illich argued that school serves to maintain the status quo, being the way in which we are taught to accept society, its institutions, and their hierarchies as they have always existed, and as they will continue to exist. In 1970 the Brazilian philosopher and educator Paulo Freire wrote *Pedagogy of the Oppressed*. Freire attacked what he coined the 'banking' model of education, where the student is viewed as an empty account to be filled by the teacher. "It transforms students into receiving objects. It attempts to control thinking and action, leads men and women to adjust to the world [rather than transforming it], and inhibits their creative power".[38]

The American historian and writer Walter Karp believed that American schools are doing precisely the kind of job political and educational authorities desire: the primary function of schools, says Karp, is to "habituate students to unfairness, inequality and special privilege".[39] The purpose of education is to "stifle self-government", to ensure a public that is docile and mindlessly deferential to authority; it is no accident that schools most resemble prisons. School teaches us to be subservient, to look outside ourselves for leadership. It has been said that the only thing a class of 30 under the charge of one teacher socialises anyone for is the military. Or as satirist and scholar H.L.Mencken put it, "The aim of public education is not to spread enlightenment at all, it is simply to reduce as many individuals as possible to the same safe level, to breed and train a standardised citizenry, to put down dissent and originality".[40] Educator Eric Robinson asked, "Is the education of the child for the sake of the child or for the sake of the state?".[41]

We should not be surprised perhaps that schools work in this way, when we understand their roots in our evolutionary history. The advent of agriculture "brought landownership, status hierarchies... servitude and slavery. In these conditions, human wilfulness and the spirit of individual autonomy were threats to survival," writes psychologist Dr Peter Gray:

> *This cultural change came about much too rapidly for natural selection to play a role. Babies continued to be born, and still are, with all of the instincts for self-determination*

and self-education that served so well in hunter-gatherer days. To get children to abide by the new rules of unquestioned conformity and obedience, wilfulness had to be beaten out of children... The same power-assertive methods that had been used to make children work in fields and factories were quite naturally transferred to the classroom... Over the past 50 or 60 years, schooling and school-like activities (such as organised, age-segregated adult-directed sports) have expanded to take over increasing portions of children's time, leaving less and less opportunity for children to bring their hunter-gatherer instincts to bear in their own education. During that same period, we have seen dramatic increases in childhood anxiety, depression, suicide, obesity, and other mental and physical ailments that can be attributed at least partly to the stress of continuous evaluation by adults and the lack of play.[42]

In their book *Homeschooling for Excellence*, homeschoolers David and Micki Colfax write, "In practice, industrialised education means that almost from the moment a child enters school he or she is age-graded, sorted, labelled, and re-sorted according to currently fashionable criteria... Control is paramount, while subservience and conformity are valued and rewarded".[43] It is rare that a child can stray from their designated place once labeled. Freire saw this traditional method of schooling as dehumanising both students and teachers, as well as stimulating oppressive attitudes and practices in society. He argued that social domination of race and class are intrinsic to the conventional educational system. It is this emphasis of conformity over critical faculty that ensures the success of the school system and the continuity of social hierarchy.

Illich notes it is ironic that schools are allegedly a preparation for participation in a democracy, but apply rules and sanctions to children which would not be acceptable to adults:

"The claim that a liberal society can be founded on the modern school is paradoxical. The safeguards of individual freedom are all cancelled in the dealings of a teacher with his pupil".[44] Holt wrote: "Education... now seems to me perhaps the most authoritarian and dangerous of all the social inventions of mankind. It is the deepest foundation of the modern slave state, in which most people feel themselves to be nothing but producers, consumers, spectators, and 'fans', driven more and more, in all parts of their lives, by greed, envy, and fear. My concern is not to improve 'education' but to do away with it, to end the ugly and antihuman business of people-shaping and to allow and help people to shape themselves".[45] It is this idea of people shaping themselves, whether as a family or individually, that is at the root of home education.

CHAPTER 2

The Control Group: Home Education

A problem well put is half-solved.

—JOHN DEWEY[46]

HOME EDUCATION FOUND A foothold in twentieth century America, in large part due to debates over the compulsory teaching of Creationism and Darwinism. Laws requiring Creationism to be taught in state schools were ruled unconstitutional in the 1960s, leading to much discontent among conservative Christians. At the same time, sociologists, psychologists, and educational theorists such as Ivan Illich and John Holt were becoming more vociferous about the failings of state education. As home schooling grew amongst the Christian community, secular families who were experiencing problems with the school system started to turn to home schooling themselves, often using the writings of Illich and Holt from the 1960s and 70s to provide philosophical frameworks.

By the late 1970s, home education started to become more common in the UK. Academics like Roland Meighan developed their own models of home education, often combining rediscovered British texts, some dating back to the 1890s (like those of Charlotte Mason) with later writers like Bertrand Russell and A.S. Neill (who had created alternative educational schools in the UK) alongside the works of writers like Illich and Holt. Whilst in the US the majority of home educators tended to follow structured curricula (reflected in the American use of the term 'home schooling'), increasing numbers of families created their own curricula or abandoned restrictive, formalised teaching methods altogether. The British use the term 'home education', distancing education from schooling, and increasingly terms such as 'unschooling' are used to distinguish those who take an entirely unstructured approach.

The true number of home educating families is unknown, but at least 48,000 UK children were known to be home educated in 2016,[47] with true figures estimated to be as high as 80,000. About 2,300,000 American children were taught at home in 2016,[48] although again it is not compulsory to register in every state, so the actual number is probably higher. Whilst there are home educators in many countries around the world, it is illegal (or effectively illegal) in many others. Estimates suggest that between 1 and 1.5% of children are home educated in the UK; this compares with less than 0.5% of children taught in fee-paying schools.[49]

The Aims of Education

Whatever method we choose to educate our children, the question behind the decision always boils down to 'What do we want to achieve?' Classical educators were as concerned with the growth of the person as they were with teaching facts; the character was as important as the intellect. "This was an education of the spirit... an education intended to teach man to serve something other than self", as David V. Hicks wrote.[50] Educators like Eric Robinson still hold this as the ideal: "Education means learning how to live and how to live better".[51] Educator and activist Bill Ayers believes "Education is always and everywhere about opening doors, opening minds, opening possibilities. Education is about opening your eye and seeing for yourself the world as it really is in all its complexity, and then finding the tools and the strength to participate fully, even to change some of what you find".[52] If this is the aim of education, then school is not often the best place to do it. You would be hard pressed to find anyone who disagreed that education should serve the person, not the other way around. More and more people are deciding that this is better achieved outside the restrictions of the classroom.

Ironically, and unsurprisingly, our pre-agrarian ancestors were much better at educating themselves than we are today, as Dr. Peter Gray explains:

Education is broadly defined as the set of processes by which each generation of human beings acquires the culture in which they grow up. By this definition, education is part and parcel of our biological makeup. An analysis of education in hunter-gatherer bands indicates that young humans are designed, by natural selection, to acquire the culture through their self-directed play and exploration... The ideal environment for such education... is one in which young people (a) have unlimited free time and much space in which to play and explore; (b) can mix freely with other children of all ages; (c) have access to a variety of knowledgeable and caring adults; (d) have access to culturally

> *relevant tools and equipment and are free to play and ex-*
> *plore with those items; (e) are free to express and debate*
> *any ideas that they wish to express and debate; (f) are free*
> *from bullying (which includes freedom from being ordered*
> *around arbitrarily by adults); and (g) have a true voice in*
> *the group's decision-making process... Our traditional*
> *schools make education difficult by removing the conditions*
> *that allow children's educative instincts to operate effective-*
> *ly.*[53]

It has been experienced time and again, in homes around the world, that once removed from the pressures of someone else's targets, exam pressure, peer pressure, bullying (both from peers and adults), grades and prizes, children cannot help but learn for the love of it. Paulo Freire noted how quickly Brazilian adults learnt to read and write when they felt that it was necessary to acquire these skills, highlighting that we learn most easily when we are genuinely interested in the topic, or when we decide for ourselves that a skill is worth acquiring.[54] Holt agreed: "I believe that we learn best when we, not others are deciding what we are going to learn, and when we are choosing the people, materials, and experiences from which we will be learning".[55] The founder of Folk Schools in the Nordic countries, N.F.S. Grundtvig, believed that obligation in any form was deadening to the human soul. He opposed all compulsion, including exams, and instead wished for a spirit of freedom, cooperation and discovery to be kindled in individuals.[56] Unschoolers feel that this is an innate aspect of ourselves, which is lost once we enter the school system. Spontaneity, self-directed study and unspecified outcomes do not fit well with the need to control a class of thirty or so students, finite resources, and the need to produce measurable outcomes for the satisfaction of others.

Holt suggested that "What children need is not new and better curricula but access to more of the real world; plenty of time and space to think over their experiences, and to use fantasy and play to make meaning out of them".[57] It is not unusual for college students especially to find that school actually interferes with their education, taking up so much of their time that they cannot study those things that truly interest them. There is little or no encouragement of ambitions that fall outside of academia, no time to study academic subjects that do not find a place within the curriculum. Many students are realising that learning (as opposed to education) does not have to be dull; it is the most exciting thing, when given the freedom, encouragement and resources to follow their own path. The 19th century educationalist Charlotte Mason desired that we "recover... the passionate love of knowledge for its own sake which brought about an earlier Renaissance".[58]

Booker Prize-winning author Dame Hilary Mantel rails against the damage done to the imagination itself by restrictive and imposed curricula:

> *Should we ask, which Gradgrind thought up the idea of set texts in the first place? Why should students be condemned to thrash to death a novel or a corpus of poetry, week after week, month after month? No novel was ever penned to puzzle and punish the young. Plays are meant to be played at... Literature is a creative discipline, not just for writer but for reader. Is the exam hall its correct context? We educate our children not as if we love them but as if we need to control and coerce them, bullying them over obstacles and drilling them like squaddies; and even the most inspired and loving teachers have to serve the system. We have laws against physical abuse. We can try to legislate against emotional abuse. So why do we think it's fine to abuse the imagination, and on an industrial scale?[59]*

The Benefits of Home Education

A fundamental motivator for many home educators is that the family is allowed to take its place as the primary unit in fostering a secure, happy, and confident child. Many families arrange their home life so that the family is together for the vast majority of the time; they make decisions together and live their life as a family. A loving, nurturing home life lays the foundations for healthy relationships, communities and societies. When school is the primary caretaker for much of the day, week and year, peers naturally become not just playmates, but the primary relationship for the child. Behaviour, judgement, values and morals are learnt from others of equal immaturity and inexperience. Social skills, traditionally learnt in the company of respected adults and the community, are instead picked up from the playground. When the child has an achievement to share, a secret or a problem, it is to their friends that they automatically turn, alienating parents and fracturing families yet further. Peer pressure, bullying and gangs are another factor in many parents decision to home educate.

The idea that it takes children many hours of repetitive exercises in order to master a skill is undermined by the experience of those who teach at home. Away from the classroom, a child has less distractions and more attention, and can master in minutes what would be drilled for hours in school, thus making much more effective use of time. When deciding whether to send her children to school, teacher Jean Bendell asked herself "Did a child really need to send the best part of every day, for a minimum of eleven years, at school? Whatever were the skills they needed and why did they take quite so long to acquire? If these skills could be learnt outside school, would it really take so many hours or was schooling an inefficient method of acquiring them?".[60] Gatto believes that "We don't need a national curriculum or national testing either. Both initiatives arise from ignorance of how people learn or deliberate indifference to it".[61] This is born out by the experience of Finland. In the PISA survey, conducted every 3 years by the Organization for Economic Co-operation and Development (OECD), 15-year-olds in different countries are compared in the areas of reading, maths, and science. Finland ranked at or near the top in all three competencies for over a decade. Their education policy is based on cooperation rather than competition between students, teachers, and schools. School is free from primary to PhD level. They have no word for accountability, seeing it as "something that is left when responsibility has been subtracted".[62] Finland has no regular exams, except for a final test at the end of their voluntary upper-secondary school. The emphasis is less on homework and more on creative play.

Curricula may be designed with the best of intentions, and to cover a variety of subjects, but the reality is that they hinder discovery of the world. Imposed ideas about what is suitable for a given age stifle the child's discovery of a huge variety of topics which are considered too advanced. Children not bound by preconceived ideas develop a wide variety of 'inappropriately' aged interests, out of step with when the curriculum dictates they should study it. This is evidenced by the difficulty in some countries in finding books for young children on topics that are not covered in school until much later. Schools all but eliminate self-directed inquiry. The core of unschooling is to cultivate it.

A benefit of unschooling is that children are able to develop in their own time, according to their own schedule. In contrast, Gatto describes his experience as a teacher:

> *David learns to read at age four; Rachel, at age nine: In normal development, when both are thirteen, you can't tell which one learned first - the five-year spread means nothing at all. But in school I label Rachel 'learning disabled' and slow David down a bit, too. For a paycheck, I adjust David to depend on me to tell him when to go and stop. He won't outgrow that dependency. I identify Rachel as discount merchandise, 'special education' fodder. She'll be locked in her place forever... In thirty years of teaching kids rich and poor I almost never met a learning disabled child; hardly ever met a gifted and talented one either.[63]*

By its very nature, a classroom environment tends to hold back the brightest as well as leaving behind the slowest. Once freed from the constraints of targets, schedules and curricula however, children are free to progress in spurts or slow patches as their natural development dictates.

Learning to Learn

In fact, many unschoolers feel that 'learning to learn' is one of the most important skills a child can acquire, and one that is not facilitated by a classroom environment. Dorothy Sayers warned that although we often succeed in teaching our pupils 'subjects', we fail in teaching them how to think: they learn everything, except the art of learning. We leave them ill equipped to learn anything new in later life, or to continue their education beyond school. Sayers believed, along with many other educators, that the reason medieval schools succeeded is that the focus was on how to learn.[64] In a modern classroom, the act of critical thinking is actively discouraged if not punished. Yet the very act of questioning of everything we come into contact with is perhaps the best way to learn.

Many parents find that once removed from the artificial atmosphere of school, children converse with adults without the inhibitions that so many school children have. They are respectful rather than deferential, comfortable joining in a conversation between adults, contribute their opinions equally, and apart from their obvious age, are otherwise indistinguishable in manners and social skills from the adults they are surrounded by. As their world is not artificially divided into separate spheres for adults and children, they are often more confident, and have friends of a variety of ages and both genders compared to school children who tend to socialise with those of the same age and gender as themselves. Far from being isolated from the 'real world' as is often suggested, it is in fact school that isolates children. In scientific studies and college interviews, home educated children have been shown to outperform their schooled peers in terms of academics, maturity and social skills.[65,66,67]

The years of compulsory schooling have increased to the point that young people who are physically and emotionally adults are still being treated as children and denied the responsibility that they crave. Teachers tell their pupils to act their age and be responsible, whilst simultaneously treating them as children and stifling initiative. Dorothy Sayers remarked on "that artificial prolongation of intellectual childhood and adolescence into the years of physical maturity... To postpone the acceptance of responsibility to a late date brings with it a number of psychological complications which, while they may interest the psychiatrist, are scarcely beneficial either to the individual or to society".[68] At a time when hormones affect students physically and emotionally, they are expected to focus wholly on studies. A recent study found that the brains of teenagers are quite different to those of children and adults, and besides needing more sleep, the development of social bonds are of prime importance [69] (although parents are by far the greatest influence still).[70] unschooling relieves these pressures, allowing the student to be responsible for their studies and schedule, and to take increasing responsibility for their own life. Independence is a gradual and natural evolution, rather than the dependency of school which abruptly ends, leaving the majority of students vastly unprepared for the world outside the school gates.

*Folkeh**ø**jskolerne*

There is one type of schooling that could be compared to the aims of many unschooelrs. Folkehøjskolerne, or Folk high schools, were created in Denmark in the 19th century by N.F.S. Grundtvig – a clergyman, poet, historian, teacher and politician. They are unaccredited educational institutions, with "an emphasis on communal learning, self-discovery, enlightenment and learning how to develop your own opinions through open debate".[71] The schools do not hold any tests or exams, education and enlightenment being seen as sufficient reward in themselves. Similar to Paulo Freire's philosophy of education, as found in *Pedagogy of the Oppressed*,[72] Folk High Schools were founded to teach people about social and democratic participation. Students are prepared for life, rather than just focusing on scholarly activity, with practical skills as well as academic subjects forming an essential part of the syllabus.

The Folk high school movement started as a reaction against a conservative ideal of both education and culture. Grundtvig fought for public education as an alternative to the university elite, where the primary relation was between the individual and the book alone, written in a language unknown to the common people. In contrast, in a Folk high school learning happens across social positions and differences – the teacher learns from the student and vice versa through mutual teaching. Folk high schools are often compared to boarding schools, as students eat, sleep, clean, study and socialise together. This is, of course, how village life has operated for much of history in most societies, and the bonds of family, community and society are strengthened in the same way through unschooling, as the family is not split up during the day at separate places of schooling and employment, only to meet together for a few hours in the evening. "Respect, equality, cooperation, dialogue and tolerance are some of the keywords in making daily life at the Folk High Schools work".[73] These are qualities found more readily in the home and community than they are amongst teachers and pupils nowadays; rather than attending a Folk high school for months as a young person, unschooled children are raised in this atmosphere from birth.

Folk high schools have been described as a place to study the art of being human, and as educating for life; Paulo Freire also envisioned an 'authentic' approach to education that allowed people to be aware of their 'incompleteness' and strive to be more fully human.[74] Whilst unschoolers would embrace these aims, how many schools could claim the same?

The Future of Education

Eric Robinson warned that "the common practice of identifying 'education' simply with 'schooling' is damaging... In evading the cultural, social and moral dimensions of education we are betraying our children and cheapening ourselves. This is a major factor in the current decay of our society".[75] In place of school, Ivan Illich envisioned a 'deschooled society', where individuals would direct their own learning, rather than their lives being directed by institutions more concerned with their own continuation. Individuals would form 'learning webs' in which everyone would be teacher as well as learner. (Several languages recognise this already, using the same word for both 'teacher' and 'pupil'). Relationships would promote self and community reliance, rather than the need to receive validation from institutions and their products.[76] Unschooling achieves all of these. And herein lies the main difference, perhaps, between schooling and unschooling: from where a person learns to find their self worth. School teaches us to be reliant on the approval and validation of others, both adults and peers, while a self-educated person forms their own opinions and finds value in their own experiences. This person is less likely to fall prey to propaganda, advertising and passing fashions, but is a leader and thinker.

American futurist Alvin Toffler describes three stages of society: The First Wave equates to the Agrarian Revolution, and replaced the hunter-gatherer lifestyle. The Second Wave equates to the Industrial Revolution; it revolves around nuclear families, factory-style education, and corporations. It is based on mass production, mass consumption, mass education and mass media. The Third Wave, which we are now entering, is a post-industrial society, and has been described variously as the Information Age, the Space Age, the Global

Village, and the Scientific-Technological Revolution. Information is key. Toffler quotes psychologist Herbert Gerjuoy, who believes that "The new education must teach the individual how to classify and reclassify information, how to evaluate its veracity, how to change categories when necessary, how to move from the concrete to the abstract and back, how to look at problems from a new direction - how to teach himself. Tomorrow's illiterate will not be the man who can't read; he will be the man who has not learned how to learn".[77] Toffler warns that schools were designed to create factory workers, but now the economy is changing we instead need people who know how to think creatively and critically.

For a long time we have been have warned that schools are failing and no longer suited to their purpose. As we move into the Third Wave, students are going to fit society less and less successfully, and it will be those who can operate in the world as it is, not as it was, who will succeed. Schools still exist in a Second Wave model, and are unlikely to be successfully changed to fit the new world. Students are taught in a Second Wave classroom, but step out the door into a Third Wave world. They are effectively operating within two paradigms, one of which is redundant.

CHAPTER 3

How School Hinders

Tis to be a slave in soul,

And to hold no strong control

Over your own wills, but be

All that others make of ye.

—PERCY BYSSHE SHELLEY[78]

THE SCHOOL SYSTEM AND the state are mirror images of each other. If we are looking to change society, we should look to schools, and vice versa. Schools are training our children to accept the world as it is: authoritarian, Darwinian and exploitative. If we want a different world, we need to raise our children in the environment we hope them to replicate as adults. We can submit to the established social system through school, or we can model democracy and freedom in our method of education, and give children a template on which to model society as adults.

Pedagogy is central to politics. Plato, Aristotle, Rousseau, Einstein and numerous others knew that education is the foundation of all society. We cannot talk about class, or democracy, without coming back to education. Those at the forefront of education reform today are vocal about the impact of education on the most pressing issues; for example a founding theorist of critical pedagogy, Henry Giroux, studies the connection between poverty, education, militarisation, incarceration, higher education, and jobs.[79] Gatto writes that "The social issues attendant upon [education] (family, workplace, prisons, the economy, social welfare, racism, industrial society, media addiction, and technology, to name a few) are all so enmeshed and intertwined with schooling that it is not possible to approach one without touching upon the others". Hitler too knew the power of education: "And this new Reich will give its youth to no one, but will itself take youth and give to youth its own education and its own upbringing".[80] (The Nazis were the first to ban home education).[81]

For Citizen or State?

Education was designed to have an impact on society, and as such, we funnel children into the system earlier and earlier. To believe that the education system was designed for the sake of children however, is a mistake. We educate now, and always have educated, for the sake of the state. Schools are modelled after a Prussian system geared towards creating compliant soldiers, modified during the industrial revolution to train people for the workforce. Schools are factories by any other name. The inherent message of school is that we - the individual, the masses - are not ultimately in control of our lives.

Mass schooling was not designed simply because children were lacking an education – literacy levels were never so high as prior to formal teaching. State schools have variously been seen as a way to make good, quiescent taxpayers out of future citizens and voters; as a way to keep children out of the workforce so as not to compete with adults; as a machine which would sort and categorise children according to the needs of industry; as an attempt to Christianise the populace; as an attack on private education; and as a way to homogenise ethnically, culturally, and religiously diverse populations. In the United States especially there is still a battle over whose values should be subsidised by taxpayers.

But however benevolent or not its origins, there exists a large volume of research showing that schools today are 'highly ineffective' in improving social mobility.[82] An adult's success in life can be predicted by their ability level on their first day of primary school. Yet home educators consistently score between the 65th and 80th percentile on standardised as-sessment exams, compared to the average 50th percentile,[83] while typically noted disparities due to gender, income levels, and ethnicity simply do not manifest in any significant way in home educating environments.[84,85,86] So why do we see these differences in our schools? It strongly suggests that school, regardless of intentions, nurtures and exaggerates these differences.

Education is politicised. But not to the ends of the people. School has been described as the most ambitious piece of social engineering in history.[87] Pedagogue Jonathan Kozol rejects the popular rhetoric of failing schools; he believes that schools "succeed extremely well in their role of national in-doctrination".[88] Education was designed to fulfil an economic need, and still does so – grade curves are adjusted constantly to relieve or increase economic pressures. Our curricula are designed with business, not scholarship in mind. From the UK Commons Select Committee:

> *"The British Chambers of Commerce (BCC) is the national body for a powerful and influential Network... Representing 100,000 businesses who together employ more than 5 million employees, the British Chambers of Commerce is the Ultimate Business Network... this is a useful opportunity to bring forward concerns that businesses have raised regarding exam procedures... Low business confidence is largely the result of poor levels of soft skills in school leavers. This often includes poor levels of literacy, punctuality and ability to concentrate. The education system works best when businesses are able to work closely with schools, colleges and the wider training system... The BCC's work with businesses... suggests that companies do not see the education system in its current form as providing young people with the "employability" skills they require."*[89]

Or as John Fowles described it in 1964: "Our present educational systems are all paramilitary. Their aim is to produce servants or soldiers who obey without question and who accept their training as the best possible training. Those who are most successful in the state are those who have the most interest in prolonging the state as it is; they are also those who have the most say in the educational system, and in particular by ensuring that the educational product they want is the most highly rewarded."[90]

The education-industrial complex increasingly displays many of the behaviours of a business monopoly. A single 'firm' (the state) controls all output in the market; it provides a unique product; and restrictions are placed on entry into and exit out of the 'industry'. Author and educator Clark Aldrich adds to this list:

- *Schools try to standardize as completely as possible the offerings. Students are expected to change to meet the needs of the offering, as opposed to the other way round.*

- *Larger administrations are created in which the middle layer does not teach but 'manages'.*

- *Many staff members within the school system (similar to the fate of people who work within such traditional monopolies such as AT&T decades ago or Facebook today) are overwhelmed by unrealistic and unfair burdens and expectations.*

- *Schools use internal metrics to evaluate success that no one outside the school cares about.*

- *The primary function of schools is to push children to consume more school hours (at the lowest possible cost of delivery), not to help them outside of the school.*

- *Schools truly believe their approach is the only approach.*

- *Schools seek to crush competition, such as vouchers and homeschooling. They will continue to employ powerful, legally enforced tools to penalize truancy and other 'anti-social' behavior. Proxies will publish reports critical of new approaches.*[91]

In comparison, an institution that is truly working for the benefit of the people should be working to make itself obsolete: Are doctors merely treating the symptoms, or are they making serious progress towards educating the population toward ideal health, such that they need treat injuries not avoidable diseases? Are we employing people to clear the rubbish or trying to avoid producing rubbish altogether? Are tradesmen fixing products or enjoying the profits of built-in obsolescence? Are governments empowering the people such that they need not be governed? Are schools teaching us to educate ourselves? We should not be investing in self-perpetuating models. We should support those who are working toward their own obsolescence. But Aldrich points out that "No monopoly has reformed itself. It is only through competition among entirely different entities that new ideas are nurtured and given the opportunity to evolve. (At first any new ideas are inevitably called 'naïve' and 'impractical' or even 'dangerous' by existing practitioners)".[92]

This economic imperative sits alongside an insidious social conditioning that goes on in schools. The emphasis of conformity over critical faculty ensures the success of the school system and the continuity of social hierarchy. School instills a belief in straightforward, right and wrong answers; in authority having the one correct answer; in authority having a monopoly on truth. It is dangerous. Society will not change significantly if children continue to be trained in the methods of the old order. School is a training ground for acceptance of the class system, acceptance of domination by illegitimate authority, acceptance of inequality, acceptance of your place in society. How pernicious this is depends on your viewpoint: at one end of the spectrum, we have to accept that any form of education is not just the transmission of information, but the enculturation, the indoctrination of a child into "a way of knowing, being, and learning", as described by anthropologist Wade Davis.[93] At the other end of the spectrum, Doris Lessing wrote in *The Golden Notebook*, "You are in the process of being indoctrinated. We have not yet evolved a system of education that is not a system of indoctrination. We are sorry, but it is the best we can do. What you are being taught here is an amalgam of current prejudice and the choices of this particular culture. The slightest look at history will show how impermanent these must be. You are being taught by people who have been able to accommodate themselves to a regime of thought laid down by their predecessors. It is a self-perpetuating system".[94]

The question is whether we can reform schools sufficiently to support a new political paradigm (one that is swiftly arriving with the mass influence of technology and automation), or whether schools are too much a part of the system itself to be rescued. Gatto does not believe that the institution of school is necessarily worth saving. "I don't think we'll get rid of schools anytime soon, certainly not in my lifetime, but if we're going to change what is rapidly becoming a disaster of ignorance, we need to realize that the school institution 'schools' very well, but it does not 'educate' - that's inherent in the design of the thing."[95] Many teachers are aware of the limitations of the current system, many try to change it with the limited power they have - to make it more democratic, less hierarchical, more student led, more reflexive and less grade oriented. But, Kozol chides, "They are not willing to confront... the one, exclusive and historic function of a system that runs counter to these goals".[96]

And so, whilst seeing the problems with schools in their entirety, the vast majority are still trying to make education adapt to the world as it currently is – reforming education to better fit the 'emerging economy', or to make students happier and less pressured by removing some tests, or to improve grades and 'success' as it is currently measured by implementing more effective teaching techniques. All these efforts are focused on re-forming education to better cope with a changing world, as if education is at the mercy of outside forces to which it must adapt. But in education, we have a tool to change the world itself. Education can train students to accept the status quo, or it can show them a democratic, humanitarian, and cooperative way of being. As long as the current value system is in place, it is nigh on impossible to separate our ideal vision of education from the conveyor belt of schooling which supports it. And yet we must. So long as we limit our discussion of education to schools, we limit our ability to imagine new ways of living and learning.

For Past or Future?

There are many voices warning that the economy is changing from an industrialised model to a more creative and technological one, and listing traits that students will need in order to be successful in the future – a future filled with jobs yet to be invented, let alone catered for in the curriculum. But education has not changed significantly since the Industrial Revolution. Not only are we failing to prepare students for a world which increasingly relies on invention, creativity, lateral and critical thinking, but we are eroding the diversity which enables us as a species to survive. We are manufacturing our own demise.

Daniel Mathews, co-founder of Wikileaks, describes the current state of the education system as it manifests in universities:

> Given that corporations are essentially authoritarian, and government is suffused by bureaucracy, that means producing workers that will obediently do required tasks. It means

instilling a culture of obedience, hierarchy, and conformity. On the other hand, to the extent they produce intellectuals, scientists and scholars, [universities] must promote free thinking, critical thinking, imagination and creativity. As long as a high-technology capitalist economy persists, there will always be this tension... when the next economic crisis comes, education is among the first to be cut. Dependency on the private sector results. In so doing education is converted into a business: students are 'consumers' exerting their 'choice', and universities provide 'products' which are courses and qualifications to certify their place in the professions... Restructuring the education system can be done... It's a matter of political struggle, as is everything else.[97]

The skills we will need to succeed in this high-technology capitalist economy are variously listed by futurists and academics as: the ability to integrate ideas from different disciplines or spheres; the capacity to uncover and clarify new problems, questions and phenomena; respect for, and awareness of, differences; understanding one's responsibilities to others (Howard Gardner)[98]; high-concept thinking, high-touch leading, the ability to build projects like symphonies; and the skills of empathy, playing (as adults) and meaning (Daniel Pink)[99]; critical thinking and problem solving; agility and adaptability; collaboration across networks; accessing and analysing information; curiosity and imagination (Tony Wagner)[100]. But none question whether this future economy, which they urge schools and universities to prepare for, is the economy that we want. Why are we moulding children to an end that they have not chosen, to an economy that they may reject (thus leaving them again unprepared), rather than giving them the tools to adapt to any economy, indeed to choose and create that economy for themselves? Educational theory focuses all too often on shaping the workforce to fit the world. But it should be about equipping the 'workforce' to create the world.

Maybe we should not even be thinking so hard about the end goal of education, so much as the process. If the process is democratic, equitable, just and co-operative, then the results will manifest these aspects too; and in a manner which we would only be constrained by dictating the end result, perhaps even distorting the process along the way. Education is not a static, perfectable endeavour. Still we put so much effort into devising standardised tests and curricula, and institutions which must be kept running beyond their prime because so much money has been spent on them, when we could be investing in open ended learning tools, technology and the internet, multi-purpose community buildings, and equipment which could be adapted to changing needs.

The debate over the 'correct' curriculum has been referred to by John Dewey as the tension between traditional and progressive education.[101] Should certain subjects be compulsory to cement the knowledge base of the population, or do all paths lead to knowledge, and a love of learning to an eventual absorption of the same information? Must we all learn the same biased histories by rote as if they were gospel? What is considered essential to learn, and how it best be learnt, changes with whoever is in power. And what of the ultimate aim of education? Endless progress? A more just society? Our aims evolve, as does society. And as our aims evolve, so must our methods of education. Michael W. Apple argues that in order to provide an education which is accessible and relevant to all students, we must develop a shared awareness of which aspects of knowledge society values, who gains from the reproduction of this knowledge, and whether this benefits everyone equally.[102] In this vein, Goan writer Joao Coutinho wrote, "There is no neutral education. Education is either for domestication or for freedom".[103]

To that end, proponents of Critical Pedagogy believe that students have been historically, and continue to be, disenfranchised by traditional schooling. Critical Pedagogy is defined as "Habits of thought, reading, writing, and speaking which go beneath surface meaning, first impressions, dominant myths, official pronouncements, traditional clichés, received wisdom, and mere opinions, to understand the deep meaning, root causes, social context, ideology, and personal consequences of any action, event, object, process, organization, experience, text, subject matter, policy, mass media, or discourse."[104] Critics interpret the goal of practitioners, such as Henry Giroux, as being "to create political radicals". Conversely then, an unquestioning acceptance of state sponsored curricula leads to political conservatives. Or perhaps merely apathetic and uninformed citizens? It is certainly true, as Kozol pointed out to the ire of many, that school teaches us how things are, but almost never how to change them for the better.[105]

There are clearly two elements of education that need to be addressed: how to best educate our children in terms of knowledge and skills to operate in the world; and how best to create the society we desire through raising our children to this end. At the moment, school takes on both of these roles, overtly or not, through the formal curriculum and through acting in loco parentis for the best part for the child's day. Children are educated and moulded to the ends of those in charge, beholden to a competitive, status-oriented system.

Should these two elements, knowledge and socialisation, be addressed together? Is it even possible to separate them?

Christian W. Beck believes the distinction between formal knowledge and cultural values is becoming increasingly blurred, as schools evolve into a power base for a globalised elite, operated by a new worldwide middle class:

> *The processes of globalisation are reliant on the development of a knowledge economy. That places education and schooling at the core of such processes. Education is needed to qualify for a globalised labour market, and to oppose and balance globalised capitalism. One has to emphasize both individual learning processes and social cooperation. The requirements of globalised schooling will be enormous. A number of people hold that school must educate human beings to become competent participants in a globalised world. This is the right wing aspect of global educational politics. The left is critical of such aims and wants school to act as a counterweight to global capitalism. They want more nationally controlled schools, including everyone and emphasizing social competence and equality. It is astonishing, how people in all countries have more or less the same understanding of school. This is also a part of globalisation. Doubtless, both the right and the left see more schooling as a positive thing... Everyone wants more education, and more education means, to them, more school. More school means that more of our social and cultural life become a matter for schools, integrated into formal educational programs.[106]*

In reaction to the increasing pressures and all-encompassing nature of school, there is a growing movement to let children develop according to their innate schedules, rather than the imposed developmental timetable of the state. Kozol argues though that "Spontaneous growth does not exist within a nation governed by stage-managed views. There is either the uncontested bias of the state or else... a number of forms of counter-imposition, competition, provocation, dialectic".[107] There is no such thing as a pure, organic education. There can be, however, a much more conscious, open-ended education than we currently have.

Revolution

Kozol, as others before him, argued "If we are to live our lives as honest people, we cannot work with teachers and develop classroom methods and materials for their use unless we simultaneously set out to introduce specific strategies for raising consciousness about the function which those teachers are compelled to carry out – and then assist them in the struggle to transform that function".[108] It is probably impossible to avoid adult imposition on the minds of children, and there is no reason we should want to avoid it. However, we have moved from the best part of our history where children were influenced mainly by their immediate community, to bombardment from every side with advertising, propaganda, and information. What children need more than anything is honesty from the adults who guide them through this world, and the ability to distinguish between that which will help them through life, and that which will hinder.

At this point in history, the adults may need educating just as much, if not more, than the children. Education has been turned into an esoteric practice, complete with rituals, doctrines and unquestioned beliefs. But we must not forget that we are all teaching implicitly, constantly, by our every word and action. Those who are consciously aware of this – for example governments, business, social media - can manipulate that fact, consciously directing words and actions to certain ends while the majority behave like unthinking automatons, expecting teachers to magically mould children into something better than the society around them. Henry Giroux calls this "pedagogical terrorism" – the preaching of certain ideals while behaving counter to our words.[109] And for children as everyone, actions speak much, much louder than words. There is a fundamental difference in the way we see education in the West – as something the state does for our children - compared to traditional cultures who see education as the entire lifestyle a community passes on for their children's survival. We grasp that adverts and politics have an agenda, but so often don't see that schooling does too.

In many countries around the world, education is mandatory; school is not. While schools fail to teach children to think critically, to innovate, to create, to cooperate, or even to learn, Gatto has a solution: "We need to scream and argue about this school thing until it is fixed or broken beyond repair, one or the other. If we can fix it, fine; if we cannot, then the success of homeschooling shows a different road to take that has great promise. Pouring the money we now pour into family education might kill two birds with one stone, repairing families as it repairs children".[110] School was the 'necessary' pedagogical tool of the industrial economy. Home education is the necessary pedagogical tool of the knowledge economy: home educated people have been shown to emphasise critical thinking,[111] to be more civically minded, and politically active.[112]

Unschooling is seen by some on the left as anti-collective and individualistic, yet it is quite the opposite – it is a move away from the isolation of children from family and society, a move to reintegrate children and families with the community around them. These families have decided that they do not wish to be part of the consumerist conveyor belt, and just as others opt out of the system by growing their own food rather than relying on supermarkets, or by using barter systems rather than money wherever possible, or by setting up a co-operative rather than accepting wage-slavery for someone else's profit, these educators are showing society that there is another way to learn. We don't criticise self-sufficiency as anti-collectivist for bypassing supermarkets, or malign co-ops for offering an alternative to the pervasive banking systems. So why fear those who choose to educate their children outside of the same system? Some critics fear the creation of a parallel society; but isn't that what many of us are trying to create in the wider world anyway, an alternative to the parasitic globalist system, an alternative which could eventually become the norm?

Some even claim that "With the evident shortcomings of many public schools, at the very least they provide a kind of social glue, a common cultural reference point in our polyglot, increasingly multicultural society".[113] If our communities are so decimated that the only way to hold them together is through a common experience of school, we have more serious societal problems than a few unschoolers. Christian W. Beck takes a more positive view: "If home educators become so numerous that they threaten public school, this can be because a school revolution has started".[114] Home education is a spontaneous, citizen-led decentralisation movement.

Education is, at root, both an economic and ideological issue: schools were instituted to fulfil a specific need (or needs) in a specific economic climate. If we do not wish to maintain this economic or political climate, or if we want the ability to change it in the future, why do we continue to educate our children to this particular end? If we do not wish to educate our children to the undisguised utilitarian ends of the school system, why do we look to reform education rather than reconsidering it from scratch? We must stop trying to reform schools to simply operate better within the existing social structure. We need to reconceive the entire system.

Currently education is constrained in the artificial way that a written language is: the structure and rules have been set, and evolution is strongly resisted if not impossible. We have made education such a restrictive endeavour that it cannot flow and adapt to changing needs. Alfred North Whitehead, a critic of those education systems which he saw as contributing to societal stagnation, wrote, "In the history of education, the most striking phenomenon is that schools of learning, which at one epoch are alive with a ferment of genius, in a succeeding generation exhibit merely pedantry and routine. The reason is, that they are overladen with inert ideas. Education with inert ideas is not only useless: it is, above all things, harmful".[115] The reason that unschooling works may not even be, as many suspect, the personal attention, support and encouragement, or the emotional stability - though these are wonderful and crucial elements not just for education but for personal development as a whole. It may actually be the freedom, the adaptation, the spontaneity of thought and focus. This cannot be shipped into schools as a useful tool, as just another idea to be incorporated. It is the be all and end all. We could help schools become more like this, but it would take mentors rather than teachers, and many more at that; a physical restructuring; the removal of delineated subjects and specified lunch breaks and start and end times; the end of grading and sorting: complete freedom.

We need to take the passion, experience and worldliness of the most motivated and dedicated adults, and combine it with the curiosity, freshness, and inventiveness of our children, allowing them to choose time, direction and depth. Gatto suggests "Independent study, community service, adventures in experience, large doses of privacy and solitude, a thousand different apprenticeships, the one day variety or longer - these are all powerful, cheap and effective ways to start a real reform of schooling".[116]

For increasing numbers of parents, the decision about how best to educate their children means making a choice about who should be in control of their children's education. Who does the child belong to, the family, or the state? Article 2 of the *European Convention for the Protection of Human Rights - Right to Education*, states that "In the exercise of any functions which it assumes in relation to education and to teaching, the State shall respect the right of parents to ensure such education and teaching is in conformity with their own religious and philosophical convictions".[117] But removing those with strong religious convictions from the equation, how many question whether state education is in conformity with their philosophical convictions, and whether that education is in their children's interest or the state's own?

In order for future voters to elect worthy, responsible leaders and create genuinely democratic structures, we have to raise our children in that very environment. We must allow children to make decisions, to take responsibility, to witness the consequences of decisions, and to work towards common goals. Most importantly, we must allow children to mature, to become adults. The only way to avoid orthodoxy is to allow and encourage freedom of thought, speech, and the ability to affect change. School, however, keeps us in a state of permanent infantilisation, reliant on and subservient to unelected authority. Our education systems treat adolescents and young adults in very much the same way they do the youngest pupils. School steals that time which in past centuries, as Gatto describes it, children and adolescents would have spent on "real work, real charity, real adventures, and the realistic search for mentors who might teach what you really wanted to learn. A great deal of time was spent in community pursuits, practicing affection, meeting and studying every level of the community, learning how to make a home, and dozens of other tasks necessary to become a whole man or woman".[118]

When the state steps in, it never fully withdraws, channeling children from school institution to college institution to corporation or welfare. Unschooling parents are freed from competing with schools for influence and authority, and life is a gradual release of sovereignty to the child as they gain independence. With the state in control, we may never become fully independent, responsible adults. Indeed, if education is central to the belief that democracy cannot survive unless the population enjoys at least a rudimentary level of education, why is the state so wary of methods of education that are not controlled by them, regardless of other systems' demonstrably superior outcomes?

It is no secret that there are inherent problems with schools; most of us can see that schools aren't working (in terms of literacy and numeracy, as well as fulfilling, educating and inspiring students). Some see that home education is working. Researchers are starting to uncover the value of home education, especially unschooling, where families reject a set curriculum, and instead make use of community resources, online classes, learning co-operatives and opportunities as they arise. There is a wealth of information waiting to be fully tapped, in the opportunities unschooling presents for comparative research into learning methods for example, or the societal impact of schools. There are less tangible but equally crucial benefits to home education, such as the impact of having families present in the daily life of the community, the strengthening of familial and societal bonds, the continuing education of the entire family through their intimate involvement with the learning process, and the fulfilment of mothers who are not relegated to mere housemaid in the raising of their offspring.

Maybe the most important thing we could do for education as a whole is to broaden our understanding of the terms 'home education' or 'unschooling'. Unschoolers simply see themselves as educating otherwise than at school; the definition is no more restrictive than this. Jeff Sandefer writes that unschoolers "are striving to evolve new approaches, not from the once-removed vantage of politicians or board members or even smart individuals grinding through the Sisyphean task of trying to get a few policies changed, but by abandoning the model and starting over. Almost exclusively, they currently represent education's real research and development".[119]

Unschooling is comparable to adult education, the only real difference being the age of the participants; in all other ways the ethos is identical: self improvement for a specified goal or for the love of the topic; groups presenting a diversity of age, gender, social background and life experience; a more relaxed and democratic classroom environment than is experienced at school; a variety of open entry, pre-requisites, accredited or non accredited courses as suits the needs of the individual. This mindset is then extended to daily life, with full advantage taken of teachers, extended family, the human and the physical communities.

Emeritus Professor Martin Rees speaks for the Council for the Defence of British Universities in saying "I believe there should be a more diverse 'ecology' of institutions, with more flexibility, more collaboration and more transferability between them".[120] This is what unschoolers are creating for themselves at a grassroots level, incorporating classes and weaving networks of education providers as they discover and need them. Gatto recognises that "Our greatest problem in getting the kind of grass-roots thinking going that could reform schooling is that we have large vested interests pre-empting all the air time and profiting from schooling just exactly as it is despite rhetoric to the contrary. We have to demand that new voices and new ideas get a hearing".[121] Reclaiming the education system is crucial if we are to stand any chance of pervasive and permanent social change. And as Clark Aldrich says, "It will not be the governments, or their school systems, or others of their institutions that will drive the real innovation in reconstructing childhood education. It will be, as it already is, the homeschoolers and unschoolers".[122]

CHAPTER 4

Finnish Lessons

There is no need to add to the criticism of our public schools. The critique is extensive and can hardly be improved on. The processes of learning and teaching, too, have been exhaustively studied... The question now is what to do.

—GEORGE DENNISON[123]

FINLAND IS RENOWNED FOR the success of its schools. Many delegations have visited the country over the past years, in an effort to understand what the Finns do differently. Interestingly, their system is perhaps the closest to home education of any traditional school. Firstly, children do not start school until 7 years of age. As is reflected in many progressive education models around the world, the Finns believe that children learn best through play, and that the early years are crucial in forming a foundation of experience and knowledge of the world. Children who have not been allowed to fully experience this crucial period find it much harder to understand abstract concepts later, as they have no real-life experience in which to ground theory. Steiner and Montessori education, and home school curricula such as Charlotte Mason and A Thomas Jefferson Education for example, all believe that the child moves through distinct stages of development, as discussed at length by Vygotsky, Piaget, Dewey and Erikson. The first seven years are a seen as a crucial developmental period, and this time is nurtured and kept free for play, in order to create a secure and happy child who will enjoy later learning. Key to both the Finnish system and unschooling is the desire for children to enjoy learning, and to come to it ready and willing, not through coercion. Several studies have found that a delayed start to formal schooling may in fact have very positive effects, to the extent that "informal knowledge gained in a supportive informal setting [may be], at least during the early years, of more consequence than formal education acquired in a formal setting".[124]

Secondly, this later starting age means more time spent with parents. Finnish parents don't see themselves as being actively involved in teaching their children, feeling that most learning happens in school, but they do have a culture of reading with children at home, as well as participation in after-school activities, trips, and community events. Families also have regular contact with their children's teachers. As discussed previously, the involvement of parents from an early age is consistent with better outcomes. Several studies have found that parental involvement in itself has more of an influence on children's intellectual and social development than the parent's occupation, education, income, social class or the size of the family.[125] Confirming the importance of parental involvement in the early years, in 2010, British MP Frank

Field conducted a review on poverty and life chances for the UK government. He found that "high-quality interventions and effective policies that begin much earlier than the first day of school really can make a difference", citing evidence that "children's life chances are most heavily predicated on their development in the first five years of life".[126] In her PhD dissertation on home education, Paula Rothermel found evidence to suggest the correlation between academic achievement and parental attention may continue until eleven years of age or even later, surmising that the success of home educated children is due in no small part to the strong bond with their parents.[127] Tizard and Hughes came to the same conclusion, after their own study on home educated children: "the key to performance irrespective of background was... the availability of parent[s] to spend time with their children, since at least one parent in each family was continually present".[128] As Rothermel found, home educating parents "see themselves as having explicit educational responsibilities at a younger age than parents of schoolchildren" and do not wait for their child to start school or for teachers to take responsibility for education, but see it as their duty from the start of the child's life.

Thirdly, primary and secondary schooling is combined in Finland, meaning pupils do not experience the disruption of moving to a new institution. Teacher Adam Lopez reports that "Many institutions are combined primary and secondary schools with no major unsettling transition stages; this also allows a consistent ethos and common language to pervade".[129] Teachers also find that this makes their job easier, developing relationships with the children based on an in-depth knowledge of their individual circumstances and personalities. Alternative schools around the world such as

Steiner Waldorf education use this approach too, with children often staying with the same teacher for the majority of their schooling. Of course in an unschooling situation, the 'teacher', in the guise of parent, is intimately aware of the child's life, health, moods etc, and there is no disruptive adjustment during the year as school terms start and end, but rather a much more integrated, continuous and fluid way of learning. Many families do follow a school year (ie those following a set curricula), but just as many do not, seeing learning as so integral to life that a schedule would be irrelevant.

Informality

Fourthly, the educational system's success in Finland seems to be partly cultural. Pupils study in a more relaxed and informal atmosphere than in many countries. This approach is also reflected amongst home educators: in Dr. Alan Thomas' studies on home educating families, he found that in the same way parents respond to signals from their newborns, home educating parents take cues from their children as regards their learning and interests, so avoiding the necessity for formal lessons. Even those families who started out using a formal curriculum became much more relaxed over time, and adopted more informal methods of learning as they grew in confidence.[130] However, even when a formal method of teaching was employed in the home, home educators were still more academically successful than schools. Tizard and Hughes found that mothers from lower socio-economic classes were more likely to use formal methods when it came to teaching maths and reading, a finding confirmed by Paula Rothermel.[131] She believes that the formal method of teaching may have better prepared lower class home educated children for the formal style of school tests, contributing to their success; but as regards the actual mastering of the subject, both formal and informal methods were more successful for home educators than for schooled students. Rothermel describes that in home educating families, "Learning appeared to be on a gentle incline from birth, a process that appears to have suited the children very well... Unlike the situation for schoolchildren, for the home-educated cohort, there was no right or wrong time to learn and it may well be that the most efficient way in which to gain skills and knowledge for life, would be to permit children to acquire information at their own pace".[132]

A significant number of home educators did not intend to reject schools, but were forced down the path by their children encountering various problems at school (bullying being a frequent factor); they did not necessarily decide to home educate due to an ideological problem with the set up of schools and formal teaching methods. These children too, as studies have shown, gradually pull their parents round to their way of learning, often becoming increasingly relaxed and less formal over time, even if they started out with a strict timetable and curriculum.[133] Both parents and children see the results of their own efforts, and trust the process of increasingly independent and self directed learning.

Parents learn to educate their children in the same subtly individual ways that they use in all interactions; this, coupled with personal attention, and sensitivity to the child's personality, produces the optimal, culturally specific learning environment. Children learning at home, under the care of those who know them best, are in the prime environment for learning without coercion; they have a dedicated and involved parent to respond to questions, note interests, introduce new topics and provide as much or as little guidance as is needed. There is no clash of culture or class in the child's primary learning environment, and when out in the world meeting new people and cultures, it is on far more equal terms than one would find in a school setting. Tizard and Hughes' summed up their research on home education: "In our opinion, it is time to shift the emphasis away from what parents should learn from professionals, and towards what professionals can learn from studying parents and children at home".[134]

Independence and Integration

Fifthly, Finland does not stream students according to ability as much as most other western nations, preferring mixed ability classrooms, and additional teachers to help those who are struggling in a particular subject. The Organisation for Economic Co-operation and Development (OECD), has found that countries that separate pupils into classes based on ability at an early age tend to have higher numbers of school drop-outs and lower levels of achievement, according to a study of 39 of the world's most developed nations.[135] Streaming by ability seems to enforce the cycle of teachers having low expectations of students with apparently low levels of academic ability; not only does the impact of low expectation hinder pupils' progress, but once streamed according to tests, there was rarely any movement between streams - pupils were "locked into a lower educational environment before they had a chance to develop ... their potential".[136] The 'best' teachers (in terms of experience and ability) were often rewarded with teaching the 'best' pupils, thus entrenching pupils' relative positions. Immigrants and pupils from low-income families were more likely to be placed in low-ability groups, exacerbating the inequalities already present for these students.

Unschooled children naturally learn in an environment which is of mixed ability, with siblings and friends of different ages, parents who are often learning alongside their children, or learning a subject for themselves in the presence of their children. Given the nature of classes that unschooled children take as they choose, which are often more of the nature of adult education classes or extra curricular classes, streaming is not an issue; a natural mixing of general abilities is always present in the class. The lack of streaming and competition found in a formal classroom situation means that unschooled children are not subject to the pressure to do anything other than enjoy learning for its own sake. This is reflected in Finnish schools, as Adam Lopez describes: "The absence of corrosive competition and an egalitarian ethos inherent in the Finnish culture has surely played a role in shaping this very impressive system".[137]

The focus on grading and streaming in schools even dictates how we relate to and judge one another. Friendships are formed with those we share classes with, extending academic streaming into the social sphere too. Publicly ranking students within groups denies a right to privacy, to learn at one's own pace, to make mistakes and to learn from them without fear of ridicule or judgement. This is compounded in lower class families, where research shows there is an emphasis on judging an action by the outcome. This is not as tolerant of creativity, invention and exploration (leading to learning through mistakes) as in middle class families, where the focus is on the intention behind the action, encouraging the child to keep investigating regardless of the outcome. In the home though, this is levelled out, as working class parents are proven to relax formal methods and allow a more natural and relaxed atmosphere to ensue. Equally, successful teachers have been found to spend more time "demonstrating, modelling, explaining, giving feedback, reviewing, and emphasizing higher-order skills, while avoiding excessive reliance on rote learning, drill and practice, or punishment" according to researchers such as Delpit.[138]

The increased independence afforded by home education, at all socio-economic levels, may be another reason for the improved success amongst lower social classes. Mental health deteriorates as we descend through socio-economic classes, linked in large part to instrumentalism – 'a sense of personal control, self-efficacy, and personal agency in affecting one's life situation'. Instrumentalism has been shown to be stronger in higher social classes, preventing or reducing depression. According to many studies,[139] happiness may well raise children's levels of learning. Thus, a learning environment which provides freedom of choice, personal control, and happiness, may well promote academic and social success. This is much more freely available to children and adults of all social classes through home education than it is in a school environment.

The Honour of Teaching

Sixthly, teaching is a highly valued and prestigious career for the Finns. Teachers must complete a Master's degree in education, after passing a selection process which cherry picks from the top 10 per cent of graduates, and only accepts one in 10 applicants. Adam Lopez describes that "Children aspire to be doctors, lawyers, scientists and in the same breath teachers".[140] Not only does this give teachers the motivation and respect needed to do their job well, but it gives the children in their charge the sense that their learning is taken seriously, and their own childhoods valued. This is in marked comparison to other countries where teaching is considered to be an easy opt-out for those who can't get a 'real' degree, summed up by the refrain "Those who can, do; those who can't, teach". Like the Finnish teachers, unschooling parents have made a huge commitment in taking responsibility for every aspect of their children's lives; it is not something they enter into lightly, and the whole family is aware of what a responsibility it is.

Again in parallel with unschooling, despite the depth of training received by teachers, or rather because of this, Finnish teachers are given much more trust and freedom to direct children's learning. Adam Lopez's description of the Finnish system has much in common with home education: "Finnish students do the least number of class hours per week in the developed world, yet get the best results in the long term. Students in Finland sit no mandatory exams until the age of 17-19. Teacher based assessments are used by schools to monitor progress and these are not graded, scored or compared; but instead are descriptive and utilised in a formative manner to inform feedback and assessment for learning... Students address teachers by their Christian names, do not wear uniforms, and are encouraged to relax in their surroundings".[141]

Lastly, Finland has low levels of immigration, especially from outside the EU. The majority of pupils speak Finnish as their native language, and are learning in a culturally congruent environment. In 2011, only 2.7% of the Finnish population were born in another country. Whilst far from classless, Finland also has one of the lowest levels of people living below the poverty line. This relatively homogenous nature of Finnish classrooms may well be a factor in their student's success (this aspect is investigated in later chapters). It is worth stating again that home educated students are more successful by all measures (academically and socially) than schooled students, regardless of economic background, social class, parental education, race and gender. Home educated students are all being taught with the linguistic accents and cultural mannerisms which are indigenous to them. Given that research shows how influential language, culture, and teacher/parental expectations are, it follows that those who can continue to learn in that environment will have less trouble than those thrust into (even a subtly) different world - one where the rules are different, where the norms and values are different, and where students are very aware of their social differences. Working class students in particular appear to benefit from a teaching style that is very clear and less dependent on culture, according to the OECD[142] – this is understandable given schools embody the values of the higher social classes; it is not such a struggle for students of higher social classes to adapt to the system.

An Equity Pedagogy

Where education is concerned, we need to accept that different social classes have different values, different dialects, different expectations and different responses; they are effectively different cultures, and must be treated with sensitivity and respect as such in an educational setting. Researchers such as James Banks have tried to counter the various class and cultural discriminations inherent in schools by creating an 'equity pedagogy', using "techniques and methods that facilitate the academic achievement of students from diverse, racial, ethnic, and social-class groups".[143] This includes having high expectations of, and believing in the potential of, all students, and working to understand how different cultural populations learn. (It seems overly optimistic however to expect that teachers will never relate better to, or expect more of, some students than others). Studies by Garcia, Irvine and Strickland all found that in classrooms with students of different cultures and native tongues, the most successful teachers, rather than trying to create a homogenous classroom (whereby one set of values will dominate), encouraged diversity, making an effort to incorporate all the various languages, dialects and cultural knowledge into the curriculum.[144]

Certain pedagogical elements produce consistently improved results: smaller schools; co-operative styles of learning; less segregation of students between different subjects and teachers; less streaming of students by ability; stronger relationships between teachers and students that extend over multiple years; greater use of team teaching; and participation of parents, teachers, and students in making decisions about schooling. Interestingly, these elements are all fundamental to unschooling. Researcher Linda Darling-Hammond and her colleagues, for example, found that when small groups of students and teachers were allowed to work together for longer periods of time, the teachers were naturally able to forge a deeper understanding of the individual students, relating to them on a more personal level and getting to know their thought processes and learning styles.[145] This highlights how hard it is for a teacher to adapt their lesson to every student in a class of 30 when they only see them for a few discrete hours a week. It is no surprise that increased time and personal attention from a teacher leads to increased results; it is why those who can afford it often pay for private tutoring. But this triad of time, understanding and genuine encouragement is provided in abundance when a child is taught at home.

Moll and Greenberg studied teachers who actively aimed to integrate the students' home lives with school, visiting families at home in an effort to understand the knowledge base that existed in each household and to get to know the families. "One teacher developed a unit on construction and building, based on her students' interests and her observation that knowledge about construction was a prominent fund of knowledge in the students' homes. Students conducted initial research on the history of dwellings and different ways of constructing structures, built model houses, and wrote brief essays describing their research and explaining their models. Parents were invited to speak to her class as experts on construction, tools, and architecture".[146] Parents were acknowledged as having equally valid knowledge, making them part of the world of learning rather than bystanders, as well as setting the student's learning in a real life context. All these things are done very naturally with unschooling, and we can start to see why it is so successful across cultures and social classes.

What is becoming clear is that while cultural differences can be catered to and integrated within the classroom, differences stemming from inequality of wealth are more entrenched in society, and again Finland provides a comparison. Finland does not have fee-paying schools. Finnish journalist Anu Partanen writes that "Only a small number of independent schools exist in Finland, and even they are all publicly financed. None is allowed to charge tuition fees. There are no private universities, either. This means that practically every person in Finland attends public school, whether for pre-K or a Ph.D.".[147] In comparison, the striking differences in opportunities offered by US schools have been shown to be the single greatest source of difference in achievement among students. When students from different social groups take courses with equally rich curricula and equally well-qualified teachers, they perform comparably. Partanen says that "The problem facing education in America isn't the ethnic diversity of the population but the economic inequality of society, and this is precisely the problem that Finnish education reform addressed".[148]

Constantly evolving curricula and teaching techniques can help to ease the differences in the classroom, but until we deal with economic disparities, those more socially advantaged will continue to be advantaged in the classroom. Unless there is a revolution in the way schools are organised - to the point that they in fact no longer resemble schools as we know them – home education is the only proven way of ameliorating differences in class, ethnicity, gender and education.

CHAPTER 5

Land Rights and Schooling

In times to come, we will have to find a responsive and sensitive balance between the still-usable skills and wisdom of the past and the sustainable products and inventions of the 20th century.

—LLOYD KHAN[149]

THE LAND TEACHES US who we are. When we lose that connection, we lose our ability to govern ourselves, and we lose our reason to teach. "Without land there is no education or customs. Land is the mother of all indigenous culture," says Maracas Pemon of Venezuela's Indigenous University.[150] Separation from the land is the central way in which education has been used to deny independence and dignity to many cultures. During the 1920s for example, around two hundred thousand people belonging to various Siberian tribes were separated when their children were forcibly sent to distant boarding schools. Dislocated from their homes, they were physically punished for speaking their own language. Stephen Corry, an anthropologist, indigenous rights activist, and director of Survival International, describes children being "taught that their own way of life is backward, and even 'sinful'... Such schools were common in much of the world until a generation ago, particularly in places taken over by European colonists".[151] The results have been damaging to say the least – that children were alienated from their own culture was the intention, but they did not become integrated with the dominant colonial society either. "The children's despair and anger led many to drugs and violence which dragged them down into domestic abuse, crime, prison, and suicide. This established a vicious cycle which still cascades down the generations".[152] In the 1960s, Innu children suffered the same fate, suffering physical and sexual abuse in the missionary schools, pushing many to drugs and even suicide. Corry asks, "If a government does not want a tribal people to carry on living as it has, and if history shows that taking its land will destroy it, then is the government guilty of genocide if it evicts the people from its lands?"[153]

Lori Johnston of the Muskogee and Yamasi People, whose ancestors once lived in areas in Florida, Georgia and South Carolina, talks of her people having been "dispossessed, silenced and buried in a 'sea of bureaucracy'. Their graves had been robbed. They were disempowered by federal structures. They had no land to preserve their traditional lives".[154] For the Aboriginal people of Australia, land is not something which can be bought or sold; it is a source of their identity, besides providing them with a livelihood. All aspects of the landscape have significance. There is a spiritual link between the person and their Ancestor via the land, which cannot be transferred elsewhere. Mick Dodson, an Australian indigenous leader says "Removed from our land we are literally removed from ourselves".[155]

Cut off From the Roots

Even when education does not involve being physically removed from the land, it still separates us from our roots. In Australia, Aborigines are fighting to educate their children as they choose. SEAM is an Australian Government initiative to ensure that children of compulsory school age in indigenous areas are enrolled in school and attending regularly. Parents who fail to enrol their children, or whose children are absent from school more than five times in any year without a valid reason, have their welfare payments suspended, amid complaints of racial discrimination, paternalism, ineffective research and a return to assimilationist policies. Many communities do feel a necessity to learn about the modern world as well as indigenous traditions, wishing their children to "understand both worlds, to survive in town and to understand the land".[156] It is not education itself which is the problem, but the manner in which it is imposed.

The Moken people, who traditionally live as 'sea gypsies' around Burma and Thailand, are being forced into a western lifestyle, as they migrate to avoid discrimination and sectarian violence. Their children are being pushed into the school system, and losing a connection with their heritage. One elder says of the children, "I don't see education as an 'option', I see it as integration into Thai society – so that they are essentially cut off from their roots".[157] Corry adds, "It is a general principle... that the closer a people feels to its roots, and the more it feels it 'belongs', the higher the self esteem of individuals, and the better their physical and mental health".[158] This should be something we all support; even from the most hardened point of view, this would save money on healthcare at the very least.

A strong connection to the land (or sea) is something associated with most, if not all, indigenous cultures; it is perhaps what defines them for those of us living Western lifestyles. It is not only to the benefit of the people, but to the benefit of the environment that this close connection with the land exists. To ensure a respectful attitude to our environment, we must have a relationship with it; a relationship based on understanding and respect rather than exploitation. Only in this way can we care for the land, protect it, judge the impact of our actions upon it, and appreciate the importance of the land of other peoples. A relationship with the land is nurtured in those myths and stories that have sprung from the people of that land. To follow this with more contemporary literature from our locale can help us to understand the cultural and political attitudes of our elders and those around us. But often we are not taught this respect for our own culture, let alone others. Stephen Corry writes, "Those [peoples] in more intense contact with mainstream society want to be recognized for what they really are, the original inhabitants. They want their story to be taught as part of their country's history, and for it no longer to be censored out and ignored... Australia did not start with Cook, nor the Americas with Columbus. Although everyone knows this, the role of indigenous peoples remains peripheral in schools' curriculums, probably nowhere more so than in Southern Africa, where the genocide of the Bushmen is barely acknowledged".[159] Whilst we have learned our lesson in relation to the environment to some extent by promoting environmental studies in schools, we are still largely ignorant of the histories and stories of the land, and of those around us.

People of the Land

By supporting those people who have lived and cared for an area over generations, we ensure its continued protection. As Noam Chomsky writes,

> *In the lead in confronting the crisis throughout the world are indigenous communities... The strongest stand has been taken by the one country they govern, Bolivia... After the ignominious collapse of the Copenhagen global climate change summit in 2009, Bolivia organised a People's Summit with 35,000 participants from 140 countries – not just representatives of governments, but also civil society and activists. It produced a People's Agreement, which called for a very sharp reduction in emissions, and a Universal Declaration on the Rights of Mother Earth. That is a key demand of indigenous communities all over the world. It is ridiculed by sophisticated westerners, but unless we can acquire some of their sensibility, they are likely to have the last laugh – a laugh of grim despair.*[160]

Through nurturing a stronger attachment to the land, we come to understand ourselves, our ancestors, our present and past. We find a sense of connection and pride, leading us in turn to take more responsibility for our surroundings, even seeking to reclaim guardianship of that land we have grown from. Many of us have lost the instinctive understanding of how impossible it is to truly 'own' land, and we fail to appreciate the control that another has over us when they control our lands. By breaking down the stranglehold of big business and property owners on our communities, we reclaim our land, our power, and our freedom to live as we choose. As long as our land is controlled by others, we cannot move freely, grow or gather food freely; voting boundaries are manipulated to control election outcomes; and we are herded around the land via house prices, our access to education, health and security dictated by the price of the land. In Britain the original Charter of the Forest imposed limits to privatisation of the land and resources. But by the 17th century, Chomsky writes, "This Charter had fallen victim to the rise of the commodity economy and capitalist practice and morality. With the commons no longer protected for co-operative nurturing and use, the rights of the common people were restricted to what could not be privatised, a category that continues to shrink to virtual invisibility".161

The Freedom of the Land

Environmentalist and lawyer William Shutkin believes that democracy and environmental protection are bound by a common destiny, though concern for the environment should be primary, being the root of all our experience. He argues "That part and parcel of [the] diminution of civic spirit and rise in economic and social inequality has been the deterioration of the American environment, both built and undeveloped".162 The relationship between land and democracy is a strong one, write George Monbiot and Simon Moore: "Those who control the land have enjoyed massive economic and political privileges... Through such ancient powers, our illegitimate rulers sustain a system of ancient injustices, which curtail alternatives and lock the poor into rent and debt".163

The Indian Land Tenure Foundation (ILTF) works to help American Indian nations in the recovery and control of their rightful homelands. "The loss of tribal lands combined with the mixed ownership patterns within reservation boundaries poses serious challenges for the sovereignty and self-determination of Indian nations. Loss of access to sacred and cultural sites makes it harder for each successive generation to remain rooted in Native culture. The checkerboard ownership pattern creates jurisdictional challenges and makes it very difficult to use reservation land for economic development. Billions of dollars in income are derived from these alienated lands, but the money goes off the reservation instead of to the Indian communities that need it most".[164] We may be well aware of land issues in regard to indigenous cultures, but most of us have forgotten that once we were all connected to the land in such a way.

Chomsky describes the importance of the land to the British in medieval times: "The commons were the source of sustenance for the general population: their fuel, their food, their construction materials, whatever was essential for life. The forest was no primitive wilderness. It had been carefully developed over generations, maintained in common, its riches available to all, and preserved for future generations – practices found today primarily in traditional societies that are under threat throughout the world".[165] Contrary to forces which would have us believe that we are nothing but parasites on the land, gradually destroying it, and that we must hand over its care to the government or environmentalists, as Nobel Laureate Elinor Ostrom's work shows, we are in fact in a symbiotic relationship with the Earth, working with it and creating with it as so many millions of other creatures do.[166] There is no pristine, perfect land, which in the absence of humans, would be free to develop unhindered. Throughout time, the land has altered by the interactions of creatures great and small, of which humans are yet another species. That is not to say we are free to treat the earth without consideration, but neither is it the disenfranchised majority who are wantonly allowing its destruction. Ostrom won a Nobel Prize in 2009 for work showing the superiority of user-managed fish stocks, pastures, woods, lakes, and groundwater basins. And as we see with the terra preta of the Amazon, where humans have enriched the - now incredibly fertile - soil over centuries, when free from the pressures of corporate greed, humans tend to affect the land in a symbiotic rather than a parasitic way.

A Necessary Change

To transition to a more (and very necessary) self sufficient and sustainable system, we need to rely much more on local food, materials and knowledge. Traditional knowledge of plants and building could be crucial in the future. Colin Donoghue writes "We are... experiencing the violence and destruction of an ongoing eviction, an eviction from the Earth... Knowledge such as what crops grow best in each bioregion and how to grow and preserve them, how to build natural dwellings, make quality clothing and pottery, knowledge of herbal medicines, etc... are not 'primitive' skills, they are valuable natural human skills that take a lot of intelligence and skill to master; modern social-systems have actually de-skilled the populace".[167] It is unlikely that we will fully value such skills however, until they can either be marketed, or save our lives.

We should be encouraging more creative, original ways of thinking; we are crippling ourselves when schools insist we all learn the same way of doing anything. Ostrom demonstrated the need for diversity through her work, emphasising "the multifaceted nature of human–ecosystem interaction" and arguing "against any singular 'panacea' for individual social-ecological system problems".[168] We cannot predict what we will need to do in the future in order to adapt, and so must preserve our myriad ways of relating to the world, and the knowledge of the different peoples. As Gandhi put it, "The essence of what I have said is that man should rest content with what are his real needs and become self-sufficient. If he does not have this control he cannot save himself".[169] To do this requires indigenous communities be given support to pass on their ways to their children, and engendering a respect of all other cultures in children of every culture.

Cross Purposes

Unfortunately, our schools do much to undermine intercultural understanding. Joel Spring gives examples of schools 'deculturalizing' students, including "the segregation and isolation of minority students, forced change of language, a curriculum whose content and textbooks reflect only the culture of the dominant group, a setting in which dominated groups are not allowed to express their culture, language, or customs, and the use of teachers exclusively from the dominant group".[170] Sonia Nieto describes a new teacher,

> *...who did not understand that many Puerto Rican children wrinkle their noses to signify nonverbally that they do not understand something. When her students did not respond verbally to her question, 'Do you understand?', she assumed wrongly that they understood. Similarly... African American children in the South did not answer obvious, factual questions to which they assumed the teacher knew the answer. This kind of questioning ('What color is the dish?' 'How many fingers do I have?'), common in many white,*

> *middle-class homes, was not part of their experience where questions were used only when the asker genuinely did not know the answer. The result was that teachers assumed the children who did not respond to obvious questions were slow or less-able learners.*[171]

Teacher expectations have been shown to greatly impact students results - significantly more so even than other factors such as race or class - so mistaking different cultural responses for a lack of ability on the student's part, ever lowers their likelihood of achieving comparably with students of the dominant culture. Pablo Yanes emphasises, "It is not enough that indigenous children attend school, it is necessary that the school be culturally and symbolically significant and that it integrates diversity instead of reproducing racism and discrimination".[172] It is debatable whether any child should be in this position in the first place; the situation is entirely a construct of a dominant order which wants to meld all cultures into one indistinct global pot, where all roots, traditions and distinct cultural heritage is lost.

It is not only indigenous peoples who are losing their ancestral knowledge. While Western cultures were responsible for colonisation across the globe, many Western cultures themselves have lost their traditions and ancient knowledge. Even within the British Isles for example, the dominant cultural values are very much those of the middle and upper levels of society, and not those of the working class. This is visible in the voting patterns where Scotland and Wales often vote entirely differently to England, yet by dint of numbers, the Celtic countries are subject to competing cultural values. The working class have been shown to have very different values to more wealthy social classes, yet it is the values of individualism and competition that prevail in schools. Many are struggling and suffering in their own ways, in the face of colonialism and the imposed values of the elite few, and many of those feeling this way are from the dominant cultures.

Dislocation

We may not think that being separated from nature and our environmental heritage has affected us deeply in the West, it is now so ingrained. But if this is true, why does our fiction evidence such a thirst to understand, and come to terms with, the world we now find ourselves in? There is a clear difference between the fiction produced by cultural groups in touch with their heritage, who produce more works of fantasy, rooted in their myths and landscapes; and those cultural groups that have become artificially separated via mass industrialisation, who produce a lot of science fiction, to the point of creating new languages to describe the new worlds they create. It appears that the language that has grown naturally from the land can no longer cope with the world and feelings it now needs to describe. While the colonised turn to their mythologies and the spirit world in the face of colonisation, the colonisers write commentaries on their separation from their own landscape and language. Science fiction is often criticised as lacking depth of character and warmth of landscape - those things that anchor us as humans. Science fiction often deals with the non-human, or how it affects the human to have our most fundamental traits removed; it describes worlds where we have become so separated from that which makes us human that we destroy ourselves. This does not sound like the writings of a people who are settled, complacent, and comfortable with their relationship to the world around them. Science fiction invents new mythologies in an attempt to create roots for a new world, increasingly separated from nature; a world which needs to be humanised. It is the job of the new fiction, with its alien languages and landscapes, to reduce the gap between the reality we find ourselves in and the world we have been separated from; it could easily be perceived as a coping mechanism for a society adrift.

When we lose our connection to the land, the connection to our ancestry fades along with it, and little of education makes sense any more. Languages become simply ways of getting by on holiday or business, no longer an ancestral tongue or a source of cultural understanding. Biology is isolated from the flora and fauna around us, as we are taken from the land to learn about it in classrooms, rather than absorbing the processes as our own food grows and our own lands change. History becomes tokenistic, and so much of our curricula is still based on the premise that if we don't learn something at school we never will, so we must have everything forced into us early on. It is a foie gras method of teaching. Somehow all this force feeding of 'facts' is thought to make us richer, when it just makes us sick. With the internet, we have more information than ever available whenever we need it: rather than needing to remember things, we need to know how to access them, and how to discern what is relevant and reasonable. Schools fill children's lives with busy work, then have to try and teach them all they have been prevented from learning by being separated from the world.

A huge amount of teaching opportunities and real life experience is lost when common stewardship of the land is lost. We are removed not just physically, but mentally and culturally. We lose a learning tool, a reason for learning and a reason for teaching. Conversely, when land rights are recognised, standards of living rise. Venezuela's Barios were once denied an identity, marked only as green space on the map. It wasn't until they were officially recognised by President Chavez that the residents could finally own property officially, and consequently receive an education. When the Nisga'a Indians of the Pacific coast negotiated their first treaty in 1999, it gave them control over most of their land, as well as their own schools. Alfredo Sfeir-Younis of the World Bank says "It is essential to understand this human rights dimension of land rights, not just as a legal obligation, but as a key element of economic and social development. Land laws in both developed and developing countries have affected the poor and the powerless the most, particularly women. These rights over the land affect other human rights; e.g., The Right To Food (security of food supplies), The Right To Housing (capacity to own a house), The Right To Health (the use of medicinal plants) and The Right To Development, to name a few".[173]

The Effects of Separation

When schools separate our children from the land they need to be learning about, and our time and access to the land is limited by corporate drives, our hands are tied. Education and work have been split into two distinct and consecutive stages. The master and apprentice model synthesises the two, but has been rejected for the most part, and dismissed as vocational training for the less academically oriented (as if professors and students are not also master and apprentice). The endless drive for progress which severs work from school, parents from children, and community from economy, stems from and concretises the separation of the people from the land. Historian Peter Linebaugh notes in *The Magna Carta Manifesto* that rights to the commons guaranteed freedom of access to local resources for everyone, in perpetuity: the land was a social safety net.[174] Meanwhile, in Bolivia there have even been attempts to privatise the rain water.

A peoples' economic sovereignty is tied to their ability to utilise their own land and resources. The security and permanence of their control and use of the natural resource base is actually more important to most indigenous groups than direct ownership of the land itself. The demand for ownership, in fact, derives from the need to ensure their access to these resources.[175] The UNESCO paper *Urban Indigenous Peoples and Migration* reports that "The main effects of building large development projects in indigenous communities is connected to the loss of land and territorial traditions, displacement and eventual resettlement, diminishment of the natural resources necessary for physical and cultural survival, destruction and contamination of the traditional environment and the tearing apart of the social organization. All these consequences drive many indigenous people into the migration movement".[176]

The UN reports that indigenous peoples typically migrate to cities as a result of a loss of livelihood, lack of social services, tribal conflicts, and land loss due to the construction of dams, mining projects or other development projects by cultures other than their own. Due to their limited skills and education, these peoples often face unemployment and poverty. Indigenous people living in cities have been found to drop out of school to seek employment earlier than their non-indigenous counterparts, leading to a pattern of working in poorly paid, low-skilled jobs. The opportunity to access a better education in the city is hindered by discrimination, cultural differences, and the high cost of education. Added to this, UNESCO reports, "the measurement of educational achievement, progress and success is dominated by ethnocentric principles that often require indigenous peoples to learn and master the cultural capital and knowledge codes of the modernised, industrialised and western worlds".[177]

The lack of access to education has far reaching consequences. A good education is credited with keeping people out of prison, but conversely, a failed education keeps certain groups of the population in. Schools control the workforce by selecting for those needed in the current economic model, and leaving the surplus to survive as best they can. This especially impacts minorities, who suffer from far higher rates of incarceration than the dominant culture. Aboriginal juveniles in Western Australia, for example, are 48 times more likely to be imprisoned than their white peers, and these disproportionate rates are reflected around the world. Not only is education failing indigenous groups, it is at the root of much of their problems, and it begins with being denied their connection to the land.

CHAPTER 6

Language and Learning

Language is the heart of our culture and the
backbone of our identity.

—MAYANS OF GUATEMALA [178]

WHEN A LAND IS invaded, language is one of the first victims, and along with it, the stories, histories and customs of the people. Aboriginal elders describe "The language belongs to the land" or "The land and the language are interconnected".[179] This is true for all languages, referring as they do to place-specific objects, which may not be found in any other language or country. Professor of Linguistics David Crystal writes, "Each language is like a key that can unlock local knowledge about medicinal secrets, ecological wisdom, weather and climate patterns, spiritual attitudes, and artistic and mythological histories... [When a language dies] what is primarily lost is the expression of a unique vision of what it means to be human".[180] Leroy Little Bear writes, "Language embodies the way a society thinks. Through learning and speaking a particular language, an individual absorbs the collective thought processes of a people".[181] Of course this applies equally to a remote Amazonian Tribe and to pupils at Harrow. Our shared language is what binds us, both at the micro and macro levels.

Colonial powers realised early on the power of language to control populations. Slave ship captain William Smith wrote "As for the languages of Gambia, they are so many and so different, that the Natives, on either Side of the River, cannot understand each other.... the safest Way is to trade with the different Nations, on either Side of the River, and having some of every Sort on board, there will be no more Likelihood of their succeeding in a Plot, than of finishing the Tower of Babel".[182] As such, a ban on a people using their own language is often one of the first results of colonisation. Louis-Jean Calvet writes in *La Guerre des Langues et les Politiques Linguistiques* that "The war of languages is always part of a wider war".[183] "Every decision about languages is political," says Linda King of UNESCO.[184] Language is used as a weapon against democracy and independence: during the systematic repression of Indonesia's Chinese community during President Suharto's regime, the use of Chinese was officially forbidden. Whilst English is an Official National Language of Wales, it is not so in England, the English never having had to impose their own language on themselves. The English Education Act of 1870 made English the sole language of education in Wales for many years, and students heard speaking Welsh were punished. In the 1960s, Innu children were punished for speaking their native language in the missionary schools. Even as recently as 1993 a Scotsman was charged with Contempt of Court for answering the judge with "Aye" rather than the English "Yes".[185]

Lesser known languages have been used as codes during wartime, for example Cherokee and Welsh, and in many ways all languages are codes, containing meanings, implications and depths of history and knowledge accessible only to the initiated. In some languages, for example, 'teacher' and 'learner' are the same word, conveying a different worldview to those languages which see them as distinctly separate. Stephen Corry suggests that "Tribal peoples, like Elizabethan Britons, generally have a more complex grammar and vocabulary – used to communicate precise information about their surrounding, societies, and ideas – than industrialised peoples do as they seek to communicate simple ideas to a large number of people from widely different backgrounds. It is difficult to see how this cannot eventually engender a corresponding simplification of the ideas that can be expressed and understood".[186] This is backed up by Lera Boroditsky of Stanford University, who studies how languages shape the way we think. "What we have learned is that people who speak different languages do indeed think differently and that even flukes of grammar can profoundly affect how we see the world... Language is central to our experience of being human, and the languages we speak profoundly shape the way we think, the way we see the world, the way we live our lives".[187]

A Common Education

Colonial conquests are estimated to be responsible for the loss of 15% of the languages that existed at the time. Each of the most endangered languages today belongs to a nation subjected to the influence of European colonial powers during recent centuries, according to Christopher Moseley, a linguistics scholar and author. "Colonial administrations seeking to unify the territory under their control needed a common administrative language", and that "usually included a common education system and featured the exclusion of anything indigenous".[188] The 'exclusion of anything indigenous', of course included the children's mother tongue.

Just as IQ tests favour those who have been raised in certain cultures, speakers of different languages will have varying levels of comfort with the dominant thought processes of an imposed language. Data from afar afield as China, Greece, Chile, Indonesia, Russia, and Aboriginal Australia shows the variety of information contained in language. "In Turkish you'd have to include in the verb how you acquired [a piece of] information: if you had witnessed this unlikely event with your own two eyes, you'd use one verb form, but if you had simply read or heard about it, or inferred it from something [someone] said, you'd use a different verb form," according to Boroditsky.[189] In Pormpuraaw, an Aboriginal community in northern Australia, inhabitants use the cardinal directions - north, south, east, and west - rather than 'left ' and 'right', to the extent of saying "There's an ant on your southeast leg". This of course requires speakers to be aware of their orientation at all times. In comparisons between Greek and English speakers, scientists found that "English speakers are more likely to be confused by distance information, estimating that a line of greater length remains on the test screen for a longer period of time, whereas Greek speakers are more likely to be confused by amount, estimating that a container that is fuller remains longer on the screen".[190] Clearly, a curriculum developed in one language will not transfer to another language or culture as straightforwardly as we might hope, and comparisons cannot necessarily be made between students from different cultures based on the same test; when the teacher is unfamiliar with the culture of the students they are teaching, they may not be explaining concepts as successfully as they think.

Boroditsky says that "In practical terms... when you're learning a new language, you're not simply learning a new way of talking, you are also inadvertently learning a new way of thinking". She describes the way artists personify concepts such as death, sin, victory, or time: "It turns out that in 85 percent of such personifications, whether a male or female figure is chosen is predicted by the grammatical gender of the word in the artist's native language. So, for example, German painters are more likely to paint death as a man, whereas Russian painters are more likely to paint death as a woman".[191] Language impacts our very philosophy of life: "Other studies have found effects of language on how people construe events, reason about causality, keep track of number, understand material substance, perceive and experience emotion, reason about other people's minds, choose to take risks, and even in the way they choose professions and spouses".[192] We need to preserve as great a diversity of languages as possible, in order to preserve diversity of thought and humanity's ability to deal with changing situations, but we must also be aware of the implications of such variety of thought when dictating how others learn.

Mother Tongue

Many studies have shown that children do better in life if they get a basic education in their own language. A study by

George Mason University in Virginia showed that "After eleven years of schooling, there is a direct link between academic results and the time spent learning in the mother tongue".[193] Around 221 million children around the world speak a different language at home to the one they are taught in.[194]

We understand a word, its depth and variety of meaning, through use and context. If a language is only heard in the classroom, and only in the context of a certain subject, it is clearly going to hinder our ability to fully comprehend the lesson being taught. It has been shown that children who speak one language at home, whilst being taught in a second language which is unheard outside the classroom, often have problems in gaining an understanding of the language taught at school.[195] This does not apply solely to children in remote areas; I have witnessed first-hand that children who are taught in one language in the classroom, but use their mother tongue at home, in the playground, and in the wider culture, struggle to both understand the lessons, and to communicate the concepts in their mother tongue, not being able to fully understand, let alone translate, the concepts they are being taught in the less familiar language.

When learning a second language, our level of competence is related to the level of competence we have achieved in our first language. A sound knowledge of one language allows us to transfer skills to another. "Successful learners capitalize on the vast amount of linguistic skills and world knowledge they have accumulated via the mother tongue", Dr. Muhammad Tariq Khan warns. "If, however, children are forced to switch abruptly or transition too soon from learning in their mother tongue to schooling in a second language, their first language acquisition may be attenuated or even lost. Even more importantly, their self-confidence as learners and their interest in what they are learning may decline, leading to lack of motivation, school failure, and early school leaving".[196] In contrast, researchers have found that first language instruction results in increased access and equity, improved learning outcomes, reduced repetition and dropout rates, socio cultural benefits and lower overall costs.[197]

The main argument raised against always teaching in the mother tongue is that of access to the scientific and academic world, the belief being that the lack of direct translations for core scientific and mathematical terms is a hindrance to students. But even English-speaking children can struggle when words have a different meaning in a scientific context as opposed to their common everyday usage - 'resistance', 'root' or 'potential', for example. Entrepreneur and writer Paul Mashegoane argues that "There can be no good reason why we should not use [English] words like oxygen, calculus and algebra, if we don't have our own indigenous names. We talk of computers, cell phones, soccer and taxi without trying to find IsiZulu, isiXhosa or Tswana translations. We will not stop using isiZulu or any other indigenous language because some technical terms are borrowed from English".[198] This argument is backed up by the case of English itself, a Germanic language that comprises Latin, Old Norse and Norman French vocabulary, plus innumerable local dialect words that can be lost in translation within a matter of miles (especially in areas which still retain a strong Brythonic influence). The important thing is not to lose the native language entirely, and it would be stronger for adopting loan-words which allow the native language to be used daily, than it would be to replace the language in its entirety for the purpose of teaching.

Language is not only an issue for indigenous cultures. A study from the Netherlands, for example, found that of a sample of 41,600 children aged between 4 and 17, about 45 per cent of pupils used a language other than Dutch at home, such as Turkish, Hindi, Berber or Arabic. The dominant nature of Western culture however, has led to younger generations viewing languages other than English as inferior. Dr Clinton Robinson warns that "Children who learn in another language get two messages – that if they want to succeed intellectually it won't be by using their mother tongue and also that their mother tongue is useless".[199] This is epitomised by the Yaqui, for whom languages do not tend to be viewed as "systems of communicative competence", but as tools to access "the socio-economic cultural domains they symbolize. The Yaqui language is perceived more as a repository for culture and heritage in a static sense, not viewed as an equally valid and viable medium for intellectual and contemporary social development. English, however, is imbued with such qualities and thereby becomes the gatekeeper for success in the European American dominated national culture".[200] Despite this, minority pupils feel more respected when their mother tongue is used as well as it having cognitive and emotional value.

Language as Resistance

Just as many imperialist powers use education to control and subdue, by teaching our own language and traditions we are asserting our independence, identity, and authority. Language is a potent tool, as governments know. A radio station in Nigeria that broadcasts only in Pidgin allows uneducated market women, bus drivers, and mechanics to listen to the news and understand what is happening in government. The authorities periodically clamp down on it, seeing "Its continued existence as a glaring symbol of a failed education system" – a failure to inculcate the masses with the language and values of the colonisers.[201] The rise of a common language is a threat to government control - effectively only those who have been through the education system and learned the language and ways of the dominant culture are enabled to participate in society, thus creating social divides. Encouraging the mother tongue can be an equally calculated political decision; one of the first moves by governments gaining independence in Africa was to re-establish their native languages, giving them official status and launching literacy campaigns. Duque reports that "Using the mother tongue at school... strengthens the student's intellectual and linguistic development, reinforces their identity, and invigorates them to enforce/practice their cultural rights".[202] As recently as 2012, the Aboriginal Warlpiri people were refusing to send their children to school as long as English-only teaching remained in place. For them, "This is just another way of taking our children away, from our language, our knowledge and us Warlpiri parents and grandparents".[203]

Even in countries where there are not different languages, there are often different dialects. In the US, opinions still differ on how best to teach students who use black dialects, with some areas teaching their students standard English as a second language. While it was once thought that black dialects would disappear as more black people were absorbed into the mainstream, inner-city youth use it more than ever, partly in an effort by young people to fit in with, and assert, their own culture. It is also a class issue, as Felicia R. Lee writes, stemming from "The increasing isolation of black inner-city residents from both whites and middle-class blacks, and stems as well from a deep cynicism about the payoffs of conforming".[204] These inner-city African-American students have to, in effect, be bilingual.

The limits of language affect the possibilities of a learning situation, in content, in the experience of the participants, and in the relationship between teacher and students, as well as placing limits on participation. Research from Israel's Haifa University looked at how well we learn when our own language or accent differs from that used by the teacher; as could be expected, the extra effort needed to understand a foreign accent or language accent means less attention can be devoted to focusing on the lesson.[205]

Used as a method of control, language enforces class differences and creates elites. When we use only one language, we have access to only that language's cannon of literature, the worldview of only that language, and the experience of only certain peoples. Multilingual Education tries to combat this, combining the theories of Freire, Gramsci, Vigostky and Piaget with the input of the community themselves, "Thereby creating a new set of people who believe in the ethics of creating and sharing knowledge for the society [rather] than to limit it to the theoreticians".[206] Students gain the ability to move back and forth between their mother tongue and other languages, rather than the mother tongue being abandoned at more advanced stages, as is common with traditional methods.

Projects such as Wikitongues, which aim to document threatened languages and dialects, are being helped massively by text and internet, as speakers develop notation systems, grammar and alphabets in order to communicate with other native speakers in written form, thus strengthening and cementing the languages. In preserving the languages of the world, we preserve our heritage, traditions and ancestral knowledge, which may have benefits for the future that we cannot foresee. Language is not just a method of communication, but a container of knowledge. Entire languages are included in UNESCO Masterpieces of the Oral and Intangible Heritage of Humanity. Ibrahim Sidibe, a specialist with UNESCO's Division of Basic Education, notes that "To be teaching tools, they must go beyond just describing the legends of the forest and be able to handle things such as scientific plant evolution and the greenhouse effect".[207] But a language unused in education is not given the chance to adapt and evolve (something intrinsic to the nature of language itself). We invent new words to describe whatever we come into contact with; as long as a language it is used, it will adapt. The best way to maintain our languages is to teach with them.

Decolonising Education

Our connection to the land, the language we speak, and our learning are all intertwined, and the first two are integral to the latter. The control of a people starts with their schools and their language. We still see this happening today, as children are removed from their traditional way of life and forced to attend schools where their mother tongue - and consequently their worldview - is rejected. As such, growing numbers of African American, Muslim American and Native American parents are choosing to home educate their children, in order to avoid the racism, rote instruction, and low expectations found in traditional schools.[208,209]

Indigenous peoples know what they want and need in terms of education. Mayan elders of Guatemala for example, say "The educational model we want to develop incorporates our culture and what our elders have taught us. We believe that education needs to take place in total harmony with the Creator and Mother Earth. Our mandate is to gather our ancestors' knowledge of science and technology". Amazonian Chief Biraci Yawanawa says "We have much to learn from the Western world and they can learn from us. Our youth has benefited from the education present in cities, but we also want Brazilians to know more about our ancient culture and the importance of preservation through mutual respect".[210] This 'two way' education, a combination of traditional and modern knowledge, is embodied in schools such as Yipirinya School, an Indigenous school in Alice Springs, Australia. The school "offers a two-way (bilingual and bicultural) education helping to keep Indigenous culture alive. It teaches literacy and numeracy and western skills following the Northern Territory/National Curriculum framework, and also teaches Indigenous languages and culture." However, alternative models of education are not globally recognised as equally valid. According to the Royal Commission Report on Aboriginal Peoples by the government of Canada, while Aboriginally controlled post-secondary institutions are valued by Canadian Aboriginal communities, they are underfunded and go unrecognised by other post-secondary institutions.[211]

Indigenous communities from Greenland to Aotearoa (New Zealand), from the Maasai to the Sami, are drawing on the knowledge of elders to create new education schemes that combine traditional knowledge with that necessary to operate on a global stage. In other places, families are turning to home education as a way to achieve this combination of traditional and modern education. The Native American Home School Association reports that "home schooling is becoming quite popular with Native American households because modern life is breaking down family ties... Native families are now feeling empowered by the ability to home school their children since the curriculum will not interfere with their values and culture".[212] Their traditional ways of teaching children do not differ in any significant way from unschooling itself. As Rita Jack, a member of the Secwepemc Nation, says, "The methods used to teach skills for everyday living and to instil values and principles were participation and example. Within communities, skills were taught by every member, with Elders playing a very important role. Education for the child began at the time he or she was born.... Integral to the traditional education was the participation of the family and community as educators." Vicki English-Currie grew up as a member of the Blackfoot Nation: "The Indian people's non-directive approach is a way of guiding offspring. It determined a basis for a future lifestyle. We matured rapidly and we became adept at determining our own actions and making our own decisions, while being sensitive to the expectations of the collective and of our elders."[213] Unschoolers would be hard pressed to describe their own approach in a better way.

As communities around the world reject a Eurocentric paradigm in favour of schools that are more oriented to their own cultural values, education may come to look more and more like indigenous teaching methods and unschooling.

The 'Right' to Education

We need little to live – sustenance, shelter, a sense of purpose and fulfilment. But we are making ourselves increasingly depressed and aimless in the West, in the same way we are destroying indigenous cultures: losing the connection to our land, language, and connection to our children.

Around the world, governments have forcibly separated parents from children under the guise of education via compulsory boarding schools. The Universal Declaration of Human Rights includes a section which according to Corry "would destroy most intact tribes within a generation or two": that primary level education be compulsory. "Enforced schooling is the most powerful weapon used by governments and missionaries to instil in tribal children values which are different, often contradictory, to those held by their own societies".[214] This brings up two immediate problems: that one world view is imposed on the colonised; and the distress caused to the individual's psyche by being caught between conflicting worlds.

Jean-Paul Restoule, an associate professor of Aboriginal Education in Canada, points out that whilst education is considered a right, traditionally it has been "provided in exchange for access to lands and resources", with education as a process of assimilation, leading to the loss of language, culture, the ability to parent, the loss of learning how to love and to be loved.[215] Bill Fogarty of the ANU's National Centre for Indigenous Studies has found that "At its worst, education can be a tool of acculturation and assimilation for remote Aboriginal people. Education can usurp local social structures, cause deep intergenerational divisions and education that is not connected to the reality of a student's daily life in remote community can seem utterly pointless, leading to dis-engagement".[216] Restoule, himself a member of the Dokis First Nation in mid-northern Ontario, says that it will take several generations to restore traditional ways of learning in relation to the social and economic conditions that his people have been left with.[217] Educators often forget what a gradual process such change must be, and expect immediate results leading to constant changes of tack.

Only One Way

Such a legacy of schooling is repeated around the world, and stems from the idea that education is only possible in the context of a school. This false premise has led us to ignore the very natural and necessary education that has taken place in all cultures since the dawn of time: that of survival, and cultural heritage. To assume that this is not a real or neces-sary education is a grave, and culturally imperialist mistake. According to Noam Chomsky, racism is so prevalent in acad-emia that it is laced into the very language used by teachers and professors. We don't question, for example, the maxim that we were all hunter-gatherers until the development of agriculture, and along with it the development of 'civilisation', of which we are either a part of, or apart from. And yet 'civilisation' has gone downhill ever since – settled agriculture and the development of surplus brought violence, alcohol, declines in height and health, lower life expectancy, increased child mortality, disease, crime and war. But still we look upon non-industrialised cultures as needing to catch up and adopt the ways of the modern world, in order to partici-pate fully in 'civilisation'. We maintain the idea that we can only negotiate when indigenous peoples are 'brought up-to-date', and we try to achieve this through the holy grail of schooling.

However accommodating education tries to be, it always revolves around modifying Western methods to integrate indigenous ones, just so long as those methods can be measured and evaluated to make sure they are succeeding on our terms. UNESCO has produced a book on indigenous education which is otherwise inclusive and progressive, yet the unquestioning acceptance of the necessity for assessment and evaluation remains, imposing on children the idea of progress and graded achievement, rather than education for its own sake.[218] Beck describes those who "hold that school must educate human beings to become competent participants in a globalised world" as "the right wing of global educational politics. The left side is critical to such aims and wants schools as a counterweight to global capitalism. They want more nationally controlled schools, which includes everyone and emphasizes social competence and equality... both political right and left find more schooling positive... everyone wants more education, and more education means to them, more school".[219]

Educating for Progress

Education is a form of cultural transmission, and as such implies a set of basic assumptions about a society's cultural interests. In this respect, the interests of the individual are subsumed into the perceived interests of the majority. Corry describes the Universal Declaration of Human Rights as a "hastily-chiselled tablet [which] concerns itself exclusively with individuals, not communities, and has almost no relevance to those living separately from the state." He continues, "in the usual developmental model, and in the minds of many Westerners, 'education' implies buildings, books, children on chairs in rows, teachers from outside the community, and a curriculum designed by city officials, often bearing little relevance to rural life. The result for indigenous peoples is that their children learn little which helps them, in an alien environment, and from unsympathetic tutors. Children sitting under a tree, or on the floor, listening to a teacher from their own community telling them things, in their own language, which are going to equip them for their changing lives, are rare exceptions".[220] Even UNESCO's publication *The Challenge of Indigenous Education* warns that "Educational materials providing accurate and fair information on [indigenous] cultures and ways of life are all too rare, and history textbooks frequently depict them in negative terms. In many cases, educational programmes fail to offer indigenous people the possibility of participating in decision-making, in the design of curricula, the selection of teachers and teaching methods, and the definition of standards".[221]

Schools are predicated on values of individualism and competition rather than cooperation or communalism. This creates a fundamental clash of cultures for those who are raised to look after others before the self. The United Nations report *Urban Indigenous Peoples and Migration* reports that inner conflicts are experienced by those caught between the expectations of the dominant culture and those of their own subculture. "In addition, role conflict can be expected to arise between the personal aspirations of an individual and appropriate behavior as defined by the person's cultural group".[222] Missionaries and government officials, for example, see the Amazonian Pirahã society as impoverished, giving them money and modern technology in an effort to help them. But

Daniel Everett, the only outsider to speak their language, has lived with them for years, and says "The Pirahã aren't poor. They don't see themselves as poor". He believes capitalism and religion are manufacturing desires. "One of the saddest things I've seen in Amazonian cultures is people who were self-sufficient and happy that now think of themselves as poor and become dissatisfied with their lives. What worries me is outsiders trying to impose their values and materialism on the Pirahã".[223] The Hadza of Tanzania place such value on equality that "differences of power, wealth and status are systematically subverted"[224] according to anthropologists, with merciless teasing employed when anyone tries to boss the others. Yet the schooling that is imposed on such communities across the world inculcates the seeking of extrinsic rewards, pits students against each other in a competition to get the top grades, and promotes the idea that success is measured in terms of money and status.

To School or not to School?

By enshrining the right to education in the United Declaration of Human Rights, governments have effectively been given carte blanche to impose Western-style schooling on their populations, without examining the question of whether it is in fact in the best interests of the people concerned to be schooled. We cannot conceive of schooling being anything other than progressive, and we have successfully embedded in mainstream consciousness that lack of access to schooling is an indicator of poverty and oppression. It is certain that it is a hindrance to self determination to be denied access to education in its broadest sense; but equating education with schooling alone, and imposing Western values on other cultures, is one of the main ways that minority cultural values and histories are obliterated. It is a striking example of double speak that we have effectively enshrined as a human right, the right to impose our values on other cultures, the right to obliterate their worldview in the guise of progress and equality.

The problem is not with education, so much as our conception of what education means. As long as we restrict our vision of education to schooling, we restrict the right to self-determination. What constitutes an education is still a subject of contention in the West, with the Swedish and German governments, for example, making home education illegal, and state schooling compulsory. This is a dangerous precedent, implying that the education has set parameters, set subjects, set methods; anyone who does not fit into the system is lost. So long as everyone, male and female, young and old, has the opportunity to study anything and everything without hindrance, can we justify any imposition of curriculum at all? No one should need a state-sanctioned education of a specific type in order for them not to be impoverished and marginalised; that we do, is a sign of how tightly controlled and monopolised our world is.

Educational Servitude

Slavery has been made illegal in theory, but continues in many guises, including compulsory education. While convincing us it is a privilege, we are enslaved into an economic system. This was exactly the basis of the school system, and why it was fought against, yet we have been convinced otherwise. It is a brilliant Orwellian trick, whereby education is the right of all, but only certain types of education count. People are impoverished by not knowing English, computing and modern subjects - if you are not versed in these things, you cannot be involved in the modern world. How can we contribute to policy decisions on genetics for example, if we do not understand the basics? But under the guise of welcoming everyone into the global marketplace, we are really forcing our values on everyone else. Only through a Western-style education, can tribal peoples discuss with us their lands and their rights - through the lens of our values which they have learned by rote in schools. UNESCO talks of the necessity "to provide and develop the knowledge and skills that enable indigenous peoples to participate fully and equally in the national and international community".[225] In other words, *they* must be initiated into *our* way of doing things. We must turn this on its head: support intrinsic motivation, independence of action, satisfaction through cooperation and solidarity. Then we may develop a society which judges itself on the welfare of all, not the 'successful' few; a world which eliminates poverty because it has eliminated greed. And as Professors Angayuqaq Oscar Kawagley and Ray Barnhardt point out: "Many of the problems that originated under conditions of marginalization have gravitated from the periphery to the center of industrial societies, so the pedagogical solutions that are emerging in indigenous societies may be of equal benefit to the broader educational community".[226] Those pedagogical solutions have notable parallels to unschooling, again suggesting reasons that the unschooling movement is experiencing such success.

CHAPTER 7

Class and Culture

In order to teach you, I must know you.

—NATIVE ALASKAN TEACHER [227]

IT IS NOT JUST indigenous people who are affected by cultural differences in education. Minority groups often fall into the lowest socio-economic class, and as such, could be said to suffer twice, as children from lower social classes, like indigenous children, are at a disadvantage in educational terms, regardless of their racial origin. Socio-economic class has been shown to correlate with IQ tests and exam scores, and is the most significant factor in determining success in school.[228] It is said that we have more in common with others of the same social class - regardless of nationality - than those of our own nationality but a different social class.

The Myth of Mobility

Social class affects all aspects of life, not just education - higher levels of illiteracy, mental illness, homicide, infant mortality, obesity, teenage pregnancies, depression, teenage suicide, and incarceration all correlate with lower social class - but it is through education that we seek to level the playing field. Time and again, however, it has been shown that schools simply don't achieve this. Professor Leon Feinstein has shown that adult success can be predicted by a child's ability level on the first day of primary school,[229] and UK government bodies have admitted "If you turn the clock back on pupils in school today 15 years and predict their outcomes from where they were born, you can do it".[230] A review conducted by British Member of Parliament Frank Field found "A large body of research concludes that schools are highly ineffective in improving the life chances of poorer children... By age three there are significant ability differences between children from lower and higher income families. These gaps persist throughout childhood, widening during school years (especially after age 11)... It would of course require a big and bold shift in the status quo to accept the evidence that schools have been ineffective in improving life chances and that for many children outcomes are unfortunately decided much earlier in life".[231]

In their study *The Constant Flux*, Erikson and Goldthorpe looked at nine industrialised countries, and found that regardless of education, relative differences among social classes have not substantially changed over time.[232] This is confirmed in comparative studies by Shavit, Blossfeld, and Müller, who all found that social class is a predictor of educational attainment.[233] The UK's Department for Work and Pensions reports that "Evidence on trends in social mobility suggests that the introduction and expansion of universal education systems in the UK and in Western Europe have not led to increasing levels of relative social mobility.... They do not indicate that there has been any major positive shift in relative social mobility over the last decade". Even where upward mobility between classes did exist, it was "found to be largely independent of the acquisition of high levels of education", according to Payne.[234]

Social mobility is often unrelated to education. Researchers Iannelli and Paterson found that changes in the labour market, from a preponderance of manual jobs to expansion in the service sector, have meant increased opportunities for people from a variety of social backgrounds to find non-manual work. "More recently, however, the rate of expansion of non-manual employment has slowed down, and so the children of parents who had been upwardly mobile between the 1950s and the 1970s now have less chance to be upwardly mobile or even to maintain their middle-class status than their parents had... In accordance with studies of other countries, we found that changing patterns of social mobility were due to changes in the occupational structure and not to changing patterns of social inequalities". They warn that an increase in the numbers of people achieving higher educational qualifications, without comparable job opportunities, leads to credit inflation, whereby there is little way to choose between many equally qualified applicants. "This may bring the offspring of middle class families to rely on alternative resources (such as social capital), which are not equally available to other social classes... employers may decide to recruit on the basis of workers' characteristics other than formal attainment... such as communication ability or capacity to work in a team, which may be more likely to be acquired in a middle class family than in less advantaged families". The researchers also cite "Certain kinds of inter-personal skills or 'emotional intelligence' that may inadvertently favour people of middle-class origin", and finish that this has "Rather serious implications for education policy... For over a century, the goal of reducing class inequalities in educational attainment has been based at least in part on the belief that this would help to equalise life chances... Education cannot be used, on its own, to eradicate social inequalities, and is relatively powerless to counter the middle-class strengths of effective networks, self-confident aspirations and sheer wealth".[235]

Rather soberingly, Prof W. W. Charters Jr. states,

> *Social class position predicts grades, achievement, and intelligence test scores, retentions at grade level, course failures, truancy, suspensions from school, high school dropouts, plans for college attendance, and total amount of formal schooling. It predicts academic honors and awards in the public school, elective school offices, extent of participation in extracurricular activities and in social affairs sponsored by the school, to say nothing of a variety of indicators of 'success' in the informal structure of the student society. Where differences in prestige value exist in high school clubs and activities, in high school curricula, or in types of advanced training institutions, the social class composition of the membership will vary accordingly.*[236]

It would seem that higher class students make their mark from day one, being more involved in the life of the school as a whole, having more contact with teachers, and as teachers subsequently develop increased expectations of these students, so they rise to the challenge, and the cycle is entrenched.

Conversely, there is no shortage of examples of people who excelled despite never attending, or having been removed from, school. The world's most prolific inventor Thomas Eddison was taught at home after the school told his mother the boy was 'addled'. Noted surgeon and anatomist John Hunter made little progress at school, but flourished once free. The author Alexandre Dumas refused to go to school, while Blaise Pascal was educated at home, as was Virginia Woolf. Yehudi Menuhin, C.S. Lewis, Florence Nightingale, Charles Dickens and Alexander Graham Bell all spent time being taught at home. Many notable people were dismissed as failures by their teachers, only to flourish once free of them.

Class as a Cultural Attitude

Is the link between social class and achievement inevitable, or is there something intrinsic to in the nature of schools that means education benefits certain classes over others? Sociologists and psychologists accept that social class is a cultural phenomenon; the different social classes move in different worlds, according to their role within the economic system. This is both a reality in the work place, as some give orders and others take them, and in the home, as different political beliefs, religious denominations, and social attitudes are intertwined with social class. "These class-specific ideologies are not learned by experience, but rather are passed down over generations within families and communities through socialization and enculturation practices", says Bill Gabrenya.[237] This is not fundamentally any different to the varying ideologies found across cultural groups, which educators have accepted they must cater to. "In the same manner that children born into different societies grow in into different sorts of adults, children of different social classes are sent on divergent life trajectories".[238]

Professor of Sociology Melvin Kohn has shown that due to the relative stability of class over generations, it is natural for parents to transmit their values to their children, as we must teach our children to operate in the both the culture they live in, and the culture that in all likelihood they will exist in as adults.[239] It would be hard for us to teach our children any other cultural values. Our values are consistent with our experiences: working class people tend to have physically hard and dangerous jobs, closely supervised by others, in an atmosphere of obedience; these parents demonstrate a comparable level of discipline in raising their children, valuing conformity and judging their children's actions on the outcome rather than their intentions. Middle class parents, meanwhile, have been shown to encourage self-direction, independent thinking, and show much patience as the child finds their own way, disciplining their children according to the intent behind their actions (this raises interesting questions regarding the impact of social class on our attitudes toward politicians, and how we judge our government's decisions).

It may seem then, that schools would in fact benefit the working class, given schools also place a high value on obedience, subservience and conformity. But the deeper message in our education system is one of competition and the inevitability of the success of some at the cost of the rest. The school system as we know it depends on creating an internal stratification, a reflection of the class structure outside school walls. From early on, children are graded according to ability, tested, labelled, given different opportunities according to their level of success. It is rare that a child can stray from their designated place once labelled. As Clark Aldrich says, "This also means that (massive amounts of) taxpayer dollars are supporting institutions that will necessarily classify and even create 'losers' of at least a third of all students. Resources are being dedicated to creating an institutional underclass".[240] During the 1970s, many prominent voices began to criticise schools as being a tool of oppression employed by the ruling class to ensure their dominance. Ivan Illich showed that schools are used to teach us to accept society, its institutions, and their hierarchies as if they have always existed, and will continue to exist.[241] Paulo Freire saw this traditional method of schooling as dehumanising both students and teachers, as well as stimulating oppressive attitudes and practices in society. He argued that the social domination of race and class is intrinsic to the conventional educational system.[242]

This is surely by design – it is no secret that schools were intended to produce a docile, obedient workforce, and public education caused mass debates as it was introduced. Chomsky says of the public, "They knew it and they fought against it. There was a lot of resistance to mass education for exactly that reason. It was also understood by the elites. Emerson once said something about how we're educating them to keep them from our throats. If you don't educate them, what we call 'education,' they're going to take control – 'they' being what Alexander Hamilton called the 'great beast,' namely the people".[243] Hierarchy thrives on withholding privilege and making the underclasses compete for it.

Slotted into Place

One of the main gatekeepers of social stratification in schools is the use of exams and streaming. While in theory giving feedback to children, teachers and potential employers in order to help them, they actually limit our perception of our own abilities. Only certain kinds of intelligence can be measured in an exam setting, which is often an unrepresentative situation in the first place. A comparison is made between students, according to that year's exam paper, that year's cohort and that year's teaching expertise, yet these grades are with us for life, and lead us and others to base our human value on a rather fleeting moment in time. Moreover, the system must create many 'failures' for every 'success', breeding disappointment, shame and disaffection.

This supports the status quo of a stratified society, as students are pitted against each other. Those at the top of the class come to identify with being the best academically, and maintaining this position becomes their primary motivation for success, although sometimes, the resentment of other students leads more able students to hide their talents for fear of bullying. The top students are inclined to help only those who are not a threat to their superior grades, and the benefits of success mean that the lure of cheating becomes worth the risk. Not only are all students expected to try their hardest knowing that the majority will only be mediocre at best, but we teach them that this is how society works. Robert M. Hauser of the University of Wisconsin describes schools as "The primary agencies of social selection for children and youth in the United States",[244] while Illich warned that "People who submit to the standards of others for the measure of their own personal growth soon apply the same ruler to themselves. They no longer have to be put in their place, but put themselves into their assigned slots, squeeze themselves into the niche which they have been taught to seek, and, in the very process, put their fellows into their places, too, until everybody and everything fits".[245] Thus, we continue to promote social hierarchy from within. It is this emphasis on conformity over critical faculty that ensures the success of the school system and the continuity of social hierarchy.

Not only do schools suppress rather than promote social mobility, but there is a clash of class culture where competition itself is concerned. A study published in 2011, *Social Class as Culture*, came to the conclusion, based on surveying numerous previous studies, that different social classes have fundamentally different ways of seeing the world, and that our social class is a "profound part of who we are"[246] (not that most of us need studies to tell us this). The authors say this fact alone should affect debates on public policy. "People who come from a lower-class background have to depend more on other people. Wealthier people don't have to rely on each other as much. This causes differences that show up in psychological studies... wealthier people don't read other people's emotions as well. They hoard resources and are less generous than they could be".[247] The author Alan Moore has never moved away from his working class roots, despite many opportunities to make a fortune in Hollywood. He credits his parents with instilling in him "The conviction that money is of secondary value in life. It was my class. The only thing you could pride yourself on, in the Boroughs, was to be decent people".[248] In contrast, finds Paul Piff of the University of California, Berkeley, "The relative privilege and security enjoyed by upper-class individuals gives rise to independence from others and a prioritization of the self and one's own welfare over the welfare of others". His studies found "More positive attitudes toward greed and the pursuit of self-interest among upper-class individuals".[249]

A Natural Solidarity

A study from the University of Chicago found that rats would release another rat from a cage without being given a reward, even when they were denied a reunion with the rescued rat. When presented with two cages, one containing a rat, and the other some chocolate, they opened both and "typically shared the chocolate".[250] The only reward was that of helping the other rat. Neuroeconomists argue that this shows our brains have evolved to get feelings of pleasure from empathy and trust, probably as a result of selection pressures, and that studies such as the caged rats provide "strong evidence for biological roots of empathically motivated helping behavior".[251] In light of all this, a school culture which is by its nature competitive and individualistic rather than cooperative, may well be causing working class children - raised to depend on each other rather than promote their own success to the detriment of others - to suffer disproportionately.

Worryingly, a series of studies by psychologists at the University of California and the University of Toronto found that those of a higher social class are more likely to engage in a variety of unethical behaviours, including lying, cheating, and breaking the law while driving.[252] A comparable change in behaviour from the natural empathy more frequently found in the working class, to a more variable morality typical of the higher social classes, has also been observed in children moving through the school system. Over the past century, various ideas have been developed and improved upon by psychologists seeking to understand why we make the moral choices that we do. For a long time, theories were based on interviews with boys only, but when women's responses were finally included in the debate, a new pattern emerged. Carol Gilligan and her team have found two types of moral response in any given situation: a 'justice' response based on fairness, personal rights, rules and set standards of behaviour, with individual welfare a secondary concern; and a 'caring' response which is simply a concern for the welfare of other people, regardless of rules. Though neither sex reacted in one manner only, time and again, males made choices based on the justice response, and females reacted with a caring response. Gilligan noted that children are also more likely to choose a caring response than a justice response. Using Peck and Havighurst's five categories, the highest of all choices, rational altruism – placing the welfare others above all else – is understood by children as young as 2, and there is evidence that even babies respond to the distress of others.[253]

But as author and educator David Gribble writes, "The very young have a natural altruism, but then they go to school. Traditional schools are usually rule-based, and encourage conformity and irrational conscientiousness to the exclusion of other moral considerations. They are dominated by a masculine way of thinking. A child's natural altruism is crushed rather than developed... If you obediently accept the authority of your school and allow it to completely govern your life, your own innate altruism is suppressed".[254] Again, this would require more of an adaptation on the part of lower class children than middle to upper class. David Graeber writes that,

> *To some degree this seems to reflect a universal sociological law. Feminists have long since pointed out that those on the*

bottom of any unequal social arrangement tend to think about, and therefore care about, those on top more than those on top think about, or care about, them. Women everywhere tend to think and know more about men's lives than men do about women, just as black people know more about white people's, employees about employers', and the poor about the rich. And humans being the empathetic creatures that they are, knowledge leads to compassion. The rich and powerful, meanwhile, can remain oblivious and uncaring, because they can afford to. Numerous psychological studies have recently confirmed this. Those born to working-class families invariably score far better at tests of gauging others' feelings than scions of the rich, or professional classes. In a way it's hardly surprising. After all, this is what being 'powerful' is largely about: not having to pay a lot of attention to what those around one are thinking and feeling. The powerful employ others to do that for them.[255]

Powerful people have even been compared to those who have suffered a traumatic brain injury, lacking the skill of mirroring others' emotions, something crucial for empathy.[256]

Another factor affecting academic success is motivation. Melvin Kohn found that the middle class work for intrinsic rewards, but the working class for extrinsic rewards such as money.[257] In a study published December 2011, researchers who wanted to understand the poor test performance of children from lower socio-economic classes (SES) examined two conflicting theories: the early damage theory, which holds that lower-SES children have undergone such early and intensive deprivation that they cannot perform in testing situations, versus the alienation theory, contending that public schools are middle-class institutions with middle-class intrinsic rewards which do not motivate children from lower socio economic classes. They found that "When faced with the testing situation the children choose not to perform". Tests demonstrated a "significant" improvement "in the test performance of lower-SES children when extrinsic (money, food) rewards, as well as conventional rewards, are offered. Extrinsic rewards did not significantly improve the test performance of upper-SES children".[258] In this respect, there is a clear clash of cultural values between lower and higher classes, and belonging to a higher social class is a distinct advantage for success in school. Working class children quite fairly expect some return for their effort in the more immediate moment, while higher class children are more secure in the belief that they will be rewarded later in life.

The Home Supporters

Parental involvement also plays a large role in children's success, and again, this is much more common amongst the middle classes from a very early age. In *Educational Failure and Working Class White Children in Britain*, anthropologist Gillian Evans writes "My own experience suggests that middle class mothers, who are usually educated to degree level, take it for granted that formal-learning-type skills, such as those associated with literacy... numeracy... arts and crafts... and science... should be incorporated, in an informal, playful way, into the caring relationship with the child at home. In this way middle class children often come, early on in their lives, to love formal learning because formal-learning-type tasks are what the loving relationship with the mother largely consists of".[259]

Conversely, parents who left education earlier tend to feel less involved in their children's education. According to the London Institute of Education, "Research has consistently shown that parental involvement in children's education does make a positive difference to pupils' achievement",[260] but again, the degree and type of support varies between social classes. Middle class parents tend to intervene more than working class parents in terms of correcting speech, developing skills through playing games, encouraging hobbies and a wide range of interests, as well as building 'culture capital' through activities such as music, travel, and extracurricular classes. Middle class homes have been found to offer more intellectual stimulation in the form of magazines, newspapers, art, technology, and the type of programmes on the television or radio. Much of this, of course, costs a not insignificant amount of money, again making it easier for middle class families to provide an educational advantage for their children. Stanford University School of Education teaches in their workshops the value of personal connections between students and teachers, relationships often forged via extra-curricular activities – again an aspect more often encouraged by middle class parents. Given that stronger teacher-student relationships lead to a better rapport in the classroom, plus increased attention and raised expectations on the part of the teacher, middle class students are again at an advantage, teacher expectation being the most important factor in student success.

The higher level of parental input evident in the middle classes is in part a reflection of differing class attitudes toward education and intellectual matters, and differing cultural definitions of success. According to the London Institute of Education, "The attitudes and aspirations of parents and of children themselves predict later educational achievement. International evidence suggests that parents with high aspirations are also more involved in their children's education". Given the same research found that "Higher parental education is significantly related to having higher expectations of children's achievement",[261] yet again middle class children are at an advantage, coming from a family likely to have more educated parents with associated higher expectations and involvement. These expectations and aspirations are academic in nature. Those traits which are not measured by standardised tests are not valued in the same way by society, so different cultural values will translate to 'lesser expectations' and lower levels of achievement on such tests. Gutman and Akerman believe that most parents have high aspirations for their children when young, but due to economic constraints, their children's apparent abilities, and limited opportunities, these aspirations change over time.[262]

It Doesn't Always Pay to Succeed

Children are either supported or hindered by the cultural attitudes they are surrounded by, whether those of adults or peers. It is not just the attitudes of parents that play a role in children's success; peers have a huge impact on the attitudes and choices of young people. Indigenous educators point to the impact of peer pressure as a factor in both low retention rates, and high rates of unqualified indigenous peoples, especially amongst the young. The UN report *Urban Indigenous Peoples and Migration* notes that "The reluctance of some young people to excel academically for fear of cultural ostracism and bullying is under-reported in the education discourse. For some youth who want to achieve, the pressure to engage in criminal activity and lifestyle cannot be undermined".[263]

Moreover, sociologist Mark Bracher explains that when a student does not receive the recognition they crave, they can

"Feel depressed, anxious or angry and as a result be less effective in their learning, or pursue non-educational means of achieving recognition".[264] This can take many forms including crime, drugs, or even pregnancy (gaining recognition and status through parenthood). When a student's peer group or family do not value being smart or intelligent, the student will be less likely to seek recognition in these areas, and more likely to seek recognition in the areas that are important to those closest to them, for example athletics or parenthood. Bracher found that those students who cannot derive recognition for being intelligent, athletic or attractive, will turn to more antisocial activities in search of status.[265] Of course, given the nature of schools, where only a certain number of students can achieve the position of being best academically, a lot of students are forced to seek recognition in other ways. For middle class children who are engaged in many extra-curricular activities, there are more opportunities to form an identity in a non-academic setting, but for working class children with limited opportunities and less parental support, the likelihood of succeeding in any way in a school environment becomes increasingly less likely.

Gillian Evans found that in a working class area of London, "Tension is created in this social class structure... because the system for establishing value through formal educational qualification... conflicts with other means for gaining status that depend on completely different kinds of social participation about which working class people might be fiercely proud". Evans suggests that not only are schools failing working class children, but that working class life presents an alternative means for gaining social status that conflicts with what it means to do well at school. The children she got to know through her anthropological work sought "acceptance and prestige in their locality through whatever means possible, and often in conflict with the requirements of school, because society at large offers them little hope of anything better".[266] As French philosopher Jacques Ellul noted, prosperous children are more susceptible to the effects of schooling because they are promised more lifelong comfort and security for yielding wholly to the system – viz. the 'old boys' networks of Eton and Oxbridge for example – while working class children have less expectations placed on them, and so have less to lose by not conforming fully.[267]

Not The History of the World

Traditional curricula also favour the upper classes, just as they favour the dominant and colonial cultures in relation to indigenous groups. In both cases, the school system promotes the history of the dominant group, whether dominant by population or by wealth. Some African Americans are turning to home schooling in the face of mainstream history lessons; as one mother said, she wanted her sons to learn about their African roots and not "to believe that their history begins with slavery".[268] Noam Chomsky reminds us "how efficient the educational system has been, and the propaganda system, in simply destroying even our awareness of our own immediate intellectual background". He continues "There was a real battle fought by working people in England and the U.S. to defend themselves against what they called the degradation and oppression and violence of the industrial capitalist system, which was not only dehumanizing them but was even radically reducing their intellectual level".[269] The 2012 Olympic opening ceremony caused delight and controversy amongst the British, simply because it was so unusual and enlightening to see an inclusive history of Britain. Danny

Boyle's display included all that isn't taught in schools, from the history of the working class to popular counter-culture music; even the seating lit up to reveal the caption 'This Is For Everybody!'

But the history taught in schools is no more a representative history of the majority of children than the history of colonialists taught to indigenous children. This in itself is a distancing experience, which is likely to alienate working class children from education just as it does indigenous children. The Native American Home School Association says that "Many Native Americans... are able to remember how embarrassed they were, as children, to admit that they were Native American because of what they were being taught in history classes. Unfortunately, these classes were teaching them that they were savage Indians. This caused a real sense of shame in many of these children, even though their families took great pride in their culture".[270] Dr. George Dei, born in Ghana and now working at the University of Toronto, describes an alternative Africentric paradigm, which

> *provides a space for African peoples to interpret their experiences on their own terms rather than through a Eurocentric lens. Of course, students need to know about European history. But they also must understand that African history is central to the construction of European history. You cannot present world history in a way that leaves out a group of people or says that their history doesn't matter. Cry Freedom is about a white man who fights apartheid. Maybe he did, but what were the Africans doing? Were they just standing there watching him fight? Or were they central to the story? I can see how subjects such as history and English can be taught with an African point of view. What about math? There's a whole literature on ethno-mathematics and indigenous conceptions of science and mathematics. To use just one example, look at the textile patterns*

used by African peoples. What are their conceptions of geometry? You'd still teach students geometry as we know it. But you allow for multiple ways of knowing.[271]

When teachers seek out alternative ways of approaching a subject, and present a variety of viewpoints, students learn to think critically about the inherent bias in any account, and to accept differing ways of thinking and being. But until alternative attitudes to a subject, and alternative ways of approaching life, are given equal credit in relation to qualifications, we are in effect asking all children to become middle class, in attitudes and culture, in order to succeed. This is epitomised in the experience of a Native community in Arizona, in the 1970s. When the authorities noticed that 97 % of pupils were of 'minority' descent, they decided the students should be split up and integrated into seven other local schools – a move that many parents felt was an attempt to assimilate the children into the dominant culture. Eventually the community opened their own school, 'I'tom Escuela' meaning 'Our School' in the Yaqui language. Octaviana V. Trujillo writes,

The alternative school prided itself on building on the cultural heritage students brought from home. The instructional program was not oriented to tests or grades, rather it helped students establish positive self-concepts through learning about their culture and those of others. Three languages were taught, English, Spanish and Yaqui. The curriculum included the unseen components of language that structure the way people view themselves, each other and the world around them. It also addressed many injustices, the most glaring being the placement of children in classes for the mentally retarded on the basis of IQ tests administered in English.[272]

Social historian Eva Swidler explains that a child must feel an emotional connection to their community, and identify with their teachers, in order for any lasting education to take place. Without a connection and sense of identification with those providing and demonstrating information or a way of thinking, no real learning will ever occur:

> *This observation explains, for instance, how boys and girls may grow up in the same family, but by identification with different family members learn to talk, walk and think differently. It explains how members of different races may go to the same schools, watch the same media, spend most of their waking hours exposed to the same accents and teachers as each other, but maintain very distinct subcultures; they each identify with different people in their cultural surroundings and educate themselves in the ways of those they identify with. Naturally, the identification process results partly from some kind of choice by the learners and partly from processes of society that tell them that they belong to some groups and not to others whether they like it or not.*[273]

The Dangers of Inequality (or Home Ed Kills Fascists)

Poverty hinders success in education at every level – from those who can't afford shoes to attend school, to those who can't afford the best tuition. But entrenched inequality and low levels of education have a more dangerous side than we may consider: they breed fascist ideologies.

After WWII, social scientists sought to understand why some people would adopt fascist ideologies. The traits they labelled as comprising an authoritarian mindset include an extreme conservative ideology; dominance of inferiors and submission to superiors; stereotyping other groups; cynicism;

'projectivity' (seeing your negative characteristics in others but not in yourself); and valuing power and toughness whilst rejecting 'intraception' (humanistic, psychological soft-heartedness). Psychologist Bill Gabrenya says that "one of the most consistent and troublesome findings in the thousands of studies of this construct has been the social class difference: working class people consistently score higher on authoritarianism".[274] Authoritarian tendencies also correlate to racial prejudice and homophobia. These tendencies are visibly borne out when societal tensions and inequalities are high – in 2012, for example, right wing Greek party Golden Dawn saw the greatest surge in support from people with the lowest levels of education; the support in this group doubled over a five month period as the austerity crisis deepened.

Northern Irish academic Paul Connolly has established that the process of developing our attitudes to other people and groups starts at a very young age, under the influence of the family, community and culture that surrounds us. "By the age of three, children from [Irish] Catholic communities were already twice as likely to be hostile to a police force... as Protestant children; by six, a third of children strongly identified with their community, while a significant minority were already making sectarian statements".[275] Daniel Bar-Tal of Tel Aviv University found similar attitudes developing amongst young Israeli children toward Arabs.[276] Peter Beaumont explains that in situations such as Nazi Germany, Rwanda, Syria and Serbia, people seemingly have little compunction about killing "because they have persuaded themselves that their victims' humanity is of lesser value than their own.... when conflict comes, it imposes its own explicit values – a 'conflict culture' that values in-group cohesion and out-group hostility, which not only plays on these existing tensions, (from negative stereotyping to the dehumanisation of the other), but actually ascribes to them a positive value".[277] Those attitudes which view other humans as so very different to - and worse than - us, which make us less critical of orders from above no matter how immoral, and which value force over mercy, are found more frequently in less educated people.

Amongst their own cultural group, however, people from lower-class backgrounds are better at reading other people's emotions, more likely to act altruistically, and more likely to help someone who is suffering. "They give more and help more" according to Dacher Keltner of the University of California-Berkeley. "When poor people see someone else suffering, they have a physiological response that is missing in people with more resources... there's all this strength to the lower class identity: greater empathy, more altruism, and finer attunement to other people".[278] These are the very attributes that are dismissed by a competitive, individualistic school system. The best of human values are confined to groups which have the least direct influence on government, and who are the most likely to follow authoritarian, closed rank ideologies. We need a system that educates all social classes to the extent that such fascist ideologies no longer flourish; but we also need a system which protects and values the empathy and altruism which lends such a sense of community, solidarity and humanity to the working class.

Unschooling is a valuable safeguard against fascism, allowing working class children to achieve comparably with their middle and upper class counterparts, resulting in higher levels of critical thinking than traditional schooling, whilst retaining the cultural values of their class by existing outside of the damaging school culture. Unschooled children are also more aware of what it is like to exist at the margins of the dominant culture, as well as being frequently judged by those unfamiliar with the concept; it is conceivable that these children may have increased sympathy with other minority groups.

We know from studies (and anecdotally if we read the news), that having significantly more wealth and resources than the majority correlates with a propensity for lying, cheating, stealing and breaking laws.[279] We agree as a society that we do not want people to behave like this, and legislate for it accordingly - people who behave like this are (theoretically) punished. We even do our best to create an environment where people are not pushed to behave like this, funding studies, education, and interventions for the poorest of society who are disproportionately likely to be imprisoned. But just as we do our best to prevent the poorest sectors of society being drawn into crime, why are we not taking equal steps to constrain those who, according to the evidence, are in fact more likely to behave unsociably, and with less excuse (i.e. they are not struggling to survive)? It has been calculated, for example, that one third of the cost of education in the private sector is recouped through tax avoidance.[280] The healthiest way for all of society to be safe from the abuse of power disparities is to prevent anyone having excessively more wealth than others. Is this unfair to the well off? No more than it is unfair to anyone to prevent them behaving in an unsociable manner for the benefit of others. We agree as a society that it is in the interests of all of us to help the poorest, whether out of compassion, or to protect our own interests in reducing the likelihood of crime. Why would we not agree that it is in the interests of all of us to prevent others amassing a level of wealth that invites immoral and illegal behaviour, and impacts and impoverishes the rest of society, especially when that wealth protects them from justice? That accumulating unending amounts of wealth is anything other than a good thing, is never questioned by a system which trains us from the day we enter school to climb the ladder of qualifications that leads to as much wealth as we can muster.

A World Beyond Class

All the elements discussed benefit middle class students in a competitive environment, where there is a limit on the amount of children who can succeed in academic terms. But what of children educated outside the traditional school environment?

Incredible as it seems, in light of all that has just been written, social class simply does not appear to be a factor in the achievements of children who are educated outside the school system. Dr. Brian Ray states that "Homeschool students score above average on achievement tests regardless of their parents level of formal education"; "Homeschool students score above average on achievement tests regardless of their family's household income"; and "Whether homeschool parents were ever certified teachers is not related to their [children's] academic achievement".[281] Paula Rothermel from the University of Durham has conducted several studies on home educated children; her results confirmed that neither social class, religion, parental level of education or having qualified teachers as parents were indicators of the children's attainment. Even gender differences were minimised, and while girls still outperformed boys, the difference was not statistically significant in contrast to UK samples in general. Home educated children outscored their schooled counterparts on standardised tests, and those from lower socio-economic groups actually outperformed their middle class peers. None of these findings could be predicted from studies based on schooled children, and strongly suggest that it is something in the nature of schools which causes class differences to impact educational achievement so strikingly. Rothermel concluded that given findings "contradict the many studies linking social class to low attainment... policy makers might do well to study the home-education model and explore ways in which the benefits could be adapted into mainstream education".[282]

There are many differences between home and school which may contribute to the comparative success of home educated children. There is no immediate clash of cultural values between child, parent and environment in an unschooling situation, and children are not routinely pitted against their peers from a young age. As published in the *Journal of Early Childhood Research*, Paula Rothermel found "The most obvious reason for their doing well, and one that is supported by evidence from other sources, is that home-educated children are, at least amongst their own ranks, free from the stigma of being poor, simply because they are not learning in an environment where affluence and labelling are an issue".[283] This is backed up research from Goldthorpe, Galloway, and Tizard and Hughes amongst others.[284] Clearly, the competitive nature of schools - whether formally via examinations and suchlike, or informally via peer pressure and social expectations - is detrimental to the very children they are meant to be helping.

CHAPTER 8

Herding Humanity

Squinting all the while in the glare of a culture that
radiates ultraviolet consumerism and infrared
celebrity. That daily, hourly, incessantly enforces the
egregious, deceitful message that you are what you
wear, what you drive, what you watch and what you
watch it on, in livid, neon pixels. The only light in
their lives comes from these luminous corporate
messages. No wonder they have their fucking
hoods up.

—RUSSELL BRAND [285]

AN EMPHASIS ON INDIVIDUAL achievement at the cost of
all else is destroying society, and placing soul-destroying levels of pressure on children. The competitive nature of
schools is ingrained in the system, from streaming to exams,
comparing children to their peers based on having been born
within a given twelve-month period in a small geographical
area - with no regard for unique aptitudes, abilities or individual background. Instead of focusing on the value of mistakes, learning to teach themselves, and helping each other

find their niche, children are forced to compete for grades, university places, jobs and social prestige. Open-ended debate and enquiry are stifled for an obsession with right and wrong answers, memorising facts, and ticking boxes.

In the 2010 documentary *Schooling The World*, the people of Ladakh describe that "With modern schooling, the old values of co-operation and compassion are starting to decline".[286] Children are raised to aspire to being doctors or engineers, with the emphasis being on material success. In all too familiar a way, education, for them, has come to equate to making money. The feelings of the Ladakhi people are reflected in our own society's complaints. Clinical psychologist Linda Blair writes of the problem with our results-driven society, "Our current education system totally reinforces this unhappy attitude, focusing as it does entirely on results rather than on the joy of learning. And it's no different when we start work. 'How much do you earn?' 'When's your next promotion?'" [287]

Not only does grading define our place in the educational and economic hierarchy, but it also affects how we relate to and judge each other, as well as – perhaps most damagingly of all – our own self image. Non-academic traits are at best unequally valued, or more often entirely ignored. Whilst close friends may appreciate the myriad aspects of our abilities and personalities, without a way to measure and assign economic value to all of our abilities, they are often not even valued within our own families. Economic historian Jerry Muller coined the term 'metric fixation' to describe the pervasive belief in test-based metrics across society:

> *Companies, government agencies, educational institutions and philanthropic organisations are today in the grip of a*

> *new phenomenon.... The key components of metric fixation are the belief that it is possible – and desirable – to replace professional judgment (acquired through personal experience and talent) with numerical indicators of comparative performance based upon standardised data (metrics); and that the best way to motivate people within these organisations is by attaching rewards and penalties to their measured performance... At the same time, rewarding individuals for measured performance diminishes a sense of common purpose, as well as the social relationships that motivate co-operation and effectiveness. Instead, such rewards promote competition.*[288]

Competing with your peers is counter-cohesive in many areas. It has been demonstrated that equality leads to friendship, whilst competition leads to disunity, so competition both in school and the wider society will inevitably cause rifts and separation. The motivation to excel in school is always going to benefit a certain cultural niche over others, and especially in strongly bonded communities, school children are being expected to behave counter to their cultural norms.

Not only are we becoming alienated from each other, but as Gregory Cajete argues, the construction of society in the West has lead to a crisis of identity: "Those who identify most with the 'bottom line' more often than not suffer from image without substance, technique without soul, and knowledge without context: the cumulative psychological results of which are usually unabridged alienation, loss of community, and a deep sense of incompleteness".[289] Author and journalist David Brooks believes that to counter this alienation, we must turn to selflessness as a path to truer success:

> *You could say there are two kinds of virtues in the world: résumé virtues and eulogy virtues. The résumé virtues are*

the ones you list on your CV, the skills that contribute to external success. The eulogy virtues are deeper. They're what get talked about at your funeral and they are usually the virtues that exist at the core of your being – whether you are kind, brave, honest or faithful; what kind of relationships you formed over your lifetime. We live in a culture that encourages us to think about how to be wealthy and successful, but which leaves many of us inarticulate about how to cultivate the deepest inner life.[290]

The irony for humanity of course, is that competition is less effective than altruism. Maslow's hierarchy of needs, describing those things that humans need to survive and flourish, starts with the basics of life itself – food, water, shelter – building up through security and love, to fulfilling our unique potential. But Maslow's hierarchy itself comes under fire for the reasons above – there is an innate ethnocentrism in self-actualisation being the peak of achievement for human beings. Whilst this may be true for an individualistic society such as those found in the West, collectivist societies place far higher value on acceptance and community than on freedom or individuality (and judging by the soaring rates of mental health disorders, loneliness and isolation in Western society, they have a point).

There is a strong argument to be made for the benefits of competition, as well as our innate propensity to compete against one another. The difference between healthy competition and the kind of competition we experience in school, however, is choosing when to compete. It is a necessary part of a successful life to feel the need to push ourselves, to set targets to aim for, to use competition to hone our skills and prove to ourselves we are progressing - but we need to freely choose in which areas to compete according to our own needs, interests, and readiness. We need to know that regardless of the outcome, competing will be of benefit to us in some way. Then we can enter into the challenge willing, motivated, and getting the most out of it. But feeling we are endlessly competing in every area of our life, against every member of our peer group, is draining, pointless, a losing battle, and a recipe for the depression, anxiety, and addiction we see manifest across society today.

Not only are children competing in every subject area during their school hours (with all the pressure of knowing that this will very likely dictate their place in adult society), but they are trying to find their place in the social hierarchy too. England's Children's Commissioner Anne Longfield carried out a study of the effects of social media on school children, finding that many eight to twelve year olds were anxious about their identity, craving likes and comments for validation, and crucially, finding it hard to manage the pressure.[291] Do we really think this problem does not exist within schools anyway? Social media may have brought it to the surface in a far more tangible way than we have previously seen, but when children exist within a system that demands their every intellectual, sporting or artistic effort be judged, is it any wonder that those who do not feel successful will turn to areas in which they can potentially regain some sense of self worth? We have trained our children to seek external validation from authority figures (whether adults or peers); trained them to judge their worth by the number of points they score – how is this different to judging their worth by the number of likes or comments they receive from their peers? And given the nature of schools, we have placed the peer group in a position of ultimate social status. Social media has simply made overt what has been happening for years anyway.

Separation

Dr. Gabor Maté has spoken about the rise in bullying, ADHD and other mental disorders in American children, which he believes are the result of our disconnected society and the loss of nurturing, non-stressed parenting. We live in a society where for the first time in history, children are spending most of their time away from nurturing adults. Maté asserts that nurturing adults are necessary for healthy brain development. He says, "the essential condition for the physiological development of these brain circuits that regulate human behaviour, that give us empathy, that give us a social sense; that give us connection with other people, that give us connection with ourselves, that allows us to mature; the essential condition for those circuits, for their physiological development, is the presence of emotionally available, consistently available, non-stressed, attuned, parenting caregivers".[292] In this respect, it is obvious that home education is superior to a class of up to thirty (or more) children, sharing the attention of one teacher and perhaps a couple of class room assistants, who change every lesson if not every year, and who cannot possibly give every child the attention and nurturing that a parent would, no matter how dedicated the teacher may be.

A study by Notre Dame University found that the conditions of child development that our hunter-gatherer ancestors provided are no longer present for our children, "depriving them of the practices that lead to well being and a moral sense".[293] For most of human history, children have been nurtured and raised by a small, consistent group of adults. To remove children from their home environment and family, for the best part of the day during their formative years, is bound to have significant repercussions. Today's children are more heavily influenced in their social development and behaviour by peers than parents. Not only does this mean emotional maturity is regressed, but we are increasingly having to replace dopamine in the brain chemically, because it is missing due to lack of nurturance. Infant monkeys separated from their mothers lost dopamine in 2 - 3 days, while mice lacking dopamine lose the will to eat and live. We are simply not designed to be separated at a young age from those we are bonded to.[294]

Maté also explains that in order for a child to feel curiosity about the world, to be vulnerable enough to try things and to feel confident to make mistakes, we must have a secure attachment to a caretaker. Schools are not providing this environment; peer pressure and bullying create exactly the opposite environment. Maté even advocates playdates for younger children be in the company or presence of parents, not separate from the family. Interestingly, this is very common amongst home educated families, where it is the norm for families to meet and spend time together as an extended group. This seems to threaten some people, who view a strong, secure family unit as lacking individual freedom and independence, despite all evidence showing that consistent, reliable, responsive caregiving in the early years produces a more mature, independent, emotionally stable adult.[295]

The separation of the family unit by school and work is reflected in the school curriculum itself. Kozol believes that splitting the day into periods and subjects means we live our entire lives only dealing with, and relating to, things that are in our immediate presence, feeling no responsibility once we move away in time and space.[296] In school, reality is presented as a series of discrete events and specialised courses which are rarely connected together. Likewise, the news is presented as if no act is connected in any way to another. We are not taught to see the connections between various political/economic events and their human cost. Narratives of straightforward economic exploitation are ruled out. Tolstoy wrote of the necessary hypocrisy that allows us to live our lives, and "the way we train ourselves not to believe in causative connections, not to believe that our advancement rests on the soil of someone else's deprivation", although "it would seem impossible to deny that which is so obvious".[297] By discussing everything in a third person, factual, and unemotive manner, schools promote the idea that we are free to choose whether to be involved in another's desperation and poverty, and the myth that we are not already complicit in our affect on the entire world through our actions or inactions.

With unschooling, there is no separation between work and play, learning and life, teachers and friends; lives are not compartmentalised. There is not a time to switch off and a time to switch on. Education is life, a continuous conversation which has no timetable and no end point. An awareness of others' suffering has no door to close, but can be triggered at any time, rather than being something which is taught and the lesson ended. Lives are not separated into classroom, office, and home. Many unschooling families work from home, so this artificial line - where work does not affect family life - is removed. There is not such a distance between actions and consequences, and there is, in the refusal to live in the mainstream, a deeper awareness of issues relating to all aspects of life. Without the peer pressure to have the latest clothes or gadgets, it is easier to explain why we are not willing to partake in the exploitation of others, and easier for our children to accept.

Schools often recoil from the idea of dealing with emotions at all. Kozol belived that "Most great fiction, almost all important verse, are written [about] one of three essential truths: love, death or pain. None of these three is ever consciously conveyed within the public schools".[298] This is not entirely true, but we are certainly taught to discuss those emotions in a mature academic style that is cold, intellectual, and objective, and that this is superior to an emotional response. The preferred style is to use 'one' instead of 'I', and a conditional syntax - 'as if' rather than 'it is'. Kozol believes that without true knowledge of suffering, death or human love, a child cannot possibly develop or maintain a sense of injustice or outrage.[299] Within the family, the everyday experience of death, love, and suffering are part of life which does not have to be submerged in order to attend work or school; they are not something we feel the need to separate into a compartment, but can be dealt with and experienced fully and in depth as we have the time and support. A family which is close discusses these things without hesitation, and thus becomes closer again. Home educated children are often noted to be more emotionally mature; this may be in large part to tackling those emotional aspects of life which school relegates to childish distractions, pranks and gossip rather than central motivators for life. By removing the discussion of such topics in school, we have no way to relate our emotions to world events. This is not the case in the home, where emotional responses to something are often the prime consideration in discussion of literature or news.

Author and journalist Dan Hind says "We urgently need a public culture in which we are able to discuss imperialism, the economy, and the environment in ways that connect meaningfully with the facts. The existing arrangements seem designed expressly to prevent the emergence of such a public culture".[300] An unschooling environment does much to express this at the grassroots level, with the time and flexibility to respond to anything that comes up in discussion, and to follow it to its conclusion, however disruptive to the status quo that may be. School, in contrast, presents life as a path of inevitable progression for all people. There is no natural rise and fall shown, or discussion of those that are left behind. Kozol writes, "Each subsequent age is studied, not for anguish, passion or for moral evolution, but for 'Major Contributions'".[301] We are given the impression that human transformations are inevitable and do not call for our participation - in great contrast to Venezuela for example, where under President Chavez, everyone knew that it was up to them to make the revolution work. In our schools, we are given the impression that the big decisions, those that count, will happen regardless, without our input. When we see poverty, we think it will improve somehow, sometime... if we just wait, someone will do something because it is inevitable. It is a myth of progress without danger or pain or sacrifice. We are not taught that we need to make it happen, or that maybe it just won't get better. Often, conditions have gotten worse. "That we do live with it, and do so moreover with a fair amount of ease and skill, and even with a certain amount of self-congratulation on the reasonable nature of our response, is just one index of the real success of mass indoctrination in this land", writes Kozol.[302]

Grading

The stratification of society, whether locally or globally, is reflected in the microcosm of schools. An OECD study published in 2012 listed the UK as continuing to have one of the most segregated school systems in the world. Children from poorer or less educated families tend to go to the same schools, and as the study points out, the educational and economic profile of students' families "exerts a strong influence on the likely outcomes for pupils".[303] This despite a 68% rise in the amount spent on individual pupils in the previous decade - clearly spending does not equate to equality.

This stratification is compounded by the ubiquitous grading of students. Grading compounds differences in social class. This is especially noticeable when using grading on a bell curve, as many schools and universities still do. This is when the grades are distributed on a curve, with the average score becoming the average grade (typically a B- or C+); scores above and below the average are distributed accordingly, with percentages of students being pushed into highest and lowest categories simply to fill out the curve. Students are thus assessed relative to their peers, which makes their grades meaningful only within that particular class - one year's class of particularly good students will demonstrate the same spread of grades as another year's class of struggling students. When those two groups come to compete for jobs or university degrees however, they are judged comparably by their grades, even though one student's A (achieved in a class with poor exam performance overall) may be the equivalent in learning and ability of another student's C (achieved in a class where the standard was much higher, but only a limited number of A grades were allocated). Regulators try to ensure a parity of grades year upon year, but this compounds the problem, not allowing for some year groups to be better or worse on average than others.

Most importantly, grading has very negative affects on a student's sense of self. In his book *Making the Grade*, Martin V. Covington writes "When conditions of scarcity [of A and B grades] prevail, failure is more likely to be interpreted [by students] as a matter of personal inadequacy, whereas success was often seen as the result of chance or good fortune... Failure created self-loathing, especially in those students who were high in self-perceived ability. This suggests that under competitive goals, individuals are likely only to continue striving only for as long as they remain successful. No one wants to continue if the result is shame and self-recrimination".[304] Another academic, Adam Grant, writes in the *New York Times* that "The more important argument against grade curves is that they create an atmosphere that's toxic by pitting students against one another. At best, it creates a hyper-competitive culture, and at worst, it sends students the message that the world is a zero-sum game: Your success means my failure".[305]

There is also manipulation of grades (via curbing grade inflation) for economic and political reasons. Just as greater success rates raise students' expectations of what they can expect to achieve in life, so lower rates depress expectations. If young people fail their exams, they may then blame a lack of opportunity on their own lack of ability, rather than on politicians' misguided economic policies. In this way, students' success and self esteem is dictated by the economic needs of government and business. The main effect of increasing access to A-levels and degrees is not, as originally intended, to ensure that elite jobs are open to talent from all backgrounds. On the contrary, longer periods of education and extended hurdles of certification favour the offspring of advantaged families, with their greater financial resources, greater reserves of cultural capital and greater access to elite institutions. By paying private school fees (or higher prices for houses close to favoured state schools) and supporting postgraduate study, today's middle classes buy prestigious jobs for their children just as elite families once bought army commissions and civil service positions.[306]

Standardised testing is becoming introduced at increasingly younger ages in our schools, leading to children as young as five being sent for extra academic coaching. In the United States, policies such as 'No Child Left Behind' and 'Race to the Top' have proved extremely controversial. Bruce E. Levine writes in *8 Reasons Young Americans Don't Fight Back*:

> *These policies are essentially standardized-testing tyranny that creates fear, which is antithetical to education for a democratic society. Fear forces students and teachers to constantly focus on the demands of test creators; it crushes curiosity, critical thinking, questioning authority, and challenging and resisting illegitimate authority. In a more democratic and less authoritarian society, one would evaluate the effectiveness of a teacher not by corporatocracy-sanctioned standardized tests but by asking students, parents, and a community if a teacher is inspiring students to be more curious, to read more, to learn independently, to enjoy thinking critically, to question authorities, and to challenge illegitimate authority.[307]*

This is exactly how unschooling ideally works, as described for example by Thomas Jefferson Leadership Education, who believe that if a child is not motivated to learn, it is directly due to a lack of inspiration and motivation in their immediate environment. The parent's job is to be inspirational, to be a role model and to provide visible motivation as to the joys and rewards of study and effort (in whatever area is relevant to that particular family and child). In comparison to this ideal, grading harms the relationship between teacher and student by turning their relationship into an authoritarian and judgmental one.

Author and educator Alfie Kohn reports the findings of educational psychologists, who studied the effects of grading on students from elementary to college age. They came to three conclusions: grading tends to diminish students' interest in whatever they're learning (grading and learning have been shown to be inversely related); grading creates a preference for the easiest possible task (the logical thing to do – put in the least work on the topic you know best rather than risking innovation or experimentation); and grading tends to reduce the quality of students' thinking (the focus is turned to picking out those elements that will be on the test and memorising them, rather than questioning, researching and theorising).[308] On these three elements alone, it is clear that an unschooling environment, free from exams and grades, is far more motivating and conducive to a student actually wanting to learn, than a school environment.

Free to Fail

Rousseau wrote that the child must be guided to suffer from the experience of the natural consequences of his own acts or behaviour. When he experiences the consequences of his own acts, he advises himself. This amounts to the freedom to fail, and to learn from our mistakes and experiences. Creativity comes from experimentation; experimentation comes from freedom to fail. In contrast, publicly ranking students within groups denies their right to privacy, to learn at their own pace, and to make mistakes from which they can learn without fear of ridicule or judgment. The psychological manipulation of grading means our children endure a process that reduces their ability to form judgments and to value themselves and others. Schooling must not harm any child in the long run, in order that each may grow and contribute to the world. Jerry Muller writes:

The source of the trouble is that when people are judged by performance metrics they are incentivised to do what the metrics measure, and what the metrics measure will be some established goal. But that impedes innovation, which means doing something not yet established, indeed that hasn't even been tried out. Innovation involves experimentation. And experimentation includes the possibility, perhaps probability, of failure... Mental stimulation is dulled when people don't decide the problems to be solved or how to solve them, and there is no excitement of venturing into the unknown because the unknown is beyond the measurable. The entrepreneurial element of human nature is stifled by metric fixation.[309]

Failure is an important experience and students need chances to try things that may not work, without penalties. In the best classrooms, grades are only one of many types of feedback provided to students. Music teachers and athletic coaches routinely provide abundant feedback to students and only occasionally associate a grade with the feedback. Teachers in visual arts, drafting, culinary arts, or computer programming allow students to create a portfolio to show their best work, knowing that the mistakes made in the course of the semester were not failures, but lessons learned on the way to success. In each of these cases, 'failures' along the way are not averaged into a calculation of the final grade.

Write Your Own Curricula

Unschooling is a much-needed antidote to the disintegration of society, at the forefront of rebuilding our communities and social structures. Learning and passion is valued over grades, and a loving, nurturing home life lays the foundations for healthy relationships in the future, at all levels of society. Far from being isolationist, unschooling is a group effort - between the family, the neighbourhood, wider learning networks and online support. Streets semi-deserted during the day are revitalised with home-based families of all ages, making use of community resources, classes and clubs, and setting up learning cooperatives. It is a communal effort in all ways.

Educator and author Michael Horn writes, "In 1900 only 17 percent of all jobs required knowledge workers, whereas more than 60 percent do today. We now ask more students to master more challenging subject matter and develop more specialized skills. In the knowledge economy, people need to be more flexible on the one hand, while on the other they benefit from cultivating their individual talents and interests. Factory-style education falls short, therefore, as it is an ineffective way for most children to learn and to maximize their potential".[310] This is simply not possible within a structured, pre-conceived curricula, which takes years to design, write, and implement. In contrast, unschooling is flexible, adaptable to the moment, and personally tailored at all stages.

Once we step outside of subjects as discrete entities, any given topic can stretch as far as our imaginations and curiosity can. One simple question can cover many 'separate' subjects, integrating them, placing them all in a unified context, opening up links and causalities that would be lost when restrained by the official 'topic at hand'. Education in a home environment becomes a conversation. Whilst school expects questions and answers to flow immediately or to be lost forever, unschoolers experience a very different temporal style, where subjects interconnect, tangents and random situations combine and re-form over nights, weeks, and months, with no boundaries. It is a continuing conversation which is not limited and delineated by bells. The line between teacher and student is blurred, as both learn and explore a given topic. And this is as it should be - in many languages 'to teach' and 'to learn' is the same word, and it is to our detriment that these languages have often been replaced by English in the education system, along with the nuances of the relationship between teacher and student.

This also reflects the atmosphere that worked best for us for most of our evolutionary history. "Intellectual development occurs best in a setting where people can share ideas freely, without censorship or fear of being ostracized. According to anthropologists' reports, hunter-gatherers were non-dogmatic in their beliefs, even in their religious beliefs. People could say what they please, without fear, and ideas that had any consequence to the group were debated endlessly... In this kind of environment, an idea is something to think about and debate, not something to memorize and feed back on a test" writes Gray.[311]

False Authority

But of course there is a vested interest in the idea of promoting constraints to dialogue, and maintaining authority on a given topic. As David Graeber[312] and many others point out, any authority must always be examined critically to justify its legitimacy; but our society is oriented generally around the perpetuation of expertise and power, rather than working form the basis that all power should be working towards its own demise, in order that all take responsibility for themselves. This self-subverting authority is a type of authority which undermines its own basis, e.g. the teacher who willingly teaches everything they know, making them no more powerful than their students; the patient who is cured by the doctor and no longer has need of the doctor's authority over them. But when we are invested in maintaining our power, it makes us reluctant to share our knowledge for fear of losing our superior status. Noam Chomsky believes,

> *People who are really sincere about the belief that a better world is possible will refuse to take power. In fact, they will try to undermine institutions that even grant power. Maybe to some extent, certain kinds of authority are required to delegate responsibility and that sort of thing, but one who is really interested in a decent world would want to reduce that to the absolute minimum, in fact to constantly be challenging authoritarian relationships and institutions and require them to justify themselves. Sometimes they can be justified, but the burden of justification is always on authority and domination. It is never legitimate in itself. That's true even if it's a family or an international society.*[313]

Unschooling is very different to school in this respect. While the power structure of a classroom is clearly delineated, in the unschooled home, parental authority tends to be exerted as little as is necessary. Education, when child-led, naturally places the child in charge of their learning, with the adult in a supportive, mentoring role. The parent will of course be the authority in the capacity of protector, provider and moral guide, but it is a noticeable tendency in unschooling families that there is a level of democracy and compromise between parents and children that is more self conscious and deliberate than is generally found in the population. The trust in the child that is founded upon seeing how well they learn and grow when given free reign, translates to a trust in their ability to make balanced, sensible and responsible decisions in other areas of their life. The home is often a democracy in as many ways as possible, and compromise a fact of life. The effects of decisions as to what to study, where to visit, or whose turn it is to do something around the house, are immediate and tangible in a way that the illusory choices of school are not.

This level of personal responsibility is in stark contrast to the children in school who are not even allowed to chose their own clothing or attend to their bodily needs without permission. Uniforms and schedules may be justified within the military or prison system, but they have no place in an environment of growth, creativity and learning. Whilst the ostensible excuse for school uniforms is to hide social differences and reduce the distractions of social preening, in reality of course it has the has opposite effect of students trying to find gaps in the rules to express their individuality - not always in healthy ways, as they are pushed to extremes in an attempt to differentiate themselves within the confines of strict regulations.

Uniforms cohere us into one recognisable brand, a symbol of the reach of the owner (whether it be military, penal, governmental or corporate) and do very little indeed to hide economic differences from the pupils. Your body no longer belongs to you when authority can punish you for your hair style, jewellery or piercings (it remains to be explained to me how any of these non-permanent things affect a child's ability to learn, rather than affecting their willingness to conform to arbitrary and evolving rules). Even the prison system came to the conclusion - decades ago - that uniforms are counter-productive: "By the late 19th century, itchy, woollen uniforms with broad arrows (to show they were the possession of the Crown) were used throughout the country, and on convicts sent to Australia to work in chain gangs. But by 1971 women's uniforms had been abolished in UK prisons because research showed inmates responded better to rules if they were allowed to wear their own clothes. Men's prison uniforms followed in 1991".[314] To quote Clark Aldrich, "Monocultures seldom work in nature".[315]

The Lie of Genius

Another way that authority is used to control us is the idea that only certain great minds have the answers, and that those who discover new answers have done so in a vacuum and due to some inherent genius that is not available to the average person. David Graeber gives an example: "Foucault's ideas, like Trotsky's, are never treated as primarily the products of a certain intellectual milieu, as something that emerged from endless conversations and arguments involving hundreds of people, but always, as if they emerged from the genius of a single man (or, very occasionally, woman)".[316] None of us exist in isolation from our environment, nor from all those who have come before. It would be far more inspiring and instructive rather, to emphasise the years of practice, mistakes, failures, apprenticeships and mentors, conversations, study and soul-searching that it took to make great leaps in our development. Linda Blair suggests that,

> *Most of the information we receive is obtained remotely, and when we receive information in this way, we inevitably receive only a small part of the total picture. So, for example, when we watch the Olympics, we see the race, but not the months and years of training that went into preparing for that race. When we watch a film, we see only the successful shots, not the hundreds of takes and retakes. Yet there's so much more to life than just the finished products. To maintain a realistic view of what success involves, we need to meet up more regularly with people we love and trust, and share experiences honestly – the successes, sure – but also, and more importantly, the failures, for these create the foundation for success.*[317]

The real lesson is that advancement in any arena takes effort and dedication. A random selection of examples may emphasise this point:

Mozart, Composer: *"People make a mistake who think that my art has come easily to me. Nobody has devoted so much time and thought to composition as I. There is not a famous master whose work I have not studied over and over".*[318]

David Almond, Writer: *"People say to me, you're so prolific, and I think, now I am! It's the payoff for all the time I spent getting sentences to work properly. Like anything, you develop a skill through hard work".*[319]

Judy Chicago, Artist: *"The difference between me and other artists is that I acknowledge the people who work with me. Henry Moore had hundreds of 'assistants'. But they were really collaborators. They brought their skills and knowledge, but when he was interviewed, he made them leave while he jumped in front of the best sculpture in the room. It's a whole unexamined area of the art world, this hidden collaboration".*[320]

Grant Cardone, Entrepreneur: *"The most successful CEOs are reported to read an average of 60 books and attend more than six conferences a year—whereas the average American worker reads an average of less than one book and makes 319 times less* *income... [the media] frequently fail to cover the amount of time and energy the wealthy have committed to reading, studying, and educating themselves".*[321]

Examples of great genius abound through history, but far too often, recounting of their achievements neglect to tell us of the years and years of practise, of their assistants (who often did much of the work), and their apprentices – these great people were mentors too, just as they had their own mentors. It serves authority to teach that geniuses are rare and self created. Professor Mark Brake demonstrates that the problem is not confined to the arts:

> *This brief portrait [of a Great Men history of physics], in which three hundred years of physics is reduced to the distilled essence of the work of just four men, highlights a problem. Communicators of science should be sceptical of the conventional view of the advancement of science... The view fails to consider two essential elements... The first is long periods of investigations, which rely upon a gradual advance of tradition and custom. This first element is the fruit of many ordinary thinkers and workers. The second element is the revolutionary tipping points. In spite of all gradualness, an innovatory leap leads to decisive change. This element is usually associated with the 'great men of science'. The 'great men' myth has led to a false idea of science, one which suggests that progress in science is due solely to the genius of great men, irrespective of factors such as culture, society and economy... No effective discovery can be made in any field without the necessary groundwork of thousands of relatively minor workers. It is on the basis of this painstaking work that great 'men' make crucial discoveries.*[322]

Denaturing Heroes

Rather than emphasising the potential for greatness that comes with dedication and passion, schools revise history and decontaminate heroes and heroines. The 'subversive' nature of prominent figures as diverse as St. Francis of Assisi, Helen Keller or Martin Luther King Jr. are neutralised by well-meaning teachers. We are taught that they should command our respect and admiration, but live beyond our dreams, where we can never hope to imitate them. Kozol highlights schools' "quite remarkable success... in getting across the message of inherent impotence to earnest children".[323] Peter Van Greenaway satirises this habit of the establishment in his book *The Man Who Held the Queen to Ransom and Sent Parliament Packing*, where a government minister explains to his inferior how the unfolding coup must read in the press: "I know as well as you do that these men aren't a pack of ignoramuses... but by the time I've done with him and the rest of them, the fiction will read that they could be nothing else. We must establish that one man only had the brains, energy, drive and capacity, was solely responsible in the long run. If not, what happens? Every Tom, Dick or Harry will consider himself a potential thinking machine able and willing to follow in Wyatt's footsteps".[324]

It suits authority to martyr the one, rather than emphasise the team who worked together. One impressive man is a lot harder to replicate for a youth than the thought that if a group of us worked together we could do something equally impactful. Cultural gatekeepers idealise the one, at the cost of the many, to keep the masses in place. School, far from being a bastion of cooperation, is where the cult of the individual begins, where we are pitted against our peers and elders. The internet is changing this - it is undermining the cult of the individual, and demonstrating the power of working together. And it is creating change, because people have the chance to be powerful as a unified group.

But of course discussions about the true context of a hero's life brings up uncomfortable truths. We enter other countries to bring 'new methods,' 'modern technology' or financial aid, never to make money, operate a missile base, put down social revolution or impose modern technology and schooling. We are only taught to abhor certain types of violence – those deliberate acts of terror and revenge. Those deaths that abound in society due to poverty, neglect or corruption are ignored. Schools cannot touch this, as they have to maintain 'objectivity' and 'academic neutrality'. Unschoolers however, do not have a school board looking over our shoulder telling us that we must be unbiased, neutral, apolitical. In the postmodern academic milieu, truth is considered a matter of opinion; children are consequently taught someone else's opinion as truth. They are taught it in such a way that rarely do they have any desire to dig deeper and find out other truths about an event. And when do they have the time to do this anyway, in any real depth, when their days are heavily scheduled for them? When do any of us?

Of course the compressing of a person's life, or of a historical event, down to a select list of attributes is to some extent necessary when communicating an overview; complex ideas must initially be simplified. And simplification by necessity must use comparisons and shortcuts which can be misleading. The assumption tends to be though that when graduating to a more in depth study of any topic, these shortcuts and simplifications will be ironed out and corrected. But this raises two problems: who is doing the compressing? Whoever compresses the information has the ability to select what matters and doesn't matter, to simplify as they see fit and to create the version of the truth that they wish to use. This is what schools do with history and other subjects, often making them so tedious and lifeless along the way that many never look any further into it to find the truth. Secondly, the shortcuts and mistakes are often not corrected until a later stage of study, and if the student never reaches this stage, the mistakes are never corrected, thus leading to lifelong misunderstandings which make the student feel they are at fault rather than the teaching. How many students never take their studies of a subject further because they can't accept the false and compressed version of events, instinctively feeling that something is not right with it, though not knowing quite what?

Celebrity Distraction

It is perhaps innate to wish to leave our mark on the world, and this has driven people throughout history to work to this end. But the end result of our failure to examine what it takes to achieve greatness, in combination with the current media obsession with vacuous celebrity, means it is far easier for a child to try and make their mark through crass sensationalism than a deep and meaningful contribution. For philosopher Allan Bloom, the failure of contemporary liberal education leads to the sterile social habits of modern students, and to their inability to fashion a life for themselves beyond the mundane offerings touted as success. Bloom argues that commercial pursuits have become more highly valued than love, the philosophic quest for truth, or the civilised pursuits of honour and glory.[325] In a culture that reveres youth without substance, and adult celebrities behaving like teenagers, we desperately need adults who are willing to be adults, and a media which encourages our children to look to those great minds of today. Instead, we trap our children in a world of peers, and saturate their free time with endless footage of adults behaving like children. We expect children to integrate into adult society and take on responsibility, but surround them with a culture that is not mature itself. When our culture itself does not contribute to the larger society as a whole, what is there for our children to work within and towards? To quote Julian Assange: "When our media is corrupt, when our academics are timid, when our history is filled with half-truths and lies – our civilization will never be just. It will never reach to the sky... Our societies are intellectual shanty towns. Our beliefs about the world and each other have been created by the same system that has lied us into repeated wars that have killed millions... The quality of our discourse is the limit of our civilization".[326]

CHAPTER 9

The Socialisation Myth

Brian: Look, you've got it all wrong! You don't need
to follow me, You don't need to follow anybody!
You've got to think for your selves! You're all
individuals!

Crowd: Yes! We're all individuals!

—MONTY PYTHON'S LIFE OF BRIAN [327]

THE GREAT MYTH OF 'Socialisation' is well known to home educators. It is brought up, time and again, when they tell others that their children do not go to school. It is the last resort of the doubters, the fallback criticism when no other rational counter-argument is left. But what do people actually mean by 'socialised'? Many people mean "How will your children make friends?" However isolated the first home educators may have been (and it is highly unlikely they were isolated in the true sense of the word), today there are upwards of fifty thousand home educators in the UK alone, and the home education movement is flourishing. Between learning co-ops, a variety of home educating groups meeting every week, day trips, all day to play with friends uninterrupted by school bells; and with most museums, science centres etc. holding regular home educator days, not to mention those same extra-curricular classes and clubs that all school children have available, it is not unheard of for home educators to protest that they need to take a break from socialising to spend some time on projects or just have some quiet time. Moreover, why would a home educating parent themselves want to spend all day, every day, shut away from other parents, friends and sources of social support, any more than their children would? Yet this is the implication of the question.

All too often, however, the question means "How will they learn to behave like everyone else?" Socialisation, in this context, is a code word for submission, peer pressure, toeing the line, even obeying without question. At worst, it can lead to an undemocratic forcing of conformity on all members of society. Yet society is crying out for people who *don't* conform, who *are* critical, who *don't* accept the norms and peccadillos of our world without question. Home educating families and children have been found to be more independent minded, more critical, less susceptible to peer pressure, more open to unconventional views and more politically radical, according to research by Dr. Paula Rothermel and others.[328]

Dr. Larry E. Shyers compared homeschooled children with traditionally schooled children as part of his PhD thesis. He found no difference between the two groups in relation to self-esteem. Shyers also examined the behaviour of homeschooled children in relation to others. Using the Children's Assertive Behavior Scale, he found no significant difference between his study groups. However, "direct observation by trained observers using a 'blind' procedure, found that home-schooled children had significantly fewer problem behaviours, as measured by the Child Observation Checklist's Direct Observation Form, than traditionally schooled children when playing in mixed groups of children from both kinds of schooling backgrounds".[329] Shyers concluded that contact with adults, rather than other children, is the most important aspect of developing social skills. The study indicated that home-schooled children behave better because they tend to imitate their parents while conventionally schooled children model themselves after their peers. Shyers states, "The results seem to show that a child's social development depends more on adult contact and less on contact with other children as previously thought".[330]

For his master's degree research, Thomas Smedley conducted a similar experiment. He used the Vineland Adaptive Behavior Scales to evaluate the communication skills, socialisation, and daily living skills of home schooled children and schooled children. According to his results, the home-schooled children were more mature, scoring in the 84th percentile, while the public school children scored in the 27th percentile.[331] The forced socialisation of school is also coming under fire from psychologists, who emphasise the crucial nature of time for reflection, the benefits of solitude for creative development and mental health, and the higher success rate of introverts.

More often than not, unschooling is far more than a statement about schooling; it is a choice about how to live. Once freed from the rigidity of schooling, families are freed from so much else. Not only are their days freed up to rise, sleep, eat and organise as they choose, but they no longer live according to the need to compete against others in the overt and subtle ways that being part of the system promotes - whether it is academic competition between children, or consumerist status symbols. Whether the decision to home educate came easily or had to be won in the face of pressure from others, the strength of making a decision against the mainstream frees unschoolers to question many other accepted doctrines, and forge their own path in myriad ways besides schooling.

Times Have Changed

The world for previous generations of home educators was very different to today, where universities actively encourage applications from home educators*, where schools share after-school activities with local home education groups, and where there are enough of us in a given locality to start weekly learning co-ops. The unschooling movement is growing by the day. There are endless online forums, subscriber-groups, formal organisations and informal support networks. There are play dates, park meet-ups, beach days, wildlife walks, bush craft weekends, camping expeditions, computer clubs, music lessons, language classes, arts groups - you name it.

* The high achievement level of American homeschoolers is recognised by recruiters from some of the best universities, where homeschooled children graduate, and attain a 4 year degree, at much higher rates than their counterparts from both public and private schools. MIT, Harvard, Stanford, and Duke Universities all actively recruit homeschoolers.[332]

Add to this all the regular opportunities any child has available to them - their neighbours, local parks, scouts, music classes, sports clubs, dance lessons, extracurricular clubs of all sorts - and lack of opportunities to socialise really is not an issue. And yet we are still faced with same tired phrases about socialisation that have been picked up from the media, when often the questioner doesn't even fully understand what they are asking. The common perception of a family opting out of the school system, with all its attendant social aspects, only to be isolated in their home, has never been true, and certainly bears no semblance to reality these days. Again, why do so many people assume that any parent actually wants to spend all day, every day, shut up in a house never speaking to any one else in society? Parents need social contact too! The problem no doubt lies in great part in the 'home' part of 'home education', leading some people to adopt the terms 'unschoolers', 'world learners' or a variation on this theme. All we mean by home education is not school. This leaves an entire world as our classroom, and we would be hard pressed not to become 'socialised'.

Socialisation or Peer Pressure?

So what do we actually mean by 'socialised'? Able to talk to others with the correct manners and etiquette? Children should pick this up from their parents as they go about life, whether schooled or not. Able to make friends? Unschooled children are certainly not short of interests or the ability to play, and connect with people of all ages and genders. Able to sit still in a classroom and be talked at? Our children are quite aware and capable of taking part in classes, participating and waiting their turn to talk, just as any child who learns by witnessing the behaviour of others. In fact many teachers comment that the home educated children they meet are far better behaved than schooled children, more mature, more interested and motivated, and less prone to behaving like children who have just been let out of a classroom. Perhaps the term socialisation really means 'How will they learn to behave like school children?'

For developmental psychologist Dr. Gordon Neufeld, socialisation is more accurately defined as being able to get along with others, while at the same time being true to oneself. "You have to be separate enough so you can be with your equals without losing your distinctiveness". But the way we structure our society is detrimental to this. "Premature socialization," says Neufeld, "was always considered by developmentalists to be the greatest sin in raising children". He continues,

> *The chief and most damaging of the competing attachments that undermine parenting authority and parental love is the increasing bonding of our children with their peers... For the first time in history young people are turning for instruction, modelling and guidance not to mothers, fathers, teachers, and other responsible adults but to people whom nature never intended to place in a parenting role – their own peers... children are being brought up by immature persons who cannot possibly guide them to maturity. They are being brought up by each other.*[333]

When our children start school at an increasingly younger age, they spend so much time with their peers that their sense of self does not get a chance to develop, and they come to resemble each other rather, crushing their individuality rather than honing it. Neufeld and Maté explain, "Children cannot be oriented to both adults and other children simultaneously. One cannot follow two sets of conflicting directions at the same time. The child's brain must automatically choose between parental values and peer values, parental guidance and peer guidance, parental culture and peer culture whenever the two would appear to be in conflict".[334] Whilst this is a clear problem for indigenous or migrant children caught between the contrasting cultures of school and home, it is also a problem for children taught within their own culture, even if the nature of the problem is not so clearly defined.

To combat this, children need to form strong attachments to adults who will be present consistently. Children whose foremost teachers are other children are not learning how to express their individuality in a confident, secure, and humane way, but simply copying the behaviours of their equally immature and ignorant (as in the opposite of wise) peers. "No matter how well intentioned, skilled, or compassionate we may be, parenting is not something we can engage in with just any child... A child must be receptive if we are to succeed in nurturing, comforting, guiding and directing her"[335], says Neufeld. How many people can say they have this relationship with their teacher? And how many relationships of this nature can a teacher possibly maintain at once? It takes all of a parent's energy to maintain this properly with their own children, let alone a class full of very different personalities and individual needs, a class which changes every school year in most cases.

It is notable that so many unschoolers reject the notion of the stereotypical teenager with attitude, as they simply don't experience this for the most part. This is understandable when we appreciate the impact of a consistent, permanent caretaker from the child's first days through to adulthood. Psychologist John Bowlby developed the idea of parent-child attachment, emphasising that early attachment is necessary for healthy adult emotional development. As Andrea Mrozek puts it, "Our high priority attachment figures (aka the people we see the most of and really love) are intended to be enduring. These are not people who should disappear from our lives, neither are strong attachments something small children should 'grow out of'...The three-year-old who can't wait to be with his friends in daycare may in fact be on his way to becoming peer rather than parent attached, because being attached makes us want to be with those we are attached to".[336]

Introversion: The Opposite of Socialisation?

The other main criticism of home education is that children do not have as many friends as they would in school, and that this is detrimental to their psychological health and development. Firstly, the opportunity to make friends is generally available to unschooled kids in a more varied way – we still live in the same neighbourhoods as schooled children, our children still play outside with others, they still go to extracurricular classes and clubs, and they have local groups of home educators to meet other home educated children, who are also available to socialise at any time of day or week. Their friendships are based on age, family proximity, shared interests etc. just as schooled children's friendships are, but with the added benefit that there is not a restriction on our children meeting only those of the same age and even gender.

Secondly, it is no revelation that fewer close friends are better than myriad acquaintances; or that befriending people you generally dislike is better than being on your own every lunch time, but no basis for strong lasting friendships. Our culture is very much of the view that the more friends you have, and the more time you spend socialising, the more successful you are. But the idea that children work better in groups or need to be around others for the majority of their day is seriously flawed. Children need time to process activities, says Clark Aldrich. "A critical part of the learning process is time for quiet reflection about activities – both before and after they are were undertaken. So the busier children are the less they may be actually learning".[337] Children need to dictate this quiet time for themselves – for introverts this will be far more often than for extroverts. As home educating parents know, development goes in leaps and bounds. There may be weeks of seemingly nothing happening, and then an intense month of learning, and then another few weeks of quiet time. Only the child really knows what they need, and must be allowed to trust themselves in recognising their own needs.

Susan Cain, author of *Quiet: The Power of Introverts in a World That Can't Stop Talking*, shows that introverts (whom she estimates to make up a third to a half of the population) are more successful academically, and that solitude is crucial to creativity. She

> *presents a history of how Western culture transformed from a culture of character to a culture of personality in which an 'extrovert ideal' dominates and introversion is viewed as inferior or even pathological... Asserting that temperament is a core element of human identity, Cain cites research in biology, psychology, neuroscience and evolution to demonstrate that introversion is both common and normal, noting that many of humankind's most creative individuals and distinguished leaders were introverts. Cain urges changes at the workplace, in schools, and in parenting.[338]*

Indeed, psychiatrist Anthony Storr pointed this out in his 1988 book *Solitude*, demonstrating "how many of the creative geniuses of our civilization have been solitary, by temperament or circumstance, and how the capacity to be alone is, even for those who are not creative, a sign of maturity".[339] Scientific breakthroughs often occur after intense independent thought, followed by taking a break alone, to wander in nature or do something else unrelated to the problem, at which point inspiration suddenly occurs. We do not allow for this to occur generally however, schools and workplaces being dominated by the idea of team work, group brainstorming and arriving at a conclusion without time for independent thought. Storr points out that "Those who are not too dependent upon, or too closely involved with, others, find it easier to ignore convention" allowing for original, creative thoughts.[340]

Lack of time to work alone stifles both creativity and sound judgment. Cain demonstrates that a given group of people will follow the beliefs of the most charismatic and dominant person, regardless of whether this person's arguments are the best. There is no correlation between being a good speaker, and having sound, well thought out ideas.[341] Brian Walsh writes,

> *It's not just introverts who suffer when work becomes an endless series of meetings and brainstorming sessions. Anyone who has spent time in any organization knows that there is rarely a correlation between the quality of an idea and the volume at which it is presented. Defying the loudest speaker - and the groupthink that tends to build around that person - can be painful for anyone. Gregory Berns, a neuroeconomist at Emory University, has found that when people oppose group consensus, their amygdalae light up, signalling fear of rejection. The risks of groupthink are per-*

haps most apparent in criminal juries, where the desire for social cohesion can sometimes short-circuit justice.[342]

The rise of the extrovert as the ideal can be traced to the late 19th century, a time before which the culture of character dominated, with people making their name by their work, ideas and integrity. But with the rise of industrialism, mass immigration and burgeoning populations, a culture of personality started to take precedence. Men of Action replaced Men of Character, appearance replaced truth, or as journalist Zosia Bielski writes, "The rise of the salesman" and "The move from morals to magnetism".[343] No longer do we have the freedom to prove ourselves gradually through life amongst a group of people known to us; now we must stand out immediately from a global population competing on social media. Barely a chance is given to be recognised for our subtler talents and virtues. The rich and famous are given so much apparent worth that we try to become famous for anything other than long term effort and behaving with integrity. These pressures are no less severe in the peer pressure of schools.

Cain challenges the paradigm that the best students and leaders are extroverts. But even extroverts are not served by constantly working with others. The very way our society is set up dictates an increasing busyness and emphasis on socialising, perhaps because, as Sir Joshua Reynolds wrote of many educational systems, "A provision of endless apparatus, a bustle of infinite inquiry and research, may be employed to shuffle off real labor - the labor of thinking".[344] Does it not suit our schools and society to have free time simply to think, to deepen our understanding of a topic, to reach our own conclusions?

It is no wonder that unschooling parents react so strongly to the question "What about socialisation?" Clearly the question stems from a fundamental misconception of both how home educator's days are structured, and of the assumed benefits of being constantly surrounded by a large group of people. Donald Winnicott, the paediatrician and psychoanalyst, warns that we need to be able retreat into our inner worlds without feeling that we will be interrupted, such 'impingements' being very disruptive to the self. Storr, writing in *Solitude*, agrees. "With few exceptions, psychotherapists have omitted to consider the fact that the capacity to be alone is also an aspect of emotional maturity," as well as inner security, and "some of the most profound and healing psychological experiences individuals encounter take place internally, and are distantly related, if at all, to interaction with other human beings".[345] During her research on home educated children, Rothermel found that "If the children were lonely they soon adapted and generally appeared to prefer their own company and that of a few friends, to being in school... The results from the RRS in particular, indicate that children can actually benefit from living without mass peer socialisation such as that experienced in school".[346]

Bullies

Another worryingly common comment we hear in tandem with the socialisation question is that children must learn to deal with bullies, and that school is the place to do this. This rings so many alarm bells I don't know where to start. It would be laughable were it not so common. The idea that our children should learn to accept bullying as a part of life is sad. The reality of their learning that it is 'just a part of life' is to normalise it, to perpetuate it generation after generation.

Children have less protection from bullies in school than they will do at many other stages in life. There are numerous children who are home educated precisely because they were being bullied in school. Bullying kills, both directly and indirectly. Why would we consider this a reason to place our children in school, in some Spartan, survival-of-the-fittest Hunger Games?

We meet plenty of rude, 'unsocialised', antagonistic and even bullying adults without the school system to add to it. They exist out there in the world, the products of unhappy home-, school-, and life-experiences. We learn to deal with them. Sometimes they become teachers. We have the luxury of walking away from their classes when they refuse to behave like pleasant human beings. School children don't have that luxury, whether their bullies are children or teachers. We meet bullies online, whether on kid's sites or general forums. They exist in parent and child form in groups of home educators. Home educators do attend classes and groups and play dates just like 'normal' people. If that isn't enough socialisation in the ways of the meaner people of the world, one wonders how much is enough. Do our children really need to spend the best part of every day, five days a week, in school, just to learn to deal with bullies? If so, it would seem that they spend more of their time in school learning to deal with 'socialisation' issues than actually learning (while children in school are repeatedly told 'You're not here to socialise'). No wonder schools are failing.

Ironically, Dr. Gordon Neufeld has found through his research, that "Peer orientation breeds both bullies and their victims. We have been dangerously naïve in thinking that by putting children together we would foster egalitarian values and relating. Instead we have paved the way for the formation of new and damaging attachment hierarchies... Peer orientation is making orphans of our children and turning our schools into day orphanages".[347] A study led by Professor Dieter Wolke of the University of Warwick found "that children who were bullied were five times more likely to experience anxiety and twice as likely to talk of suffering depression and self-harm as those who were maltreated at home".[348] This is even more alarming when 'maltreated' includes "any physical or emotional ill-treatment, sexual abuse, neglect, or negligent treatment resulting in actual or potential harm to the child's health, survival, development or dignity" - yet bullying by other children causes *more* harm.

A child who has rarely been treated unkindly, unfairly or bullied, will have certain expectations of how the world should work. That may mean they are shocked when they discover that people can behave otherwise. That is how we all should feel, but we have become so inured to it we accept it as the way it is. An unschooled child is more likely to be the person in society who says "This is not okay". I, for one, would like these children to exist.

The Dangers of Socialisation

Along with the issue of socialisation, there is a fear amongst some people that to allow home educators to exist is to allow the potential development of parallel societies. The National Education Association, a United States teachers' union and professional association, opposes homeschooling on the basis of the potential for the development of parallel societies "That do not fit into standards of citizenship and the community".[349] Are home educators themselves not a part of the community? Are their personal standards of citizenship not equally valid? Given studies have shown that home educated students are more civically minded, more likely to be involved in voluntary and community work, and more socially and emotionally mature than their counterparts,[350] it is ironic that they are the ones seen as a potential threat to civilised society. Regardless, a well developed critical faculty is necessary to discern that which benefits the whole of society from that which is simply expedient - something which is not encouraged in school. An understanding that our own culture's way of life is not the only way, and that there have been better and worse ways throughout history, broadens the perspective, and opens the imagination to other ways of living, as well as encouraging the child to choose the ways of being that resonate with them personally. None of these are encouraged within a school system that uncritically promotes the values of the faux-democratic state and monopolies. Having to uncritically, and forcibly, conform to 'standards of citizenship and the community' is undemocratic. John Stuart Mill wrote in *On Liberty*: "A general State education is a mere contrivance for molding people to be exactly like one another: and as the mold in which it casts them is that which pleases the predominant power in the government, whether this be a monarch, a priesthood, an aristocracy, or the majority of the existing generation in proportion as it is efficient and successful, it establishes a despotism over the mind, leading by a natural tendency to one over the body".[351]

Another objection by The National Education Association is the "lack of socialization with peers of different ethnic and religious backgrounds". This claim is not upheld: individual schools do not automatically represent a cross section of society whether racially, economically, religiously or culturally, and even in schools where a diversity of social class and ethnic background is present, pupils rarely mix with an entire cohort, but rather socialise with a limited selection of children sharing a common parental background and living within close proximity to their own family. Moreover, school is stifling in its relationships and peer pressure. Unschooled children meet others at extra curricular classes, home education groups, in their community, and all the places other children make friends. Unschooled children also benefit from having more time to meet others in their area, and indeed often have friends of a wider variety of ages and backgrounds than schooled children.

The atmosphere of a home where responsibility for learning is taken seriously and is integral to daily life, often leads, as might be expected, to an entire lifestyle change. "Very 'normal' families, once home-educating soon changed, sometimes quite radically, as a result of their decision and their mixing with other home-educators," Rothermel found. "From personal experience this is likely to mean a questioning of many previously accepted conventions, from traditional medicine to attachment parenting to vegetarianism to more left leaning political views... The interviews found that more often than not, home-educating was a lifestyle decision. It was a choice about how to live far more that a statement about schooling".[352] By stating our identity so firmly as outsiders, we do not feel such a pressing need to conform or to identify ourselves through more materialist methods. In this way, it is easy to understand why home educated children have been found to be more independently minded than their schooled peers.

This raises questions both of how deeply schools inform our political and cultural attitudes, and why we may become so 'radical' when freed from traditional societal norms. Under 'common concerns' with home education, Wikipedia previously listed "the potential for development of religious or social extremism" (this reference has since disappeared). Besides the fact that many schools are overtly founded on their religious beliefs, the fact that families freed from schooling tend to experience a relaxing and evolution of political and cultural attitudes, could easily be read to show that schools are as guilty of indoctrinating children with their own worldview as any parent. We are oppressed and infantilised through education. Opinions are judged and labelled, discussions are limited to narrowly defined sources, and peer pressure constrains freedom of thought. True self government requires responsible, free and sovereign adults.

I think we would all agree that it takes educated people to maintain a free society. However, it also takes people who understand the nature of freedom in order to maintain our basic natural rights. While this once may have been the preserve and intention of schools, author and homeschooler David Guterson points out that "We now have, for better or worse, television, newspapers, magazines and the cinema exerting themselves as powerful forces from which we take our cues as a people. If we have a consensus at all, it is generated and sustained primarily by these forces – they do the job given over to schools in the century preceding this one".[353] We should add social media, mainstream and alternative media, and incessant advertising to this list. Guterson goes on,

> *Schools have not been effective agents of consensus building. Nor must a society in which families take primary responsibility for education - a homeschooling society, if you*

> *will, based on cooperation between families and govern-*
> *ment - invariably become fragmented. On the contrary,*
> *homeschooling can do much to promote the process of*
> *building a national consensus, beginning, of course, by in-*
> *spiring a consensus about the importance of family life. A*
> *homeschooling society might also nurture the kind of inde-*
> *pendent-minded, critical electorate our republic desperately*
> *needs; it might infuse our tired democracy with a new,*
> *grass-roots energy... All of this, of course, is speculative and*
> *utopian. It is also worth considering.*[354]

There is much philosophical and political diversity within the home educating community, if not severe splits. The idea of there being one organised home educating community pre- senting a threat to society as a whole is laughable in the face of a group which has no clear creed, no consistent ideology, and no cohesive political attitude. The real reason for such a variety of parenting techniques and philosophies (and there are many, many more than you would find amongst the par- ents of an average school) is because there is no One Way. The only thing that home educating parents have in common is that they are home educating. Why they are doing so, their feelings about it, their methods, their family environment, and their aims for their children are as almost as numerous as the families themselves. And this is a huge strength: while it causes groups to split, to reform, to regroup, it also provides a wealth of checks and balances on our beliefs and thoughts, and as a whole, unschoolers constantly wonder whether they could be doing things even better.

Invisible Children

The real Bogeyman - one that seems to be more commonly perpetuated by the media than anyone else - is the idea that home educated children are 'invisible' to authorities, and at higher risk of harm or abuse due to the lack of supervision from authorities outside the home. This stems in part from the fact that in the UK for example, parents who have never sent their children to school do not have to inform anyone that their child is being home educated; only those who withdraw their children from school have to inform anyone of their decision. However, statistics show that far from being invisible, home educated children seem to attract disproportionate scrutiny, being twice as likely to be referred to social services as schooled children (this could be due to genuine concerns, misunderstanding the nature of home education, or even being picked up by truancy patrols during school hours). Moreover, once social services have visited the family, home educated children are found to be at less risk of harm than their schooled peers (in Wales for example, the home educated are between 1/7th and 1/3rd at risk compared to schooled children).[355]

The idea that school children are less likely to be abused because a teacher will spot it, or conversely, that abuse of home educated children is less likely to be spotted due to their 'isolation', has never been anything more than urban myth: home educated children at are on average 5 times *less* likely to be served with a Child Protection Plan (CPP) by social services (home educated children are between 3.5 - 5 times less likely to have a referral lead to a CPP than are schooled children aged 5-16, and 5 - 7 times less likely than children aged 0-4 years).[356] Dr. Brian Ray conducted a literature review to see if there was any basis for claims of homeschooled children being at risk. He found only one report utilising original data directly related to homeschooling and child abuse. "That study asked one question regarding sexual abuse and found that adults who had been home educated reported being abused at a lower rate than those in two other groups and at the same rate as a third group... Based on this very limited base of information, one might say that there is no reliable, empirical evidence that homeschooled children experience any more abuse, neglect or fatalities due to neglect than do children who attend public or private institutional school".[357] The bastions of community - school and church - are certainly no strangers to scandals of child abuse.

Legally, as regards all home educated children, The Education Act 1996 "provides a duty for a parent to cause every child to receive efficient and suitable full-time education 'either by regular attendance at school or otherwise'. The serious character of this duty is reflected in criminal penalties attached to breaches. Local Authority education officers are supported in challenging any such breach by legislation and guidance, together with the financial resources necessary to their role. Those authorities also have qualified legal professionals to advise them in fulfilling this role".[358] Home education activist Wendy Charles-Warner points out that "Although there have been some high profile cases involving EHE children it is clear that in every one of these cases the child was known to social services before becoming EHE and that in many cases a large number of professionals were already involved with the child".[359] These children were failed due to authorities not performing their due diligence, not due to any lack in the existing home education legislation. Sadly, and somewhat ironically, Charles-Warner notes that "Teaching staff with responsibility for caring for children during school hours, were found to be more likely to be guilty of abusing those children, than a home educated child was found likely to be abused. Clearly, the risk of a home educated child being subject to abuse is lower than the risk of an educational professional employed in a school being found guilty of abusing a child or children in their care". [360]

A Secret Persecution

A worrying trend in the reporting of home education is currently the (perhaps one might suggest intentional) confusion of the terms 'home educated', 'missing from education', and 'known to social services'. Home education is the conscious choice to take full responsibility for your child's education. Children Missing from Education, or CME, refers to those children who have dropped out of the school system for various reasons including geographical isolation, truancy, bullying, illness, caring duties, and being suspended or expelled from school. These children have not been officially deregistered from school (as their parents have not elected to home educate their children) and therefore fall under the protection and guidance of the Local Authority. 'Known to social services' can be cover a variety of circumstances, and caused confusion after the Badman Review, a report on home education commissioned by the UK government in 2009. The Action for Home Education website reports:

> *A very serious example of this is the reporting of the Graham Badman Review of Elective Home Education. We have collated the statistics on child abuse in the EHE population and find from the Local Authority submissions to the review... that the EHE population have less than half the rate of abuse of the general public. However, it is reported that EHE children are twice as likely to be abused... Many complaints are being processed by the PCC [Press Complaints Commission] (regarding TES, Independent, Guardian, etc.)... The problem is that the journalists reporting [the Badman Review] have taken 'known to social services' to be*

synonymous with 'on the at risk register' because they have not read the review and have misunderstood the reasons children may be 'known to social services' such as being in receipt of a disability allowance.[361]

The truth did not perhaps make for such sensationalist headlines though, and the unfounded news reports remain in the public domain, regardless of any upheld complaints.

One of the few public figures to even note the threat to home education in any mainstream publication is journalist and author Peter Hitchens, who recently wrote "Now the freedom to educate children at home, always a barometer of liberty, is being seriously threatened for the first time in our history. The pretext for this is supposed fears of child abuse or 'extremism'".[362] One lady wrote to her Member of Parliament to complain about press coverage of the topic: "The latest wave of articles started in October [2017] with a program on the BBC on children missing education. It chose a case of a young man from an ethnic and religious minority who had been failed by his school and tried erroneously to present this as the failure of the family, as typical of home education and to conflate a child being educated otherwise than at school with neglect and exposure to radicalisation".[363] As it stands, we have no government or other officially recognised independent body on our side to protect our rights, although organisations such as the Home School Legal Defense Association in the US charge an annual membership fee in exchange for legal support, and Education Otherwise in the UK has some level of influence, though it is by no means supported by all home educators, and is a divisive issue. As with many minority groups, an extremely rare problem with one member of the group becomes grounds to persecute the whole. To suggest that home educators are using their deep involvement with, and responsibility for, their children's education as cover for abuse (as did a 2014 report by the NSPCC[364]), is as ridiculous as assuming all Muslims are terrorists, or that all competitive athletes are drug addicts, or that anyone with a tattoo is a thief. It is based on sheer ignorance and prejudice. And yet the media continues to do just this.

According to the now infamous (and widely discredited) report by the NSPCC, home educated children currently "have no right to independent access to friends, family or professional agencies". No child has the 'right' to independent relationships outside of the family, and any parent who does not know who their child is associating with, or how and where they spend their time, could equally be accused of neglect. Implications that parents are forcibly keeping their children at home are almost laughable - the fact that it is for parents to decide the best way to educate aside, the vast majority of home educating parents regularly check that their children are happy to remain out of school. The same cannot be said for school children, who are rarely if ever asked their opinion on how they would rather be educated, whilst no criticism is made of parents who decide to send their children to school without ever considering if it is indeed the best option for their child. As author and home educating parent David Guterson writes, "Abstractions about what works universally in education are best made secondary to the real needs of each child, while knowledge about what nurtures each should be acted upon by those in a position to do so – whether they be teachers or parents or both together".[365]

So why are governments around Europe trying to curtail the freedom to educate as we choose? Child abuse is often used as an excuse, but statistics do not hold up this contention, as discussed above. It is not an 'easy option' to remove your children from school, to take on the responsibility and cost yourself - there is no monetary gain from doing this, and if you are not committed, then having your kids in school all day and off your hands is a much easier option. In cases where children are being abused or made to work, home education has rarely if ever been used as an excuse - these children are missing from education, and this is entirely different to being home educated. Regulations are already in place to catch these situations, as they are for regular checks that home educated children are being cared for and taught properly. If we weren't lacking strong communities, perhaps children wouldn't go so easily unnoticed. The alternative - compulsory schooling - is no guarantee of safety. There is no shortage of teachers jailed for abusing children, whether it is reported at the time or years afterwards, and children abused at home outside of school hours are not remotely guaranteed to be spotted by their teachers or friends.

The fundamental issue here is the right of parents to direct the education of their own children. If you limit the rights of parents to home educate due to their own beliefs, the next step is to require private schools to conform to the government standards too. That was the path taken by the German government in the 1930's:

> *With the rise of the Weimar Republic and the Nazi regime, homeschooling was seen as an anti-nationalistic and subversive practice that could undermine children's loyalty to their country. The Reichsschulpflichtgesetz, implemented in 1938, effectively banned all homeschooling with criminal consequences for anyone found practicing... It wasn't until the unification of Germany in 1990 that education law was reformed and homeschooling was allowed under strict ob-*

servation and extreme circumstances. Today, however, homeschooling remains illegal.[366]

Do we truly believe that government schooling is the only way to safeguard our children's freedoms in the face of parental opinions, whatever they may be? Do we trust government run schooling to dictate the correct way to think? Guterson writes, "The risk that such coercive power could be dangerously misused, and the fact that it strikes many people as a violation of freedom of thought and conscience, cause people in most countries to shy away from this use of schooling. When an opinion poll asked the Japanese public if their nation's Fundamental Education Law should be amended to include teaching 'patriotic loyalty to Japan', for example, they rejected the idea".[367] Yet in the face of home education, some seem to believe that the only place children are safe from extreme or bizarre points of view is in the safety of schools. Homeschooling author Peter Darby points out "I think you'll also find that most people who believe the world is truly ruled by Jew hating lizards from outer space were, in fact, schooled, along with the vast majority of British Islamic extremists, BNP supporters, climate change believers/deniers (delete where you agree) and people who vote on Britain's Got Talent. Being schooled does not, on present evidence, inoculate you in any way against collective insanity".[368] Of course the majority of people are concerned by home education due to genuine care for others - but they should remember to turn an equally critical and educated eye toward schools.

CHAPTER 10

The Teaching Species

And man NEEDS to teach, not only for the sake of
those who need to be taught, and not only for the
fulfilment of his identity, but because facts are kept
alive by being told, logic by being demonstrated,
truth by being professed.

—ERIK H. ERIKSON [369]

UNCHOOLING'S BASIC TENET IS that the desire to learn is
innate. Children do not need to be manipulated, coerced,
threatened or bribed to learn; they cannot help but do so, and
we only hinder the process by interfering. When children are
allowed to explore in an inspiring environment, they cannot
help but develop passions, be inquisitive, creative, and inven-
tive. If the drive to learn is such an intrinsic part of us, it follows that the drive to teach is highly likely to be an integral
part of us too – though the way we should understand 'teaching' may be very different to our modern notion of a teacher.

The psychologist and psychoanalyst Erik Erikson - the man who coined the term 'identity crisis' - called humans the 'Teaching Species', writing that a need to teach and help others grow is at the very centre of an adult's identity.[370] This has been demonstrated by psychologists who found that when we play games, we derive as much enjoyment from mentoring others as from playing the game itself. But crucially, unless we have helped and encouraged the other person in their success, we may instead feel jealousy or resentment toward them.[371] Our investment in those around us, in the form of mentoring, is essential if we are to develop a healthy and supportive community, rather than one which is rife with resentment and envy. Yet this is what the worlds of school and work are currently based on - individual achievement. We invest resources in our children to help them achieve, but rarely do we conceive of this in a communal or global context; rather we aim to ensure our own children are equipped to survive in a modern, competitive economy, at the expense of everyone else.

In contrast, unschooling's non-competitive, communal approach enriches everyone, and embodies the traditions found around the world that the teacher should be as much a student as the student themselves. Many indigenous traditions view education as a communal endeavour and a collective responsibility. Everyone is a potential teacher or mentor. A society that genuinely wants to educate everyone starts by educating the adults, and allowing them to teach the children themselves, fulfilling everyone's needs through the process. When our role in raising the younger generation is replaced by the state, we are denied a vital part of ourselves.

As the global population has tipped into being more urbanised than rural, increasing numbers of us work merely to make profit for others, in a manner that leaves us disconnected from our home and community life. Unsurprisingly, we suffer feelings of alienation and other mental health problems, as we are no longer able to address our needs for creative, fulfilling and worthwhile work. David Graeber, in *On the Phenomenon of Bullshit Jobs*, writes that "Huge swathes of people, in Europe and North America in particular, spend their entire working lives performing tasks they secretly believe do not really need to be performed. The moral and spiritual damage that comes from this situation is profound".[372] In contrast, when we undertake a job that absorbs us, and gives us a feeling of fulfilment, it is often hard to stop us sharing that with others: teaching our children how to service a bicycle, to sew, to plant a garden, to balance an equation or fill in a crossword – it doesn't matter the task, it is our personal enjoyment of it that is infectious and lends itself to teaching others. By teaching and learning on an intimate level, we are tapping into that part of our nature which connects generation to generation, passing on the knowledge of culture and society that makes us who we are.

We Exist to Educate

Erikson felt that one of the deepest impulses of adult human beings, in contrast to children, is not so much to learn, as the impulse to teach. It is this need, he believed, that defines us: "Human beings need to teach not only for the sake of those who need to be taught but for the fulfilment of our identities".[373] We are not talking only about copying the basic survival skills of our parents before being left to fend for ourselves, but about a thirst for knowledge which has led the human race to achieve all it has. Our current level of knowledge has been made possible by our ancestors, who felt a compunction to record their knowledge and pass it on for posterity. Erikson used the term 'generativity' to describe the instinct which drives us to selflessly care for others. Psychologist Mark Bracher writes, "This generative impulse - this need to teach, to help others thrive, develop, and flourish - is a fundamental and central component of adult identity".[374]

Children too have the need to teach, and take immense pleasure in demonstrating to others how to do something. Psychologist Dr. Peter Gray studied the play of children in hunter-gatherer groups, which almost always occurs in mixed age groups, of any age from four to fifteen.

> *In an age-mixed environment, all children have the opportunity to practice being mature - to practice leading, guiding, and caring for others - through their interactions with younger children... The presence of younger children seems to draw out the nurturing instincts in children and adolescents of both sexes and to promote the development of nurturing behavior... As all teachers know from experience, explaining a concept to others is often the best way to stretch and consolidate one's own understanding of that concept". He goes on, to explain that "age-mixed play is qualitatively different from same-age play. It is less competitive, more nurturing, and offers unique learning opportunities both for the older and younger participants.[375]*

This is likely to be one of the reasons that firstborns achieve disproportionately in the West compared to their younger siblings. A review of studies relating to the subject found that "the teacher gains more than the learner in the process of teaching".[376]

Teaching another person gives us a sense of accomplishment and respect which is crucial to our psychological health. Schools that employ the mentoring of younger students by older students provide a valuable opportunity, and mentoring has been shown to have a beneficial impact on both those being mentored as well as the mentors themselves.[377] As Erikson pointed out, "The teaching passion is not restricted to the teaching profession. Every mature adult knows the satisfaction of explaining what is dear to him and of being understood by a groping mind".[378] This is encapsulated in the Yiddish word 'naches', which describes the pride felt when a protégé succeeds. The emotion of naches has been listed in the top emotions produced by successful video games. Cognitive psychologist and game designer Christopher Bateman found that game players frequently derived enjoyment from mentoring others on games they had mastered, as much as from playing the game themselves.[379] Psychologist Paul Ekman believes that we have evolved this emotion as a group survival mechanism: "Naches ensures parental investment in facilitating the growth and achievements of their children".[380] The drive to teach others is a manifestation of our need to be needed, and teaching can fulfil this need, whether as a parent or otherwise.

But as renowned author and game designer Jane McGonigal warns in her book *Reality is Broken*, "We don't naturally explode with pride at someone else's success if we haven't helped and encouraged them; too often we feel jealousy or resentment... To generate the emotional reward of naches, we have to throw ourselves into the act of mentoring". Yet in the modern world, the incentive to encourage others is lacking, especially in school or work. McGonigal writes, "For the most part, we live in a world of individual achievement, or what Martin Seligman calls 'the waxing of the self' and 'the waning of the commons'. He explains, 'The society we live in takes the pleasures and pains, the successes and failures of the individual with unprecedented seriousness.' And when we see success or failure as an entirely individual affair, we don't bother to invest time or resources in someone else's achievements".[381]

Meaning and Responsibility

Erikson believed that our identity as teachers is also fundamental to our work: "The ideological polarization of the Western world which has made Freud the century's theorist of sex, and Marx that of work, has, until quite recently, left a whole area of man's mind uncharted in psychoanalysis. I refer to man's love for his works and ideas as well as for his children, and the necessary self-verification which adult man's ego receives, and must receive, from his labour's challenge".[382] As our lives become ever more compartmentalised and our work ever more anonymous, society is moving further and further away from this 'necessary self-verification' through work.

People need to feel valued and necessary, part of a community, and part of humanity. Teaching others is a crucial drive for us, a drive that is lost when we are denied responsibility for others or for our work. We seek to find a new justification for our work, new reasons for our existence. Perhaps this is why we are so ready to accept the Myth of Progress. We have replaced the responsibility of providing for our family through the teaching of skills and knowledge (which in turn leads to independence), with the responsibility of providing through accumulation of goods and social advancement. We accept the Myth of Progress in order to feel some level of control over our lives, replacing the role of Teacher with the role of Facilitator. No longer the provider of our children's nourishment in all its forms, both physical and mental, we become the facilitators of access to material goods and benefits. The need to see an immediate and relevant return on any task - referred to as fiero in games and psychological theory - is provided by seeing an apprentice 'get it' and succeed (as shown in studies on gamers), but lost when we are wage slaves. Mothers particularly suffer when they are isolated and no longer rewarded by whole tribe witnessing the progression of their children, no longer rewarded by seeing the larger context of their impact on society in terms of where their children will fit in and grow. This in turn has led to women leaving the home to find more 'rewarding' work.

The Architecture of the System

While the current pattern of work continues, we are prevented from truly fulfilling our inner need of generativity, or teaching. The industrial Revolution started to alienate workers from the product and impact of their work; schools as we know them were also a product of the industrial revolution, designed to feed the machine itself. In the seminal *A Pattern Language*, Christopher Alexander writes, "To organize work in such a manner that it becomes meaningless, boring, stultifying, or nerve wracking for the worker would be little short of criminal; it would indicate a greater concern with goods than with people, an evil lack of compassion and a soul-destroying degree of attachment to the most primitive side of this worldly existence".[383] Yet this is not only how work is structured for the vast majority, but it is just what schools do to our children.

In contrast, if we can combine work and leisure in a way that is both enjoyable and productive, we feel we are truly living in a way we control - and this enjoyment of work is what unschooling achieves. When work is undertaken for the pleasure of the act and the product itself, no coercion is needed; it is not even understood to be work. In this way, unschooled children are not subject to that feeling so common to many in school – in Erikson's words, "the ambivalence adhering to irreversible obligation".[384] This is very much the difference between fulfilling work that includes passing on knowledge to others, and working for some distant corporate organisation.

In his book *Deschooling Society*, Ivan Illich wrote "Schools are designed on the assumption that there is a secret to everything in life; that the quality of life depends on knowing that secret; that secrets can be known only in orderly successions; and that only teachers can properly reveal these secrets. An individual with a schooled mind conceives of the world as a pyramid of classified packages accessible only to those who carry the proper tags. New educational institutions would break apart this pyramid. Their purpose must be to facilitate access for the learner".[385] This access could be facilitated massively in comparison to current society, simply by having adults working within the community in an accessible and integrated way. Children and adults would see what others' jobs entailed, appreciate the value of the effort going into the work, feel more connected to the items created – and more fundamentally would appreciate the human difference between 'production' and 'creation'. Christopher Alexander et al describe the problem:

> *The artificial separation of houses and work creates intolerable rifts in people's inner lives. In modern times almost all cities create zones for 'work' and other zones for 'living' and in most cases enforce the separation by law. Two reasons are given for the separation. First, the work places*

> *need to be near each other, for commercial reasons. Second, workplaces destroy the quiet and safety of residential neighborhoods... But this separation creates enormous rifts in people's emotional lives. Children grow up in areas where there are no men, except on weekends; women are trapped in an atmosphere where they are expected to be pretty, un-intelligent housekeepers; men are forced to accept a schism in which they spend the greater part of their waking lives 'at work, and away from their families' and then the other part of their lives 'with their families, away from work.' Throughout, this separation reinforces the idea that work is a toil, while only family life is 'living' - a schizophrenic view which creates tremendous problems for all the members of a family.*[386]

Even when updated for a culture where women are as likely to go out to work as men are, the empty communities and the work-life schism remain. The most obvious way to rectify this schism is to reintegrate work and home, distributing workplaces throughout communities as far as possible. Not only would this reunite community and family, but would make it much more possible for children to learn about their world in a natural, fluid way. Currently we isolate children in schools, and then attempt to artificially create that which the school environment lacks.

In our society there is an argument to be made that there are jobs that need to be done which no one actively chooses to do, and that these are not jobs we can take pride in so easily. But this is because we have set up a society which does not question what we do and the consequences of our activities. Would it not be better to create a society where no one had to clear other people's rubbish, because we compost or recycle what little excess packing we produce, and because businesses took the lead in reducing unnecessary packaging? A society where people respect their environment enough that we don't need teams of street cleaners to make our streets presentable? A society where sewerage is directly reused as fertiliser or grey-water recycling? Rather than expect that we need the lowest achievers to fill these jobs, we should expect more of our creativity and of our society. And if a job is so crucial that it cannot be avoided, should we not be more appreciative of those who perform the dangerous, unpleasant tasks?

A Tradition of Mentors

The clearest form of student-teacher relationship is that of master and apprentice. To some extent, all learning situations fit this model, whether recognised as such or not; mother and child is the most fundamental of master-apprentice relationships. But the tradition of apprentices – a tradition which stretches back at least as far as the Ice Age - is nowadays lost from the one place it should be found: school. Christopher Alexander reports "a class in which one person teaches a small group of others is most likely to be successful in those cases where the 'students' are actually helping the 'teacher' to do something or solve some problem, which he is working on anyway - not when a subject of abstract or general interest is being taught".[387] We all know this instinctively from our own experience.

Indigenous educators point to their traditional teaching methods, which are far more comparable to a master and apprentice model than formal schooling. Kawagley and Barnhardt describe the differences:

> *While western science and education tend to emphasize compartmentalized knowledge which is often decontextualized and taught in the detached setting of a classroom or*

laboratory, Native people have traditionally acquired their knowledge through direct experience in the natural environment. For them, the particulars come to be understood in relation to the whole, and the 'laws' are continually tested in the context of everyday survival. Western thought also differs from Native thought in its notion of competency. In western terms, competency is based on predetermined ideas of what a person should know, which is then measured indirectly through various forms of 'objective' tests. Such an approach does not address whether that person is really capable of putting the knowledge into practice.[388]

This was the traditional model for much of history throughout the world. Christopher Alexander writes, "The schools and universities have taken over and abstracted many ways of learning which in earlier times were always closely related to the real work of professionals, tradesmen, artisans, independent scholars. In the twelfth century, for instance, young people learned by working beside masters - helping them, making contact directly with every corner of society. When a young person found himself able to contribute to a field of knowledge, or a trade - he would prepare a master 'piece'; and with the consent of the masters, become a fellow in the guild".[389] A good modern example would be the survival expert Ray Mears, who "Didn't go to university, and the career he aspired to in the Royal Marines was thwarted by poor eyesight. Instead, he read voraciously and taught himself about bushcraft, seeking out experts and badgering them to pass their skills on to him".[390]

Educating the Adults/ Teaching the Teachers

It's not unusual for parents to be attracted to the idea of unschooling, but to feel intimidated and inadequate when it comes to actually teaching. It is true that you need to be inspired, dedicated, and very ready to learn yourself, but this should be seen as an opportunity, not a hindrance. (Conversely, if filling gaps in your own knowledge is not something you are willing to do, then you should probably not be unschooling.) Eric Robinson believes that "Most parents want to play a part in the education of their children but feel inadequate for it. To improve the education of children we have to make up a deficit in the education of their parents".[391] Whilst improving the education levels of adults is not an obvious side effect of teaching our children, I believe it does in fact come about for several reasons.

Children are innately curious about the world. They ask questions, and they will keep on asking until they are satisfied, unless their curiosity is stifled. It is natural for a loving, attentive parent to answer these questions. The act of answering the child's questions does several things: the parent must understand the answer themselves, be able to explain the answer clearly and eloquently, and do so with consistency. The diligent parent finds the answers to questions they cannot answer (whether in books, on the internet, or by asking others), thus showing their child, by example, how to find information. The parent must then distil the relevant aspects, and explain them at a level suitable for their child. The act of discussion naturally invites input from other family members or others who may be present, thus widening the variety of viewpoints, and often leading to fascinating tangential discussions (when life itself is the classroom, the most unexpected opportunities to learn arise). The parent must constantly improve their ability to find information, refine their abilities to communicate clearly, and adapt their explanations to the maturing child. The parent learns alongside the child, and improves their own education and - crucially - their own ability to learn, accordingly. In her studies of home educated children, Rothermel confirmed that home education educates the whole family, as parents often learned in tandem with their children.[392]

Many people considering home education worry about how they will teach their children certain subjects, or what happens when the child's thirst for knowledge outstrips the parent's ability to answer. The fallacy here is the assumption that 'home education' means the parent is the sole teacher; it is quite the opposite. The world becomes their teacher. Courses and classes, apprenticeships and mentors, work experience and volunteering, neighbours, family and tutors are all available. The student is not confined to the expertise of those in their school during restricted hours and according to the motivation of a teacher. Their opportunities to learn are limited only by their imagination and budget (this should not be a reason to see school as a better option – many a child is forced to limit their opportunities much more severely when their parents do not have the means to choose a different school). And many a student has accessed courses by working to fund themselves, often by setting up their own business in an area they are passionate about, learning much about business and economics along the way. Home educated students have worked as volunteers in return for tuition, or by being so motivated that they have been awarded scholarships or won higher education entrance despite a lack of conventional qualifications.[393]

It is common that a parent whose primary role is to raise their children (I use 'raise' specifically, not only caring for or minding the child, but actively raising them to adulthood), tends to find new passions or rekindle old ones. As their children become more independent, parents often pursue their own interests in a variety of ways, whether through formal accredited courses, dedicating more time to hobbies, or deeply researching a certain subject. This creates an atmosphere of learning within the home, seeing a parent learn for the love of it, seeing learning as a lifelong pursuit, not something confined to childhood and to be escaped from at the earliest opportunity, or as merely a means to an end. Rothermel recounts that in working class families who had to withdraw their children due to problems at school, the parents often had no education themselves beyond the age of 16. But when they came to sit down and help their own children learn, the parents themselves often continued on to college or university. Some parents that Rothermel met had even sent their children back to school eventually, as they had qualified as lawyers and wanted to practice full time![394]

Then there is the perhaps less urbane matter of wanting to keep up with the Joneses, which may be an innate human trait. When unschooling parents meet up, it is natural to want to ensure their child is on a par with their peers, taking into account their different interests, abilities and developmental age. Resources are shared, books discussed, tips given on learning methods which worked for one or another child. Education is something all are involved in, all have ownership and control of. It is a family and community matter, and one which those involved take very seriously – it is they who are responsible for their children's success. When raising a child is the responsibility of the parent, rather than being handed over to a teacher at 9am, the parent takes a much more active role and they rise to the challenge. They have been given a reason to care about their own level of education in a way that is not present when the state takes responsibility for their children. When a child is home educated, the entire family is educated.

Some educational philosophers strongly emphasise the need for the parent to lead by example when it comes to education. The authors of the Thomas Jefferson Education philosophy, for example, argue that if children are not enthused by learning, parents should look to themselves to see whether they are modelling a 'love of learning' in their own lives.[395] Developing our own identity and interests is inspiring for our children, and also an acknowledgement that we should be constantly growing and learning throughout our lives.

The Personal Relationship

There appear to be two versions of a certain phrase, depending on your attitude: "Those who can, do; those who can't, teach" versus "Those who can, teach; those who can't, do". As with the master and apprentice model, to train until one has the experience and knowledge to teach others is the ideal, making teachers true masters of their knowledge. There are two elements to traditional mentoring: helping to create something that actually matters, and that will be used in the real world (rather than abstract busywork); and a personal relationship and attention, something that is replicated on a temporary basis by tutoring.

It has long been known that smaller class sizes mean more dedicated individual attention, and improved student success. Yet we keep building schools so large in scale that they cannot provide the resources to give students what they need. Funds are eaten up by administrative costs and overheads;

economics drive the teaching experience rather than the other way round. Charles Rusch founded 'MOBOC' or the Mobile Open Classroom in the seventies. Instead of a dedicated school building with all the associated costs, they based their classes in an old school house on wheels, or in public libraries. The mornings were spent on the traditional school curriculum, while the afternoons were free for field trips. Rusch found that "By eliminating the building and the salaries of all those persons who do not directly work with the children, the student/teacher ratio can be reduced from something like 35/1 to 10/1. In this one stroke many of the most pressing public school problems can be eliminated at no extra cost to the school or school district".[396]

Many variations on this theme have been tried, including Shopfront Schools and Street Schools. In *The Lives of Children*, George Dennison wrote an account of the first Street School in America, where overheads such as "Vast administrative costs, bookkeeping, elaborate buildings, maintenance, enforcement personnel" were removed from the equation, again through the rejection of a centralised school building, instead allowing instead a much higher ratio of teachers to students. Through his teaching projects he found that the reduced student-teacher ratios "make possible the human contact capable of curing the diseases we have been naming with such frequency for the last ten years". Dennison was a strong believer that "relationships, not instruction, promoted real learning".[397] Certainly home educated children – a group with dedicated, very personal attention - have been found to be happier, more satisfied with their lives, and have more feeling of control over their lives than the general populace.[398]

Progressive and experimental educators throughout recent history have come to conclusions regarding the ideal teaching environment as being one which is very reminiscent of the unschooling environment. American pedagogue William Heard Kilpatrick, for example, saw the role of the teacher as guide rather than authority figure. He thought that children's interests should lead their learning, gaining knowledge and experience via the senses while exploring their environment.[399] This is reflected in the beliefs of unschoolers who see the parent's primary role as facilitator and mentor, and who find that their children learn best when free to follow their own interests. In common with many progressive educators today, Kilpatrick objected to those elements of traditional schooling such as memorisation, rote learning, rigidly organised classrooms, and traditional forms of assessment – forms of learning which are based on regurgitating memorised facts rather than genuine understanding and application. To counter this, Sal Khan of Khan Academy coined the idea of 'flipping the classroom': students study lessons where and when they choose by watching videos, while working through homework together with their classmates and teacher.[400] This method has been shown to be successful, and many unschoolers across the world integrate Khan Academy into their learning.

Strikingly, in his survey of hunter-gatherer societies, Dr. Peter Gray found that "Self-education through play and exploration requires enormous amounts of unscheduled time - time to do whatever one wants to do, without pressure, judgment, or intrusion from authority figures. That time is needed to make friends, play with ideas and materials, experience and overcome boredom, and develop passions. In hunter-gatherer bands, adults place few demands on children and adolescents, partly because they recognize that young people need to explore and play on their own to become competent adults".[401]

Back to the Village

Illich imagined the ideal pedagogue as an adviser, or intermediary, who matched students with the most suitable mentor and resources. A sort of pedagogic 'fixer', this role would require a broad knowledge of subjects, resources, and available mentors. Unschooling advocate Grace Llewellyn uses the term 'Glorious Generalist' to describe such people, while the founders of Thomas Jefferson Education have a similar vision of 'Master Mentors', who can help students make connections with other people, make connections across history, and connections between different subjects. For this to be implemented on any scale, we must know our communities well enough to know who can help us on any given topic. In *A Pattern Language*, the authors proposed:

> *Arrange the work in every workgroup, industry, and office, in such a way that work and learning go forward hand in hand. Treat every piece of work as an opportunity for learning... decentralize the process of learning and enrich it through contact with many places and people all over the city... In short, the educational system so radically decentralized becomes congruent with the urban structure itself. People of all walks of life come forth, and offer a class in the things they know and love: professionals and workgroups offer apprenticeships in their offices and workshops, old people offer to teach whatever their life work and interest has been, specialists offer tutoring in their special subjects. Living and learning are the same. It is not hard to imagine that eventually every third or fourth household will have at least one person in it who is offering a class or training of some kind.[402]*

Whilst this may sound utopian, a quick list of just some of the skills offered in my village would include mechanic, chemist, bee keeper, astronomer, farmer, organist, nurse, journalist, chiropractor, photographer, horticulturalist, author, electrical engineer, builder, ex-city tour guide, artist, environmental health inspector, local councillor, and until recently, a BAFTA award-winning writer and scientist. Not to mention those who have a wealth of knowledge on local history and other skills, regardless of official qualifications. This is not a wealthy area; it is one of the most economically deprived areas of Europe, and is not particularly unusual or notable in any way. If I extended my list to include those within thirty minutes - the distance to the nearest city - I could probably find someone who could mentor in any given area of knowledge, or put me in touch with someone else who could. Leroy Little Bear describes how this works in a traditional Native American setting:

> *Teaching through actual experience is done by relatives: for example, aunts teaching girls and uncles teaching boys. One relative usually takes a young child under his or her wing, assuming responsibility for teaching the child all she or he knows about the culture and survival. This person makes ongoing progress reports to the group, friends, relatives, and parents, resulting in praise and recognition for the child. There are many people involved in the education and socialization of a child. Anyone can participate in educating a child because education is a collective responsibility.*[403]

Home education is communal in that we are forced to learn to live together, compromise, and work as a team for the benefit of the family, and the family within society, in a way that students in school are not required to. Within the dictates of the classroom there are set structures which absolve us of these responsibilities. Many families find they struggle to be around each other full time during school holidays, and look forward to the children going back to school; the British government has even touted shorter summer holidays as a way to attract female voters.[404] By removing children from the family, and work from the home, we are destroying the most valuable place we have to learn how to live communally, how to compromise and negotiate. A common phrase unschoolers hear is "I could never be with my family all the time!" So many of us find it easier to avoid each other than to work together. It is undeniably a challenge, but if this is how we feel about our own families, how can we expect to live together in society generally?

We tend to think teaching as an isolated event, happening at set times and places. Whilst this is true to an extent, it distracts from the fact that we are all teaching constantly, by our every word and action. Too many people expect teachers to magically mould children into something better than the society they exist within. There is a fundamental difference in the way we see education in the West – as something the state does to our children - compared with traditional cultures who see education as the entire lifestyle a community passes on for their children's survival.

Traditional Ways of Teaching

Professors Angayuqaq Oscar Kawagley and Ray Barnhardt write of the difference in attitudes toward schooling between the West and Indigenous peoples: "Whereas western-derived practices tend to focus on individually-oriented considerations and goals, indigenous people are more likely to seek a community-oriented approach, focusing on the commons as the basis for individual sustenance, and the individual as the basis for the strength of the commons. The educational practices associated with such an outlook are grounded in the same premises as the African proverb, 'It takes a whole village to raise a child'".[405] This emphasis on the commons and communal solidarity is more culturally similar to the working class in the West, and more evidence that schools most harm those who do not grow up in an individual-oriented household.

The similarities between indigenous styles of teaching and unschooling are strong: the importance of play; that learning cannot be forced; letting children learn at their own pace; introducing materials as children are ready and letting them take what they need from them; letting children make mistakes; non-interference parenting; the use of knowledgeable adults to act as mentors; and the environment and community being the classroom. According to many Aboriginal traditions, children are gifts from the Creator. As a result, parents take a long term view of the child's development, which includes a sense of destiny, and which means that the parent's role is not to shape and create behaviour but to provide a context for its expression. This can also be seen in Aboriginal parents preferring non-verbal teaching and learning styles where they observe their children's behaviours rather than intervene.[406] This is a very good description of the way unschoolers see their role.

Learning Without Formal teaching

Many people's doubts about the efficacy of home education stem from their brainwashing that children must be formally taught in order to learn. Researcher Alan Thomas found that over time, most home-educating families adopted less formal learning patterns than those originally initiated.[407] He attributed this change to a "manoeuvre by the children, possibly without conscious intent, to orchestrate a learning programme to suit their needs: just as the parents of young babies respond to signals from their infant, home-educating parents were seen to take cues from their children beyond school age and in more advanced learning situations, avoiding the necessity of formal teaching".[408] Naturalist and author Tom Brown Jr. beautifully describes his education under the tutelage of his Native American mentor:

> *"Stalking Wolf gave me the tools to track the mystery to its source. He taught me how to teach myself. I have been using the tools he gave me ever since... He gave us questions that would lead us to our answers, but he never told us an answer... School taught me how to read. Stalking Wolf taught me how to learn... It amazes me, when I look back, how little of all that Stalking Wolf taught me was done in words, and how deftly everything was done. He never gave me a direct answer, and when he had something to teach us, he arranged it so that something we suddenly needed desperately to know... He let us go and discover the whole thing for ourselves. We learned whatever we made important in our lives... Stalking Wolf led us to situations where we could learn certain principles, but once he had shown them to us, it was up to us to put in the hours and hours of practice it took to acquire the skill... I learned more in one day with Stalking Wolf than I learned in any class during a whole year... When Stalking Wolf gave us a test, it was not a test in the sense that it could be graded. It was a way of knowing what to work on next. The importance of the test was not the results but what we did with them... All we cared about was the information, and a difficult failure often taught us more than two or three easy successes".[409]*

What Stalking Wolf knew, if not in the same terms, was that "mammals come into the world with instincts to play at the very activities that they most need to develop in order to become effective adults... our survival depends on our abilities, when young, to acquire the skills and knowledge unique to the culture in which we are born". This was the finding of German philosopher and naturalist Karl Groos, who applied Darwin's theory to an analysis of animal play.[410] Groos believed that "natural selection enlarged the play drive in humans and shaped it in a manner to include a strong element of mimicry. Human children play not just at species-specific skills (the kinds of skills that characterize the species everywhere), like other mammals do, but also play at culture-specific skills... children come into the world with an innate drive to look around and see what the adults, especially the most admired and successful adults, are doing and to incorporate those activities into their play".[411] In other words, formal structured teaching is not automatically necessary in order for children to learn and thrive, provided they are surrounded by adults performing those activities which children need to learn. This innate drive to mimicry is, of course, a double edged sword: if we surround children with less than ideal role models in prominent positions, we cannot complain when they naturally mimic the behaviours of those they perceive to be successful. If we wish children to aspire to the behaviour of people other than pop stars, models, and sports stars, why are we rewarding those people with sums of money that imply they are of inestimable value to society? Meantime we allow those who truly are deeply valuable (firefighters, paramedics, those who care for our children) to verge on poverty.

Being A Role Model

Too many adults no longer think of themselves as teachers, mentors, or as an example for the younger generation in any way. A celebrity culture increasingly oriented around youth has undermined the role of the mature adult as something to be desired and aimed for. But if we want our children to grow into the adults we hope them to be, we have to be those adults ourselves. This is of utmost importance when media culture especially surrounds with so many examples of what not to be. As pedagogist Dr Henry Giroux writes,

> *I am often disconcerted by people whom I consider thoughtful and progressive and literate, but who seem utterly unable to connect their own personal behavior to the theories and ideologies they espouse. Yes, they may be theoretically smart and yet [they are] pedagogical terrorists. I cannot tell you how many... intellectuals I know who have no understanding of what it means to mimic the theory that they write about in their own social relationships, who are mean-spirited, and even hateful.[412]*

As mature, socially responsible adults, we are role models, constantly. It is a shame it often takes having our own children to understand this, as children look up to us for social cues well before we become parents ourselves. To the founders of Tomas Jefferson Leadership Education, this is as crucial an aspect of education as anything else. It is to a large extent true that "Whatever learning activities adults want children to perform, they have to model themselves. If they want children to read novels, they have to read novels. If they want children to do science experiments, they have to do science experiments. If they want children to write blogs, they have to write blogs".[413] It is equally true that we must model the moral behaviour we would like our children to adopt. Our children model our behaviour for better or worse regardless; but how much conscious thought do most of us put in to our day to day attitudes? Charlotte Mason education also emphasises 'the atmosphere and life' a child is surrounded by. We have such a lack of role models in society that we have to teach Leadership Skills as a specific subject rather than being surrounded by genuine leaders who teach by example.

A Group Responsibility

Home educated students have been shown to internalise their parents' beliefs very strongly compared to schooled students. This is no doubt largely due to the major influence of the parents as role models, but may also be impacted by the power of witnessing people living by their beliefs – unschooling takes dedication, commitment and responsibility. Schools too have such a responsibility given the huge amount of time and influence they have on our children. When we are so programmed to absorb the received values, attitudes and standards of our care givers, is it any wonder the state maintains such a monopoly on it?

Ideological tendencies of all stripes are developed at a very young age, and place a weight of responsibility on parents and community to act responsibly. We cannot easily change the attitudes of an entire community; we can however affect the attitudes of our children in the face of environmental prejudices. Responsibility is one of the fundamental descriptors of home education. Education in its broadest sense is the responsibility of the entire community, whether we accept it or not. Children learn from those around them, in the home, the street and on the television. When we hand over education to the state, we are denied a large part of our responsibility as parents. The family unit takes a back seat, as schools raise our children and parents are left to become wage slaves. We all need reason and purpose to function fully, and eventually this can only be found in passing on our traditions, skills, and knowledge to others.

Adults as Authority

When children lose regular contact with adults through the destruction of strong local communities, it gives those adults they do meet much more power. A major difference between home educated children and schooled children is the way they react to adults, due to the nature of the adult relationships they experience. Schooled children tend to see all adults as authority figures, and become both deferential and secretive in relation to them. Home educated children can be confident to the point of unnerving forwardness with adults, because they are used to be treated as near equals, and certainly with respect, tolerance and integrity. For home educated children, adults are a resource, people who can help them in a myriad of ways. Clark Aldrich writes, "Parents often unfortunately look at any adults willing to spend time with their offspring as potential stand-in caregivers. This is robbing children of one of the greatest learning opportunities – time with the non-authority figure adult". This is inhibited when available adults are left in charge while parents attend to their own life, not only robbing children of the opportunity to engage with the adult world and with their own parents, but preventing the easy, humorous friendships that are found when parents are on hand to attend to basic needs, allowing other adults to relax and be themselves. These relationships may evolve into mentoring.[414]

Schooled children are conditioned to respond to adults as authority figures, and punished to varying degrees when they question or refuse to obey orders. This attitude is never fully remedied, so that throughout life we continue to follow orders unquestioningly from our boss, from the medical profession, from the police, from the government, and on and on. Even in adult life, those who question authority are often branded trouble makers, rather than being seen as a sign of a secure and democratic society. At the extreme, this blind obedience leads to dangerously concentrated power, as can be seen in the experiments of Stanley Milgram. The British anarchist Colin Ward wrote,

> *It is governments which make wars and prepare for wars, but obviously it is not governments alone - the power of a government, even the most absolute dictatorship, depends on the tacit assent of the governed. Why do people consent to be governed? It isn't only fear: what have millions of people to fear from a small group of politicians? It is because they subscribe to the same values as their governors. Rulers and ruled alike believe in the principle of authority, of hierarchy, of power. These are the characteristics of the political principle. The anarchists, who have always distinguished between the state and society, adhere to the social principle, which can be seen wherever men link themselves in an association based on a common need or a common interest.*[415]

The Role of Elders

Nowadays, many children learn about life outside school, and how to relate to and respond to life, from school friends. We surround children with their peers, not their elders. Yet the whole point of an elder is to be there to teach, guide, and impart wisdom. We have isolated children from their traditional source of knowledge. The children I have personally worked with who have older parents, or who have a job in the family business or who volunteer, are noticeably more mature and confident due to that responsibility and time spent with mature, responsible adults. Would it not improve our relationships, societies and culture to include the older generations as elders and keepers of history and knowledge? We train young people fresh out of university to be the main teachers of our children - yet it takes years for young people to become real figures of authority with the weight of experience and wisdom behind them. Should a teacher not evolve naturally as they integrate their knowledge and life experience, rather than being someone barely an adult themselves, trained to get children to repeat the facts they have only just learned themselves? Of course many teachers are older and experienced, but how many have entered the profession after living life, rather than their life being lived within the profession?

Look at any country that scores highly in education tables, and you will find the culture is designed around the fact that teachers are some of the most important people in society. A chapter of this book is dedicated to the Finnish example. In Germany,

> *A lot is invested in the training of the professional... a teacher studies for four years to be a teacher, then they have supervised teaching practice for a year, then they go out to a school or college and teach for a year. A report is sent to their training college and they are monitored and supervised for another year... When you look at it this way you see that teachers in Germany are educated roughly the way doctors and lawyers are in the UK. They are paid more in relative terms, as well, and they are not impoverished part*

time and supply contract teachers or outsourced peons. They are professionals.[416]

To return to the indigenous model, the relationship between elders and authority can be very different to that which we expect in the West. Author Thom Hartmann writes,

> *Leadership in a tribe is an advisory role, not an authoritarian one. (There are exceptions to this, but the anthropological record shows they are rare.) ... early European invaders of the Americas didn't understand this: in fact, they considered it a sign of backwardness, and so sought out the 'chief' or leader of a tribe, thinking that they could negotiate with that person and everybody else in the tribe would then have to comply. In fact, tribal leadership is usually held by a committee, and even that committee is more advisory than authoritarian. Power is shared among the members of the tribe, as are resources.*[417]

Who is in Control?

Society takes it as read that children deserve an education rather than having to work, but the manner in which this education is achieved means losing much knowledge of the world along the way. There is so much knowledge in culture that is only contained within the language and lifestyle itself, but does not create currency and so is not considered by the vast majority to be knowledge that is of 'value'. Stephen Corry of the charity Survival International writes:

> *I have explained already that indigenous peoples want schooling – which should include lessons for adults in some places – that is appropriate to their needs, rather than dictated by outside teachers imposing an alien and pointless curriculum. Interestingly, and completely contrary to some liberal Western sentiment, tribal peoples do not always want their children taught about their own background in*

school. Some tribal parents think they can do that better themselves: they want their children primarily to go to school to learn the new knowledge and skills needed to interact with national society. They want their schools staffed with their own teachers, not because they seek an apartheid-style separation from others, but because they know just how much damage outsiders can do.[418]

One group of sea gypsies, the Bajau of South-East Asia, traditionally passed knowledge down orally, requiring little in the way of formal education, but as Kaye and Orland report, "New economic and ecological challenges have forced the Bajau to develop specialised schooling to keep their distinct culture afloat". In their school room, is an "aquaculture fish farming lab which, along with seaweed cultivation and computer skills, figure in the Rumah Pintar curriculum".[419]

Perhaps in these situations, it must be the adults who are 'educated', not the children; adults who have more confidence to demand they be taught that which they actually need to survive in a changing society; adults who can pass that knowledge onto their children through the filter of their own society's traditions, so integrating the two cultures as much as possible. With unschooling too, it is the adults who need to be educated in order to pass knowledge on to the children in an active way, rather than in a passive classroom setting. Children learn through imitation, so always it is the adults who need to be doing while the children mimic; but it has to be in family groups or small communities, and integrated with daily life. A state which wants to indoctrinate children does it through schools, by removing children from their community and culture. A state which genuinely wants to educate everyone starts with the adults and allows them to teach the children themselves through the lens of their individual cultures. We should not assume that indigenous peoples wish for schools and teachers because they are incapable of teaching. Given access to knowledge we are all as capable as anyone of teaching our children ourselves. We should not be limiting access to education whatsoever. Education should be freely available to adults everywhere, as learning should be a life long process enabling all adults to teach children themselves, rather than it being the responsibility of the few. What everyone needs are resources, not schools, and it should remain up to the community how they use those resources.

As a teaching species, we are destroying the fundamental basis of education by separating it from the home and community. As adults, our raison d'être is to teach; for our children it is to learn. As we are removed from our roots through loss of language, loss of land, separation of family and community through work and school, so we lose our reason for being, our opportunity for teaching, and for living in a manner that matters. We lose connection to all that we are and have been. It is the disease of the West, and we are spreading it to all the corners of the world. To halt the spreading rootlessness, depression and apathy, we must give the responsibility of raising our young back to the people and the land.

CHAPTER 11

Reclaiming Motherhood

If feminism has receded in visibility and prestige, it is precisely because its vision of life's goals and rewards has become too narrow and elitist.

—CAMILLE PAGLIA [420]

THE LAST STAGE OF feminism pushed women out to work, telling them they were neither valued, nor achieving their potential, when staying at home to raise a family. As a result they have ended up trying to do both. But what if women were equally valued and respected for choosing to stay at home and teach our own children? A new generation of women are refusing to give in to the need to prove themselves equal to men by joining the workforce and sending their children to state institutions to be raised. Instead, they are actively choosing to stay at home, accepting the power and responsibility that is inherent in teaching their own children; a power that extends to influencing their community and society from the roots up. Home educators know that choosing to raise their children rather than 'working for the Man' is of equal value to society if not more. It is not sexist but empowering. Women are returning to their traditional sphere from a strengthened standpoint, accepting financial support from their partners not because they are incapable of working, but because their work is so important as to be priceless. Wendy McElroy writes in *Can a Feminist Home-school Her Child?*, "Homeschooling constitutes a revolution in education. But it is also one of the most significant trends to affect women and families in decades, especially since it is led by mother-educators".[421] Feminism in general however tends to silence or ambivalence when it comes to teaching our children ourselves. McElroy writes, "Analysis of home-schooling has focused on the children - and properly so - but the relationship of mother-educators to feminism deserves investigation in its own right".[422]

Finding Fulfillment

Many Western mothers resent giving up a career with tangible and societal rewards in order to stay at home and raise their children. Motherhood is rarely regarded as a worthy and fulfilling career in itself, and the rewards are not immediately visible. Part of our schooled brainwashing is a need for recognition and certification from outside, and can lead to looking for proof of our worth through the achievements of our children, thus presenting them with yet another source of pressure. In forgoing a salary to teach children at home, women are once more reliant on a partner, which can feel like a backwards step in terms of equality (for it is still mainly mothers who stay home, due to the inequality of wages, as much as due to biology). In many countries, mothering itself is no longer recognised as a valid choice or as integral to a successful society. Journalist Deborah Orr writes,

The trouble, of course, is that the penalisation of stay-at-home parents, still usually mothers, is nothing new. And it is not merely financial. It's all very well to make romantic speeches about the important work of raising a family. But historically and culturally, those who accept the traditional role of economically dependent spouse and parent become vastly more vulnerable themselves... giving [women] an education was not considered worthwhile, since it would be 'wasted' on bringing up children (which, far from being the most important thing a human could do, was at that time considered to be work for the ignorant)... women often find that being a 'full-time mother' is tough. It can promote feelings of lack of identity or of self-worth, sometimes depression, undermining the very role that has been so nobly undertaken. [423]

Many mothers choose to work, feeling that they are not fulfilled or valued intellectually and creatively at home. But it is not necessarily the act of motherhood itself which is lacking; it is the cultural attitudes toward motherhood which lack understanding and respect for the challenge, the responsibility, and the impact of motherhood on society. Psychotherapist Naomi Stadlen spent 20 years listening to mothers at her weekly discussion groups. She writes,

There is another way in which the prevailing disrespect affects mothers. Most of them enter the 'mother culture' from a 'work culture'. There they have already created their individual identities. Many are contracted to resume work after a few months. This makes it possible for a mother to see her work identity as her 'real' self, while the motherly one can seem an anomaly... 'You are simply 'the mum with the baby'. This role subsumes all other selves you have been or want to be. For many women, this is intolerable. A number of mothers who take short maternity breaks do not see the point of creating identities as mothers. What respect would they gain if they did? It must be the first time that a whole generation of mothers has been faced with such an acute identity dilemma.[424]

The problem lies with the way we have constructed society generally: there is a home sphere, a work sphere, a childcare sphere, all separate and distinct, so much so that one has to switch between identities. In this model, mothers simply cannot be fully attentive and also fully their own selves – we have made sure that you are either in the home/mothering sphere, or the work/independent identity sphere. Author Susan Maushart frames the problem, "To the extent that the whole feminist platform centres on empowering women, it *is* anti-family - or at the very least anti-what-we've-always-de-fined-as-the-family. Female subservience to the needs of men and offspring is not incidental to 'family life'; it is the very ground on which we have constructed family life... As a fem-inist, I am more interested to discover possible alternative foundations for family life - ones that might serve the pur-pose equally well or even better".[425] In other words, women can only be empowered if we redesign the entire idea of what constitutes family, as we cannot currently be both a mother and an independent person. Philosopher Slavoj Zizek points out that this is because our entire idea of what constitutes an independent identity is based on male traits: autonomy, pub-lic activity, competition, income. "In our societies, a sexual-ized division of labor still predominates which confers a male twist on basic liberal categories (autonomy, public activity, competition), and relegates women to the private sphere of family solidarity... Furthermore, it is only the modern West-ern capitalist culture for which autonomy, individual free-dom, etc., stand higher than collective solidarity, connection, responsibility for dependent others, the duty to respect the customs of one's community".[426] As with schooling, the aspects of life which women traditionally maintain – tradition, community, relationships, compromise – are suppressed in favour of those things which bring material progress; suppressed almost to the point of destroying them.

Mothers, as a result, become one identical mass, their time totally subsumed by all doing the same repetitive tasks for their undistinguishable offspring, with nothing to delineate us from each other. Of course this is a ridiculous characterisation, and yet this is how mothers are made to feel. It is the fathers who define the family through their occupation outside the home, and thus women feel they must also enter this sphere of individualism to find themselves. We are trying to be equal to men on their terms. Perhaps we do need to redefine the idea of the family, but not by removing ourselves from it. Equality means 'the same as', and women are clearly not the same as men, however politically incorrect it is to say so. What we really need is parity – parity of of opportunity, parity of reward, parity of respect – whilst accepting that we all have things we do well because of our gender, not in spite of it.

The Necessity of Attachment

Government itself often seems at pains to convince us that mothers are not necessary after the first few weeks of their infant's life, that any half-decent carer will do, that it makes no difference at all whether babies and young children spend their days in childcare or crèche, and that we are even benefitting our children by treating them this way. The evidence to support this view simply does not hold up however. Studies claiming that working mothers benefit their children have been shown to be misleading, with the only sector of society to actually benefit being the children of low-income single mothers, who are trying to support themselves, raise a child and run a household alone.[427] The campaign group Mothers At Home Matter believe "Mothers and fathers are not identical... Babies need their mothers. The science is starting to back up this fundamental assumption which is now being questioned in the interests of persuading mothers it doesn't matter who looks after their children so they are free to work".[428] Researchers have found that newborns prefer the sound of their mother's voice to any other voice, and prefer their mother's voice to any other sound. The mother's voice helps children manage their emotions, reduces their stress levels and increases their feeling of wellbeing. It is particularly significant in helping infants detect emotion in speech and continues to stimulate brain areas associated with social communication even at seven and twelve years of age.[429]

Home education also has a very beneficial impact on the ability of mothers to breastfeed for as long as their child needs, improving the health of both mother and child, and protecting their children against infections through natural means. The World Health Organisation and UNICEF recommend that breastfeeding extends to a period of at least 2 years of age or beyond, while the natural age of weaning in humans has been calculated by various physiological measures to be between 2.5 and 7 years of age, with a median of 5 years.[430] In England however, over 56% of mothers do not breastfeed at all.[431] In her doctoral thesis Paula Rothermel writes,

> *Noticeable... was the way in which home-educators tended towards long-term breastfeeding of their children beyond infancy... This finding was not about 'eccentric' home-educators choosing to nurse their children long term, but illus-*

trated the way in which, because the mothers were at home, day-to-day practices altered and the parameters of what was possible broadened. Where parents were not restricted by work and school they could spend more time devoted to the care of their children. It was logical that if a mother was not preparing a child for school or getting ready to 'return' to work, there was no need to wean.[432]

When mothers feel so devalued, we are deeply impacting the development a child goes through after birth. The first years are not an insignificant period; they lay the foundations for the rest of our lives. Recent research shows that the first five years of life are particularly important, and the first three critical, in shaping a child's brain architecture. Our earliest experiences determine how well we develop learning, social and emotional skills.[433] "Babies who have the right early movement experiences in their first year have better coordination, concentration, memory, behaviour and perception as they get older...Research has shown that the correct stimulation for babies can influence how well they behave, read and learn when they reach school. In addition, they have improved confidence, communication and socialisation skills".[434] Even more crucially, the number of neural connections a child will end up with for life is determined in their first year. The number of connections peaks at around one year old, after which those connections not regularly used are eliminated.[435] In more tangible terms, York University, in Toronto, found that at just 6 months old, a baby can tell the difference between an adult being unable to do something and being unwilling to do it.[436] The more attached, genuinely attentive and motivated the carer, the more a baby has a chance to develop and cement the healthy neural connections that will serve them for the rest of their life.

Conversely, Dr Gordon Neufeld explains, without the ideal attached relationship to a carer, children may struggle:

> *Developmentalists – psychologists or other scientists who study human development – call it an attachment relationship. For a child to be open to being parented by an adult, he must be actively attaching to that adult...If everything unfolds according to design, the attachment will eventually unfold into an emotional closeness and finally a sense of psychological intimacy. Children who lack this kind of connection with those responsible for them are very difficult to parent, or often, even to teach. Only the attachment relationship can provide the proper context for child-rearing.*[437]

Yet for the first time in history, the majority of children spend most of their waking time away from the care of nurturing, attached adults. For the optimum chance of success, a child needs to be raised and taught by their own parent or someone they have developed an attachment relationship with early on, in the way of the traditional village. We need, Neufeld concludes, to recreate the attachment village.[438]

The difference between the attachment village and our current society is primarily the number of adults - attached, consistent, invested adults - available at any given time. In the attachment village, which is comparable to indigenous societies today, the adults have more time to rest, interact, and share the workload, while children have more close, secure relationships with well rested, motivated adults. It is much easier to parent well when surrounded by supportive friends who care for you, your children, and who bear witness to your efforts. This is something the unschooling community goes some way to replicating, given the freedom to spend entire days together as families, whether a few or an entire home educating community (i.e. those not necessarily living in the same immediate community, but close enough to have formed a community within a reasonable geographic proximity). Given the differences too in family numbers and ages of children, stages of development, interests, passions, hindrances and talents, we are less likely to blend into the background of same-aged children, following the same curricula, during the same hours, out of necessity following the same routines outside the school gate. Freed from the factory that family life has become, we can define our identity as mothers in a way that we never could within the dictates of the school-oriented life. We witness each other's efforts, struggles, and influence on our families in a way that we simply do not appreciate when our children spend the best part of their days away from us. When unschooling, although mothers are not seen as separate from our families, we also become more whole, more unique, more recognisable as an individual, due to the very clear differences between our choices, family ethos, where we spend our energies and time, and how very different our children are from each other and from ourselves. We all bring something different to the community, and are valued for those aspects of us which are different to every other family. But bonding us always is the foundation of valuing our children and our family above all else.

The Value of Motherhood

Women have railed against traditional gender roles for good reason, not least being denied an education. But given women are still the primary carers for young children, our children are being raised in their most impressionable years by the sector of society who have traditionally been kept the most ignorant. Given the crucial nature of the formative years for young children, this makes no sense at all. The problem we face is that the end point of education is so intrinsically tied in our minds to a career and an income, that education is not valued for its own sake (or for its less quantifiable ends). There are many reasons, with many agendas behind them, which contribute (knowingly or unwittingly) to the devaluing of full time motherhood. Marilyn Waring, author of *If Women Counted*, was one of the first to suggest that a GDP based solely on production and consumption in the market sphere renders women's unpaid work invisible, thus dismissing it in the minds of those to whom money is the measure of all. Comments from prime ministers such as Denmark's Helle Thorning-Schmidt, who says "It seems a waste for society to give a woman a law degree in a fancy university and she then spends her time looking after the children",[439] show how an educated mother raising her own children is not seen as an asset, but as a wasted investment on the part of the state. It matters not which parent stays at home and which goes to work, in this respect – value is tied to a wage slip, and the importance of being available for your child is simply not quantifiable in this regard. David Graeber writes,

> *In our society, there seems a general rule that, the more obviously one's work benefits other people, the less one is likely to be paid for it. Again, an objective measure is hard to find, but one easy way to get a sense is to ask: what would happen were this entire class of people to simply disappear? Say what you like about nurses, garbage collectors, or mechanics, it's obvious that were they to vanish in a puff of smoke, the results would be immediate and catastrophic. A world without teachers or dock-workers would soon be in trouble, and even one without science fiction writers or ska musicians would clearly be a lesser place. It's not entirely clear how humanity would suffer were all private equity CEOs, lobbyists, PR researchers, actuaries, telemarketers, bailiffs or legal consultants to similarly vanish. (Many suspect it might markedly improve.) Yet apart from a handful*

of well-touted exceptions (doctors), the rule holds surprisingly well.[440]

The fact that mothers are not even mentioned by Graeber demonstrates his argument perfectly – we are paid nothing at all, and are so integral as to be priceless.

Once women were given the opportunity to be educated on a par with men, the state encouraged them to go out to work, expecting its economic investment to be repaid by women contributing to the GDP. Stay-at-home mothers became 'economically inactive'. For all the benefits of a state funded education, this is the concomitant danger - education becomes solely an economic investment in future workers, on which the state expects to see a return in the form of adults directly contributing to the economy, rather than education being of value in itself, for people to utilise as they see fit, and which can only contribute to society as a whole. In our current situation, education is driven by the needs of the economy, so business dictates curricula, and children are constrained in how they envision their future. Students become disassociated from their own education, losing motivation to learn. Knowledge is no longer their own, but some other authority's It is for this reason that many indigenous groups are wary of state funding for their schools and universities, fearing a loss of control over their curricula and methods.

When women stay at home to educate their children, they do often take on the lion's share of domestic chores, as well as expecting their children to help out. But their prime responsibility is to educate their children, not to keep house. Education, in the broadest sense of the word, is prized above all. Home educating mothers have returned to the traditional sphere, but from a strengthened standpoint. They have accepted the power and responsibility that is inherent in raising and teaching their own children, rather than being tied to the home through domestic servitude. We cannot put motherhood back on a par with wage earners until we understand both the immense value of raising secure, happy, mentally healthy children, and until we appreciate the value of an educated mother in and of herself, regardless of the manner in which her education contributes back to society. Some governments do now take the contribution of mothers into account: Venezuela offers full time mothers a pension, and the President of Russia annually awards The Order of Parental Glory to parents (including adoptive parents) raising seven or more children, ensuring due care for their health, education, physical, spiritual and moral development: "Caring for children and helping them to fully develop their abilities is one of the main incentives that take people, families and society in general forward".[441]

Generally however, we still do not fully recognise the value of parents being present during a child's first years. Our early, crucial input is devalued. We view the education of a child as something that is delayed until primary school, something professionalized, not something that as parents we do instinctively. Mothers are no longer respected and rewarded for the foundations they are painstakingly creating, but instead demoted to house maids, handing the responsibility of raising their children to others (who generally have little investment in our children personally, due to lack of a continuing and integrated community) as soon as our children are of school age, i.e. ready to be educated 'properly'. We need to understand the impact that our teaching has in the first years; understand that we are all teaching, always; that we are doing it instinctively and we are probably doing it right; and we do make a difference. But our crucial early role can remain so, beyond school-starting age. It also needs to, given that teenagers need just as much of our time, albeit in a different way, with evidence suggesting that "experiences in adolescence are at least as influential in determining adult outcomes as they are in infancy".[442]

Reconciling Work and Home

We can balance a role as a mother with working from home, as could all the community, if we choose to structure it so. The need to leave the home in order to work is gradually diminishing, ending the separation of work versus family life, and the stereotypical role of mother along with it. The split between work and home, community and school, forces parents to make a choice between work and children - a choice that in the modern world should not be so imperative and destructive. Why should parents not work from home, whether in a workshop, from a computer, or on the land? Why should children have to be sent to school, occupied with busy work and someone else's agenda, to enable parents to work for someone else, somewhere else? In fact, many unschooling families have either begun, or evolved along the way, to a situation where the entire family is at home together. This is when it works best - the whole family living, learning and working together.

It may seem counterintuitive for women to achieve a better work-home balance by staying at home to teach their children, but this may be the ideal solution, in an era when working from home and flexi-working are increasingly possible, and when technology provides so many resources (both informational and human). Both working from home, and unschooling, tend to be viewed as an isolating experience, but as with anything, it is what you make of it.

According to the UK Office of National Statistics (ONS), 4.2 million people were working from home in 2014, including those who were based entirely at home (1.5 million) and those who were based at home but travelled to various places (2.7 million). 63% were self-employed, and they tended to be well-paid and highly skilled.[443] The biggest growth in the numbers working from home over the last decade has been women, with supporters pointing to benefits such as reducing commuting costs, and helping people with caring and childcare responsibilities. Research tells us that another 4 million people would like to work from home but are refused. Phil Flaxton, who organises National Work From Home Day, says "Cultural, economic and social changes are affecting attitudes to how we balance or mix work and lifestyle, where increasing mobility and technology is shifting the acceptance or need for traditional office based, 9-5 work patterns, to be replaced by more home-based, flexible ways and periods of work".[444] And given the increasing numbers of people who work from home, culture is adapting: cafés have started to offer free wifi and extra charging points for laptops, providing for many just the right balance of being in a sociable environment with the motivation to focus on their work (a lot of people report feeling the obligation to work under the imagined public gaze!). Papers such as *The Telegraph* publish lists of the best cafes to work from in London,[445] and other cities are catching on.[446]

Those who work 'from home' (in the same way unschoolers are based 'at home'), are building communities of those who are connected primarily through locale and lifestyle. Unschooling builds communities in the same way, through connecting networks of like-minded families, and by bringing the full spectrum of ages and genders back into the neighbourhood during the day. As those working from home realise, the day itself becomes calmer as we no longer have to compete for space at peak times on the roads, in the shops, and during school holidays. We meet neighbours who are active in the community during those hours when we would otherwise never cross paths. But also very importantly, we are free to structure our time around family responsibilities, allowing work to be fitted in when it suits us best. Many unschoolers across Britain and the United States do some amount of self-employed work, whether as researchers, farmsteaders, tutors, or artisans for example. In the United States, many homeschoolers are contributing to the craft and homesteading revivals, as they have time to invest and pass on teachings, as well as the motivation of a lower income, and a generational family outlook. Many have started businesses based on a hobby, the freedom of unschooling allowing them to gradually turn it into something more profitable. We do not separate our identities of mother and worker, but see ourselves as integrated home-educating-mother-and-artist/-researcher/ etc.

It is noticeable that many unschooling fathers are also self-employed or work flexibly from home, giving greater freedom for both parents to adapt their schedules, and accommodate each other's work and family commitments. Rothermel found that "Fathers had more involvement with their children's day to day education and family life than might normally be expected had the children been in school".[447] It is a very different experience for a child to see first hand what their parents' work entails on a daily basis, rather than getting the odd glimpse here and there or hearing about it second hand. When both parents are based at home, we can appreciate the efforts of the other much more easily. No longer do we need to feel that our partner has no idea how much effort we put in during the day, how much harder we have worked than the other. The presence of two parents, however preoccupied with work one may be, changes the whole dynamic and feel of the household. The more advanced technology becomes, and the more opportunities there are for working from home, the more we can reintegrate being a fully present mother with maintaining a sense of self beyond motherhood.

For single parents it is much harder to home educate of course; most families sacrifice one steady income in order to have a parent at home. But some do manage, and feel the sacrifices are worth the time they would otherwise lose with their child. There is also a saving in not sending children to school, even state-funded school: it is estimated that raising a child born in 2016 will cost the typical parent £231,843 over the course of birth to age 21, including £74,430 spent on state schooling. A fee-paying school pushes the cost to over £373,000, and just short of £500,000 if the child goes to boarding school.[448] Dr. Brian Ray's studies show that the average American school spends nearly $10,000 per child per year, whereas the average homeschool family spends about $500 per child per year.[449]

Rebuilding the Community

A much more considered organising of communities would go a long way to enabling one or both parents to combine work and spending time with their children, as well as providing more support for single parents. While we wait for this to happen however, we can start to initiate it ourselves. Christopher Alexander writes in *A Pattern Language*, "As the decentralization of work becomes more and more effective, the workshop in the home grows and grows in importance".[450] We might switch that to say that as the workshop (or office) in the home grows in importance, the decentralization of work becomes more effective. Either way, the ONS note that "About 1.5 million actually work in their home, or in studios or workshops in the grounds".[451] Alexander envisioned this situation as the recapturing of our natural way of living and working, reminding us again of our hunter-gatherer ancestors. It is worth quoting Alexander's vision of the future community, one that sounds very like an unschooling-home-working community:

> *Make a place in the home, where substantial work can be done; not just a hobby, but a job. Change the zoning laws to encourage modest, quiet work operations to locate in neighborhoods. Give the workshop perhaps a few hundred square feet; and locate it so it can be seen from the street and the owner can hang out a shingle... we imagine a society in which work and family are far more intermingled than today; a society in which people - businessmen artists, craftsmen, shopkeepers, professionals work for themselves, alone and in small groups, with much more relation to their immediate surroundings than they have today. In such a society, the home workshop becomes far more than a basement or a garage hobby shop. It becomes an integral part of every house; as central to the house's function as the kitchen or the bedrooms. And we believe its most important characteristic is its relationship to the public street. For most of us, work life is relatively public. Certainly, compared to the privacy of the hearth, it is a public affair. Even where the public relationship is slight, there is something to be gained, both for the worker and the community, by enlarging the connection between the two. In the case of the home workshop, the public nature of the work is especially*

valuable. It brings the workshop out of the realm of back-yard hobbies and into the public domain. The people working there have a view of the street; they are exposed to the people passing by. And the people passing learn something about the nature of the community. The children especially are enlivened by this contact.[452]

Alexander continues his vision with the transformation of the school's place in the community:

Empowering corporations to sell off assets and move the schools elsewhere defeats a longer term strategy of having walkable facilities in every neighborhood that families can use. These neighborhood schools should remain vital centers for communities...Physical structures could facilitate far more than classes: they are natural sites for gardens, common workplaces and small business incubators, and recreation and fairs and markets. Our physical schools could be important places to nurture and create social networks and this is critical if we are to move toward green, local economies. That means people have to work together somehow and somewhere. This access to the physical spaces already present in most neighborhoods, could help grow wider, denser, more multi-nodal social networks and begin to replace the lost social capital of many communities. And that should enable a lot of small scale sharing and conservation to occur as we rebuild the social networks, like soil structure, at the smallest level.[453]

Working from home and educating at home are the vanguard of this movement, a way for women, and often men, to raise their children themselves whilst engaging in fulfilling work. This could apply also to higher or continuing education. Camille Paglia and Christina Hoff Sommers both argue that universities need to be much more flexible for women, given the different trajectories their lives take in comparison to men's due to motherhood.[454,455] They argue that women need to be able to take courses around their biological drives and childrearing commitments, over a longer period than men, although there is no reason this could not equally apply to everyone: to fit in learning and development as an ongoing, lifetime commitment alongside apprenticeships, career, periods of reflection, family duties, travel or whatever else helps us find who we are. To learn as we need and want.

Central to the rebuilding of communities is seeing our contribution to society as having a much longer-term impact than we currently conceive of, resounding through generations. Kawagley and Barnhardt list four crucial aspects of indigenous worldviews, demonstrating how they are expressed through education.[456] These happen to correlate very clearly with the general attitude of unschoolers. Indigenous worldviews take a long term perspective of life, meaning that education is understood, and carried out, across generations. The inter-connectedness of all things is also a fundamental concept. This expresses as knowledge being bound to the context in which it is learned, and that all elements of knowledge are interrelated, something far more tangible in an unschooled environment, where learning is not compartmentalised, and is often extremely 'tangential'. Indigenous worldviews place an emphasis on adaptation to change, and so see education as something which must continually adapt to fit the time and place – something we try to do with schools, but clearly is impossible given their structured nature. The last point is a commitment to the commons, expressed in education as the whole being greater than the sum of its parts: all have something to contribute, and it will vary from person to person, but it is the aggregate of abilities and knowledge that matters, in polar opposition to western society where the prime concern is our own destiny, not that of society as a whole.

The Balance of Power

Intriguingly, there is evidence that women and their work have been devalued by the spread of alphabetic literacy. While on holiday in the Mediterranean, Leonard Shlain, a cardiovascular surgeon, inventor and author, became interested in the connection between the demise of Goddess worship, the advent of patriarchy, and the development of literacy. As a vascular surgeon operating on arteries that supply blood to the brain, he was very aware of the different functions performed by each of the brain's hemispheres. Knowing that as we grow, different kinds of learning strengthen some neuronal pathways and weaken others, he extrapolated from the individual to the cultural level. Shlain discovered that once a critical mass of a society learn to read and write, traditionally masculine characteristics start to dominate cultural attitudes, while the associated feminine traits are systematically devalued. He believes that this shift is due to literacy's reliance on the analytic thought processes linked to the left hemisphere of the brain.[457]

Shlain agrees that we are still influenced by the original neurodesign that we inherited from our hunter-gatherer ancestors. He describes the right hemisphere of the brain as performing those functions associated with the holistic, simultaneous, synthetic and concrete, whereas the left hemisphere is associated with linear, sequential, reductionist and abstract needs. "Every newborn is endowed with a brain that embodies both modes of thought... [but] A third shaping force, almost as important, is the principal medium through which the child learns to perceive his culture's information. This medium - pictorial or alphabetic - plays a role in determining which neuronal pathways of the child's developing brain will be reinforced: those that process images or those that process words". Shlain believes that it is no accident that we have seen a resurgence of feminine values, holistic thinking and respect for nature alongside the rise in visually-oriented technologies: "I would argue that the visual media are largely responsible for this revolution... though not simply because of the information they convey. A greater factor may be the way they actually reprogram our brains".[458]

Certainly the spread of literacy is intimately tied to the development of agriculture, and the need to document, keep accounts, trade and organise. At the same time, the huge differences in life style between farmers and hunter-gatherers led to a complete reorganisation of society – one that to all intents we still live under today. Dr. Peter Gray describes the changes that took place:

> *While hunter-gatherer parents are indulgent and permissive, agrarian parents are typically strict and autocratic... While hunter-gatherers value their children's wilfulness and independence, agrarian parents value obedience. While hunter-gatherer children are free to play and explore all day on their own, agrarian children are required to work a good portion, if not most of the day, at chores in the home and field. A study of peoples in Botswana with mixed hunter-gatherer and agrarian subsistence revealed that the more a family was involved in hunting and gathering and the less they were involved in farming, the more time children had to play... Hunting and gathering are knowledge- and skill-intensive, but not labor-intensive. The adults hunt and gather with a sense of play, and they have plenty of time left over for such leisure activities as gossiping, visiting friends in neighboring bands, making music, and in other ways playing... Moreover, the birth rate among hunter-gatherers is relatively low, so there are relatively few young mouths to feed. Hunter-gatherers simply don't need child labor. In contrast, farming is highly labor-intensive, and much of that labor is unskilled and can be done by children. Farmers*

> *typically have more children than do hunter-gatherers, and to feed and care for them all the children must work.*[459]

To all intents we are still farmers, regardless of our actual jobs: we fulfil the role of production, necessitating huge organised workforces and the training of the young to take over the role.

In *The Disappearance of Childhood*, Neil Postman ties the invention of movable type printing to the invention of childhood itself (as opposed to a gradual and natural progression from infancy to adulthood). With literacy came adult 'secrets', information available only to adults who could read, and literacy required schools to teach people how to read. "Because school was designed for the preparation of a literate adult, the young became to be perceived not as miniature adults, but as ... unformed adults".[460] Children became the proverbial pails waiting to be filled, rather than fires waiting to be sparked into life. Almost overnight in evolutionary time, we upended our natural way of living and learning over generations, and created the labour-intensive, authoritarian system we maintain today. Very few truly benefit.

As Western society moved from an oral culture, with knowledge passed on traditionally through stories, experience and mentors, to the spread of alphabetic literacy and a more hierarchical and controlling approach to knowledge, so women's traditional role was lost. The current school system continues to reflect the needs of industry, neglecting our social side which seeks to nurture relationships, both human and environmental, intimate and societal. It is no wonder, then, that the further we stray from our original relationship-oriented, matriarchal model, the less we seem able to get along together on the local or global scale. David Graeber explains, "In

North America, consensus process emerged more than anything else through the feminist movement... Much of the procedure was originally adopted from the Quakers, and Quaker-inspired groups; the Quakers, in turn, claim to have been inspired by Native American practice". Graeber relates many examples of native groups who had been practicing democracy through consensus ever since they can remember, and that from their point of view, "rather than disseminating democracy around the world, 'Western' governments have been spending at least as much time inserting themselves into the lives of people who have been practicing democracy for thousands of years, and in one way or another, telling them to cut it out".[461] Schooling, of course, is one of the primary methods.

Casualties of Education

Modern Western culture likes women to go out to work. This is called equality. It also ensures that women are emasculated (or should it be masculated?) from their connection to the family. The truth is, there is a power in raising your children, rather than allowing the state to do it. A power that extends to having the time to meet other women and share opinions, to rally, control, and influence men and community. Grassroots activism throughout history has been majorly influenced by women. It is this power which is denigrated and then denied when we are subsumed into a culturally male workplace. Many indigenous cultures still recognise the power of mothers, and value it. Once the children are dislocated to schools though, culture usually disintegrates, as women and elders no longer have a reason to take pride in their work or teachings. This is compounded when children go on to higher education in more distant areas.

Our world encourages the seeking of qualifications, and measures progress by the distance we move from our roots, impoverishing communities and concentrating wealth and knowledge in exclusive geographical areas. The documentary *Schooling The World: The White Man's Last Burden*, highlights this effect in Ladakh, India, where gaining an education leads naturally to aspirations of a career and good income, causing the flight of generations away from their homes.[462] Whether in rural Ladakh or the UK, the effect is the same, splitting families up, but providing for an entire industry in care homes, childcare, and all the other all the jobs we cannot do because we have to work and our family network is too distant. Academia itself - the peak of education - all too often forces us to choose between career and roots: if we stay at our local university, try to give back something to our own community and children, we often have to sacrifice the respect, prestige and resources of a more prominent university. The most talented academics are thus tempted away from their communities, leaving a lack of local role models. This promotes the monopoly on learning where the 'best' teachers are attracted to the 'best' schools and universities, and in order to fund research and academic wages, students must pay a high fee, thus entrenching social inequality.

The UN publication *Urban Indigenous Peoples and Migration* recognises that "For practical and economic reasons the larger towns offer better educational facilities and it is difficult to attract educated teachers to smaller places. In recent years, a number of schools have closed down, which is a serious problem for those who wish to remain in their smaller communities".[463] However, the report goes on to say that "In these situations, the parents themselves become responsible for teaching their children, but this *may* pose a problem, as they *may* not hold any formal education themselves. This *may* prevent the children from continuing their education in the larger towns. The relatively low level of education in the settlements is thus maintained" (my emphases). There is a lot of uncertainty in these statements; uncertainty that could have been appeased by looking at the research on home educated children.

The educational attainment of parents is only a factor for children attending school. In a home education situation, children succeed comparably, and beyond, their schooled peers regardless of their parent's educational background.[464] The problem for the small communities discussed here is not that parents are incapable of teaching their children, but that they do not have the support - in terms of time, finance, and access to resources - to support or even learn alongside their children. Further, studies such as the Hole in the Wall experiment conducted by Sugata Mitra (where a computer with internet access was placed in a kiosk in a Delhi slum, and children were allowed to use it freely and unsupervised, teaching themselves to use the technology regardless of being able to speak English) show how little guidance children need when they are given resources such as internet access, teaching themselves to use a computer, browse the internet and learn advanced concepts without any adult interference.[465] There is very good reason to believe that providing remote communities with internet access and remote support in the form of a teacher or even simply motivated peers, would not diminish the ability of children to receive an education comparable to children attending urban schools.

The conflict between roots and career is not confined to academia of course; it has come to be seen as progress to move away from your community and youth, with the distance travelled an indicator of success. Independence from family is seen as a mark of self-sufficiency and maturity, freedom more important than responsibility. This attitude is more prevalent in middle class areas, again influencing the likelihood of the better off relocating to get the best jobs, while the working class are inhibited by income and family commitment.

Bunker Roy's Barefoot College decided for this very reason to teach the mothers and grandmothers in rural villages, rather than the men. Men are ambitious and move to the cities for work once they have qualifications - a necessary financial prerogative as provider, but this was doing nothing to raise the village's educational level as a whole, and teachers would have to teach every new generation from scratch, as any training given to the men did not find its way to the community in a lasting way. Roy says that "Women, on the other hand, are committed to staying in their communities. They have roots with their children and grandchildren and want to improve their future".[466] Once the grandmothers and mothers were educated, they took on the responsibility of teaching the knowledge to the younger generations. This is in direct contrast to Western attitudes, where investing in the very people raising the next generation tends to be seen as a waste of time. It also starts to remedy the plight of the elder generation, who in Ladakh, for example, tell how they used to be proud of their ability to manage life and of all their knowledge, but now feel inferior and worthless compared to their schooled children.[467]

Bolivia is an example of a country that has tried to tackle the problem of indigenous communities being underrepresented in higher education, without destroying the integrity of the communities themselves. In 2008, the government of President Evo Morales launched the Indigenous University of Bolivia (UNIBOL) with sites in three ethnolinguistic regions. The universities are dedicated to preserving and promoting indigenous knowledge, and indigenous histories and knowledge are taught alongside technical expertise. A Guarani oil technician, for example, would be on a par with other experts, but would also understand local indigenous issues. While oil and gas exploration, as well as ranching, logging and industrialised fishing have all affected indigenous communities in negative ways, some indigenous organisations have taken a stance of engagement rather than opposition. They hope that training in these fields will help their people monitor, mitigate, and participate in these industries, ensuring proper concern for the environmental and social aspects, as well as proper distribution of the profits. Morales intends the Indigenous Universities to stem the exodus of young people from the countryside to cities. Students are expected to return to their communities once their studies have been completed, and apply their new knowledge towards the improvement of their region.

The Indigenous University of Venezuela teaches subjects including human rights, law, and native agricultural practices. By protecting and perpetuating both ancient and modern knowledge, we ensure the potential of creativity – we cannot predict how disparate elements of knowledge may come together to promote new discoveries and solutions. Indigenous universities train community leaders to fight to protect their land and culture.[468] This idea goes back at least to the Survival Schools movement begun in the United States in the late 1960s and 1970s, as a response to the loss of indigenous language and culture in the residential schools (interestingly, this was also around the time that Second Wave feminism arose). First Nations communities set up locally-run schools where their own languages and cultures could be prominent. Many Survival Schools continue to exist today.

Home educating is a reclaiming of women's work, and a statement of communal and anti-colonial values. UNESCO asks that we strengthen the role of indigenous women as "custodians of culture, language and beliefs",[469] raising the status of women and acknowledging the responsibility women have in "transmitting cultural and spiritual knowledge and practices, and group identity in general, to succeeding generations. Because culture exists through, and is generated by, the lived experiences of people, women's role in transmitting culture also situates them as creators and custodians of culture".[470] We can make mothers feel needed and valued by allowing them to teach and to work in a way that includes their own children. Our efforts must be considered worthwhile, valuable and meaningful. Prominent home schooler Rachel DeMille reminds us that "Women have power over generations - and we must use this power or see others usurp and misuse it. In our modern world the void left by women who don't magnify this power is being filled by government... Raising children is the thing that changes the world the most. Everybody knows this, but Modern Feminism has convinced us that it's cliché, even patronizing".[471] Susan Maushart asks for a "family structure which empowers women". Many would argue that teaching our children ourselves is the answer.

CHAPTER 12

Teaching with Tech

Why would we want to limit a kid's computer time?
The computer is, without question, the single most
important tool of modern society. Our limiting kids'
computer time would be like hunter-gatherer adults
limiting their kids' bow-and-arrow time.

—PETER GRAY [472]

THE FUTURE BELONGS TO the autodidacts. Increasing numbers of entrepreneurs have not finished high school, especially in the area of technology, and a traditional undergraduate degree is not only becoming unaffordable for many, but unnecessary - online universities, lectures, and open-source content all render a campus-based education just another option, and one that comes with no guarantees of a job. More and more people are finding that the unschooler's world of intensive, passionate study is far more valuable than the mindless busy-work imposed upon students by schools, which are more concerned with hitting targets than educating students for life. Even the idea of what constitutes knowledge itself is changing, as the internet opens up access to information that was once the preserve of the academic elite, and indigenous oral traditions are finally being accepted to contain generations of scientific observation.

The Knowledge Economy

Futurist guru Alvin Toffler predicted a major powershift in society due to the sheer volume of knowledge accessible to anyone with an internet connection. Knowledge, he believed, would replace material power:

> *Knowledge itself ... turns out to be not only the source of the highest-quality power, but also the most important in-gredient of force and wealth. Put differently, knowledge has gone from being an adjunct of money power and muscle power, to being their very essence. It is, in fact, the ultimate amplifier. This is the key to the powershift that lies ahead, and it explains why the battle for control of knowledge and the means of communication is heating up all over the world... we are creating new networks of knowledge ... link-ing concepts to one another in startling ways ... building up amazing hierarchies of inference ... spawning new theories, hypotheses, and images, based on novel assumptions, new languages, codes, and logics... But more important, we are interrelating data in more ways, giving them context, and thus forming them into information; and we are assembling chunks of information into larger and larger models and architectures of knowledge.* [473]

One measure of intelligence is the ability to adapt to new in-formation, and this is where the freedom from structured curricula comes to the fore. Those who are free to adapt to, challenge, and integrate new knowledge and ideas as they arise, will be at the forefront of creating the new knowledge-based society. Various futurists have described the skills they believe will be crucial in the coming generations. These include Harvard's Professor of Cognition and Education, Howard Gardner, who lists "The ability to integrate ideas from different disciplines or spheres; the capacity to uncover and clarify new problems, questions and phenomena; respect for, and awareness of, differences; understanding one's responsibilities to others".[474] Tony Wagner, of Harvard University's Innovation Lab, lists critical thinking and problem solving; agility and adaptability; curiosity and imagination.[475] Behavioural Scientist Daniel Pink lists high-concept thinking, high-touch leading, the ability to build projects like symphonies, and the skills of empathy, playing (as adults) and meaning.[476]

When Harvard School of Government issued advice to students planning a career in the new international economy which it believes is arriving, "It warned sharply that academic classes and professional credentials would count for less and less when measured against real world training",[477] going on to list their own essential skills that future citizens will need. These can be summarised as: the ability to define problems without a guide; to ask hard questions which challenge prevailing assumptions; the ability to quickly assimilate needed data from masses of irrelevant information, and to conceptualise and reorganise information into new patterns; the ability to think inductively, deductively and dialectically; the ability to discuss issues, problems, and techniques in public with an eye to reaching decisions about policy, whilst persuading others that your course is the right one; the ability to work in teams without any guidance, and the ability to work absolutely alone.[478] James Heckman and Tim Kautz of America's National Bureau of Economic Research argue for more emphasis on 'character skills' such as perseverance, sociability and curiosity, which are highly valued by employers and correlate closely with employees' ability to adapt to new situations and acquire new skills.[479]

These 'future skills' are highly unlikely to flourish in the confines of the school curriculum, where the emphasis is on giving the correct answers to predefined questions – the polar opposite to the world described above. As Gatto writes, one of the most conflicting aspects of school in relation to the above is that "We demand [children] acknowledge they cannot solve problems by themselves, but must wait for a teacher, a social worker, a TV set, a computer program, or a government official to tell them what to do".[480] In great contrast, we really need people who can think outside the box, who believe in their own ideas passionately, who can bring together disparate elements of knowledge to create something new, who are not afraid to challenge orthodoxy, who can work flexibly with others or alone as needed, and perhaps above all, those who can entertain themselves and others in the broadest sense of the word, finding something of interest and excitement in any situation and inspiring others to see it too. This is the description of an unschooler far more than it is of any school child.

A New Operating System

In the seventies, Ivan Illich wrote the now classic *Deschooling Society*, where he proposed the idea of learning webs. These webs, Illich envisioned, would be an evolving collection of mentors and professionals, whose skills and knowledge could be matched to students as the need and passion arose. Illich wrote that "A good education system should have three purposes: to provide all that want to learn with access to resources at any time in their lives; make it possible for all who want to share knowledge etc. to find those who want to learn it from them; and to create opportunities for those who want to present an issue to the public to make their arguments known".[481] This has not only become actionable with the advent of the internet, but learning webs have effectively arisen organically due to the nature of the technology itself.

Christopher Alexander demonstrates how the internet reflects not only the ideas of the futurists, but recreates the original role of the university:

> *The original universities in the middle ages were simply collections of teachers who attracted students because they had something to offer. They were marketplaces of ideas, located all over the town, where people could shop around for the kinds of ideas and learning which made sense to them... First, the social and physical environment must provide a setting which encourages rather than discourages individuality and freedom of thought. Second, the environment must provide a setting which encourages the student to see for himself which ideas make sense - a setting which gives him the maximum opportunity and exposure to a great variety of ideas, so that he can make up his mind for himself.[482]*

This is the internet through and through, when used with intelligence and skill.

It is this aspect of technology that has allowed unschooling to flourish. Unschoolers are experts at seeking out the huge variety of resources available online, and are in no small part responsible for the early success of Salman Khan, the founder of Khan Academy, an online education site. Khan Academy has 3,500 short videos or tutorials and over 10 million students, covering subjects such as maths, history, medicine, physics, art history and computer science. They recently partnered with institutions such as NASA, The Museum of Modern Art, and MIT to offer specialised content, while the courses are available in up to 36 languages. And it is free. Prominent universities are following suit, including MIT, Harvard, Berkeley, and Edinburgh. Sebastian Thrun, previously professor of Artificial Intelligence at Stanford and the head of Google's top-secret experimental lab, resigned to work on his own project: massive scale, free to all, online education (massive open online courses or MOOCs). "The music industry, publishing, transportation, retail – they've all experienced the great technological disruption. Now, says Thrun, it's education's turn".[483] Anant Argarwal of MIT says MOOCs are "Going to reinvent education. It's going to transform universities. It's going to democratise education on a global scale. It's the biggest innovation to happen in education for 200 years".[484] In Thrun's Artificial Intelligence course, of the 23,000 students who graduated, all 400 of the top marks were online students. These courses are available to unschooled and schooled students alike, studying independently or as a learning co-op.

Many and various curricula are available online, some for a price, some for free. Many universities including MIT and Stanford post their curricula online, and entire structured courses are available from sites such as Codecademy and Khan Academy. AltSchool, a startup created by a former Google employee, "has launched a series of 'micro-schools' in which teachers help students create their own individualized lesson plans".[485] Goldsmiths, University of London has created a full BSc degree in computer science, taught entirely online for £5,650 per year over three years. The course is being produced in a partnership with one of the world's biggest online university companies, Coursera. It will include group work, live video and individual tuition, with students attending exam centres for their final exams. The chief executive of Coursera sees the new course as a game changer, allowing adults in full time work to pursue a degree without having to leave their job or pay for the costs of relocation and accommodation. He expects a lot of older and employed students.[486] Coursera itself offers a huge variety of free university courses taught by professors around the world.

Clearly, the movement is away from traditional classrooms and to a more student led, individualised method of learning. The Hole in the Wall Experiments by Sugata Mitra gained him a lot of attention for demonstrating what unschoolers have known and practiced for years and years: children do not need to be sat in a classroom, but given the environment and access to resources, will teach themselves. This is a world away from school, where children are subject to someone else's timetable, someone else's curriculum, being graded at a time of someone else's choosing, and developing according to someone else's schedule. The availability of the internet across massive parts of the world has the potential to challenge the entire educational model. Anyone can help another provided they both have internet access, breaking down the concentration of quality education in certain areas and certain institutions.

Interestingly, the trend of home educating families to become more child-led in their learning over time, has been backed up by researchers who studied the impact of widespread use of laptop technology on teaching and learning. "Researchers have documented a shift from lectures and other teacher-centered forms of delivery to lessons that are more collaborative and project-oriented. Teachers... become facilitators in

project-oriented classrooms, with students increasingly assuming the role of directors of their own learning".[487] When
given the opportunity to free themselves from the constraints of traditional schooling methods, students start to
move toward a much more natural way of learning – and one
that produces far better outcomes: "Among the many reported benefits of this project-based approach to learning are
greater student engagement, improved analytic abilities, and
a greater likelihood to apply high-order thinking skills".[488]
The Center for Children and Technology at the Education
Development Center monitored a two-year technology trial:
"The study found that after multimedia technology was
used... eighth graders in Union City, New Jersey, scored 27
percentage points higher than students from other urban and
special needs school districts on statewide tests in reading,
math, and writing achievement. The study also found a decrease in absenteeism and an increase in students transferring to the school".[489] And "In a five-year study, researchers
at SRI International found that technology-using students...
outperformed non-technology-using students in communication skills, teamwork, and problem solving". The researchers,
"found increased student engagement, greater responsibility
for learning, increased peer collaboration skills, and greater
achievement gains by students who had been labeled low
achievers".[490]

Of course, technology is a tool like any other. When used to
replicate school, it will produce the same results as school-
learning. Researcher Harold Wenglinsky "found that the effectiveness of computers in the classroom depended on how
they were used... Wenglinsky found that if computers were
used for drill or practice, they typically had a negative effect
on student achievement. If they were used with real-world

applications, such as spreadsheets, or to simulate relationships or changing variables, student achievement increased".[491] It is the manner of learning itself which defines the outcomes, and when used well, technology has the potential to allow children to learn in their own unique way, in their own developmental timeframe, and to focus on their specific needs at any given time. Schools themselves do not necessarily need to be part of the equation.

The impact of technology on learning is such that in 2007, Andrew Churches further developed and refined the traditional Bloom's Taxonomy of Learning to create Bloom's Digital Taxonomy. Where the traditional taxonomy lists, for example, 'recognising, listing, identifying, locating, finding', Churches has added 'highlighting, bookmarking, searching, googling'; the heading Analysing, including 'comparing, organising, deconstructing, outlining, integrating' incorporates digital techniques such as 'mashing, linking, validating, reverse-engineering, cracking'; whilst the category of Creating, which includes 'designing, constructing, planning, producing, inventing' has the addition of 'programming, blogging, mixing, remixing, wiki-ing, publishing, directing/producing'. Churches makes manifest the depth of learning and experience available via the online world when used interactively and constructively.[492] An extract from *The Guardian* demonstrates this in a more tangible way:

The online world offers kids remarkable opportunities to become literate and creative because young people can now publish ideas not just to their friends, but to the world. And it turns out that when they write for strangers, their sense of 'authentic audience' makes them work harder, push themselves further, and create powerful new communicative forms. Consider Sam McPherson. At 13, he became obsessed with the television show Lost and began to con-

*tribute to a fan-run wiki. 'I jumped in and just started edit-
ing,' Sam says. He developed skills in cooperating with far-
flung strangers and keeping a cool head while mediating
arguments. Joseph Kahne, a professor of education at Mills
College in California, studied 400 teenagers over three
years. Kahne found that teens who participated in fan or
hobby sites were more likely than other kids to do real-world
volunteering. Interestingly, this wasn't true of being on
Facebook.*[493]

Gaming Matters

There are two major problems with our attitudes to children
and technology: the first is the conflation of technology with
games; the second is the assumption that games themselves
are frivolous pursuits. Whilst most people can see the benefits of the internet in a general sense, many still object to
their children spending significant amounts of time online,
and especially have difficulty accepting that there is anything
of merit in video games. We have not yet accepted gaming as
a worthy tool for children in the same way that we do books.
It should be remembered that poetry, plays, books and radio
have all been seen as a threat to children in the same way the
internet is today. To be too immersed in books was seen as
dangerous to the mind, as evidenced from Plato to Dante to
Madame Bovary, and parents feared for their children who
sat in doors all day reading in the same we worry about children on laptops.

Psychologist Dr. Peter Gray asks "Why is it any better to limit
TV or computer time than to limit book-reading time? Why
do we worry about a kid's spending maybe 4 or 5 hours a day
at a computer screen, doing what he wants to do, but don't
worry about the same kid sitting at school for 6 hours a day

and then doing homework for another couple of hours - doing what others are forcing him to do? I ask you to consider the possibility that the kid is learning more valuable lessons at the computer than at school, in part because the computer activity is self-chosen and the school activity is not".[494] In comparison to books, the internet is interactive, sociable, varied in viewpoints, and contextual (whereas we can easily read a book without discussing it with anyone else, without any understanding of wider context, without invitation to critique and research the ideas, and without an audience for your inspired fanfiction).

And we certainly cannot lump video games into the same pot as television under the heading of 'Screen Time'. In Neil Postman's *Amusing Ourselves to Death*, he argues that "Television confounds serious issues by demeaning and undermining political discourse and by turning real, complex issues into superficial images, less about ideas and thoughts and more about entertainment... television is not an effective way of providing education, as it provides only top-down information transfer, rather than the interaction... necessary to maximize learning".[495] Postman refers to the relationship between information and human response as the 'information-action' ratio. Gaming has a very different information-action ratio to television: interactive, involved and democratic versus passive, submissive and indoctrinating. As Gray points out, "Systematic surveys have shown that regular video-game players are, if anything, more physically fit, less likely to be obese, more likely to also enjoy outdoor play, more socially engaged, more socially well-adjusted, and more civic minded than are their non-gaming peers".[496]

This is not so surprising when we understand the nature of playing MMORPGs (Massively Multiplayer Online Role-playing Games). Gray explains,

> *At school and in other adult-dominated contexts [players] may be treated as idiots who need constant direction, but in the game they are in charge and can solve difficult problems and exhibit extraordinary skills. In the game, age does not matter, but skill does. In these ways, video games are like all other forms of true play... Players go on quests within this virtual world, and along the way they meet other players, who might become friends or foes. Players may start off playing solo, avoiding others, but to advance to the higher levels they have to make friends and join with others in mutual quests. Making friends within the game requires essentially the same skills as making friends in the real world. You can't be rude. You have to understand the etiquette of the culture you are in and abide by that etiquette. You have to learn about the goals of a potential friend and help that individual to achieve those goals.. The games offer players endless opportunities to experiment with different personalities and ways of behaving, in a fantasy world where there are no real-life consequences for failing... Such games are, in many ways, like the imaginative sociodramatic games of preschool children, but played in a virtual world, with communication by online text, and raised up many notches in sophistication to fit the interests and abilities of the older children, teenagers, and adults who play them. Like all sociodramatic games, they are very much anchored in an understanding of the real world, and they exercise concepts and social skills that are quite relevant to that world.*[497]

Professor of Education James Paul Gee started playing video games when his young son asked for help with one. He went on to investigate the way video games help us to learn, concluding that schools are "In the cognitive-science dark ages".[498] Gee lists some of those elements found in games which have been shown to help us learn new things: well ordered problems/ problem based learning; cycles of expertise (creating a feeling of accumulating and building upon knowledge and skills); being invested in the material; co-design (players' input creates their experience); empowering learners by feeling that what you do matters; customisation (games allow you to customise according to your type of playing/learning, also inviting you to play in a new style); the freedom to explore and try things without penalties; the cost of failure is low, allowing learning through mistakes; levelled problem solving which leads sequentially to the next stage; the right level of frustration to keep you going; deep/long term learning; clear roles, allowing you to see the point and identity of who you will become if you do persevere; the further afield your knowledge extends, the greater potential you have for innovation; information on demand and just in time; and using new skills in context. In contrast, a school setting often leaves students without a feeling for the whole system which they are studying, and when we fail to see new information as a set of complex interactions and relationships, each fact and isolated element memorised for a test is meaningless.[499]

A 2014 analysis of studies on the effects of video games demonstrated the "long-lasting positive effects of video games on basic mental processes - such as perception, attention, memory, and decision-making. Most of the research involves effects of action video games... Many of the abilities tapped by such games are precisely those that psychologists consider to be the basic building blocks of intelligence".[500] Psychologists and neuroscientists found that gaming accounted for improvements in basic visual processes; improvements in attention and vigilance; improvements in executive functioning (referring to a person's ability to allot their mental resources in ways that allow for rapid, efficient problem solving or decision-making); and improvements in job-related skills. Gray adds, "It's interesting to note that video games appear to build these components of intelligence faster and more efficiently than any other intervention anyone has devised".[501] In fact, "a study commissioned by the IBM Corporation concluded that the leadership skills exercised within MMORPGs are essentially the same as those required to run a modern company".[502]

But just as important as the medium, is the content and context of the information presented. One gamer recounts the effect of playing the hugely popular *Metal Gear Solid* on their ability to recall scientific terms:

> *Two brothers, clones of the greatest soldier of all time, are doing battle. The one brother, codenamed Solid Snake, is the main character of the game and has been genetically engineered to have all the combat related genes. While Liquid Snake, the other brother and game's antagonist who received all the recessive genes, desperately tries to outdo his brother in combat. The game is the embodiment of the classical battle between nature and nurture (something that has come back to me time and again in my studies of psychology). Liquid explains in one cut-scene about how though their genotype is the same, their phenotype is different. I have never since forgotten the meaning of those two biological terms. However, the terms viviparous and oviparous which were not covered in the game but were rather included in my ninth grade biology class are completely lost on me. Why is that? Because I did not learn them contextually. I was not immersed in a world where viviparous and oviparous meant anything to me. I did not have to engage in a battle of simulated life or death over them. Thanks to this game still to this day I can recall that TNF epsilon is a type of cytokine and that it is a polypeptide bond; I can remember that apoptosis is when cells commit suicide. And I hate biology![503]*

This makes sense when we understand the way our brains form memories and new connections. Author Robert Twigger explains it well:

It appears that a great deal depends on the nucleus basalis, located in the basal forebrain. Among other things, this bit of the brain produces significant amounts of acetylcholine, a neurotransmitter that regulates the rate at which new connections are made between brain cells. This in turn dictates how readily we form memories of various kinds, and how strongly we retain them. When the nucleus basalis is 'switched on', acetylcholine flows and new connections occur. When it is switched off, we make far fewer new connections... From research into the way stroke victims recover lost skills it has been observed that the nucleus basalis only switches on when one of three conditions occur: a novel situation, a shock, or intense focus, maintained through repetition or continuous application.[504]

These three situations in which new neural connections can be formed – novel situations, shocks, and intense focus – can all be found in well designed games, which also maintain the necessary repetition of the new skill.

According to Jane McGonigal, who wrote her doctoral thesis on gaming, the reason for the mass exodus to virtual worlds is that video games are increasingly fulfilling genuine human needs, whilst reality is not engineered to maximise our potential, and does not motivate us effectively. "What most people see when they look at the game are horrible little creatures running around killing people and making crude jokes. They fail to see the little nuances of game play that provoke mental development. If we were to throw out all the educational things that have violence or crude humor then we would have to do away with the works of William Shakespeare. Yet of course, that sounds absurd, but stopping a child from playing a game that routinely challenges him to think of different ways to solve a puzzle is completely reasonable".[505] Game designer Will Wright believes games teach us in a way that schools simply cannot:

> *The problem with our education system is we've taken this kind of narrow, reductionist, Aristotelian approach to what learning is. It's not designed for experimenting with complex systems and navigating your way through them in an intuitive way, which is what games teach. It's not really designed for failure, which is also something games teach... I think that failure is a better teacher than success. Trial and error, reverse-engineering stuff in your mind - all the ways that kids interact with games - that's the kind of thinking schools should be teaching. And I would argue that as the world becomes more complex, and as outcomes become less about success or failure, games are better at preparing you. The education system is going to realize this sooner or later. It's starting.[506]*

We accept that play is a fundamental need for children in order to set the foundations for later learning, but we also know that we learn better at any age when the learning is fun and play-like. Editor of *Psychology Today*, Hara Estroff Marano, writes "Play makes children nimble - neurobiologically, mentally, behaviorally - capable of adapting to a rapidly evolving world. That makes it just about the best preparation for life in the 21st century. Psychologists believe that play cajoles people toward their human potential because it preserves all the possibilities nervous systems tend to otherwise prune away. It's no accident that all of the predicaments of play - the challenges, the dares, the races and chases - model the struggle for survival. Think of play as the future with sneakers on".[507]

Hacking Education

As might be expected given the parallels in philosophy, un-schooling is increasingly being adopted by the Silicon Valley population. "Many of those new homeschoolers come from the tech community. When homeschooling expert Diane Flynn Keith held a sold-out workshop in Redwood City, Cali-fornia... fully half of the parents worked in the tech industry. Jens Peter de Pedro, an app designer in Brooklyn, says that five of the 10 fathers in his homeschooling group work in tech, as do two of the eight mothers. And Samantha Cook says that her local hackerspace is often filled with tech-savvy homeschoolers".[508] Even Elon Musk, founder of Tesla, SpaceX and PayPal and, has rejected traditional schooling for his children, setting up a space for a small group of children under the guidance of a well paid, specially selected mentor, and letting the group "loose with all sorts of hands-on projects and experiments". There is no grading in terms age or ability.[509] De Pedro describes a mentality "within the tech and startup community where you look at the world and go, 'Is the way we do things now really the best way to do it? If you look at schools with this mentality, really the only possi-ble conclusion is 'Heck, I could do this better myself out of my garage!"[510] Whilst certain subjects have long had a strong amateur component (technology and astronomy for exam-ple), the number of autodidacts in all areas is now increasing due to the depth of knowledge available via the internet, fo-rums for the exchange of ideas, and the networking opportu-nities that allow more and more people to make a valuable contribution.

Children of the Code/ Edgewalkers

Former President of Venezuela Hugo Chavez understood the potential of technology for large-scale intellectual liberation. Mission Science aimed to train 400,000 people in the concepts and use of open source software, the fundamentals of hardware and software, their use and utilities, and the importance of information and communication technologies for communities. The project specifically targeted low-income communities with poor access to technology. The courses were entirely free, and designed according to the needs of each community. Chavez' project is not the only situation where indigenous peoples have used technology to adapt and improve their situations, preserving their indigenous identities while maximising the benefits of urban society. Using the term 'edgewalkers' to describe such youth in the Pacific region, one indigenous author explained, edgewalkers "are part of a generation of Pacific peoples who have mastered skills that have enabled them to adopt situational identities that allow them to weave between traditional indigenous contexts and the technological and information worlds".[511] "An edgewalker is resilient to cultural shifts and able to maintain continuity wherever he or she goes, walking the edge between...cultures in the same persona".[512]

In the 8th Fire television series about Aboriginal Canadians, it is said "Education is the new buffalo," sustaining and nourishing the people. The First Nations in North America are one of the growing populations in home schooling, although for them it is not a new method, but a reclaiming of their traditions. This allows them to maintain their heritage and identity whilst taking advantage of all that technology offers. Kawagley and Barnhardt write:

Unlike the western observers' tendency to freeze indigenous cultural systems in time, as though they existed in some kind of idealized static state destined never to change, indigenous people themselves, as a matter of cultural survival, have been quick to adapt new technologies and to grasp the 'new world order.' While retaining a keen sense of place and rootedness in the land they occupy, they have not hesitated to take advantage of new opportunities (as well as create a few of their own) to improve their quality of life and the efficacy of their lifestyles. This is done, however, within their own framework of values, priorities and worldview, so that the development trajectory they choose is not always the same as what outsiders might choose for them.[513]

A group of students from the Inupiaq people, for example, drew on their traditional base-20 counting system "to create a unique numerical notation and computation system that is capable of performing high-level mathematical calculations. The system has been so successful that when they were challenged by a team of oil-field engineers with electronic calculators, the Inupiaq students were able to accurately preform the calculations faster than the engineers. They have demonstrated that it is possible to adapt to the imperatives of the western educational system without sacrificing their own cultural traditions in the process".[514]

The Price of Education

Besides the wealth of knowledge and information available on the internet, its other gift is that so much information is freely available (notwithstanding the financial monopoly many academic journals hold over the results of tax-payer funded studies). This stands in great contrast to the economics-oriented system of mainstream education, whether it manifests as budgets and test scores dictating teaching methods and attitudes, or the prohibitive costs of higher education undermining aptitude being the determinant of succes. Nowadays many universities are putting their reading lists and course notes online for free. Students attending the physical lectures are effectively paying for tutor and class interaction, something else which increasingly takes place online. What is left? The certification. We end up investing in the piece of paper rather than the knowledge itself, and those who distribute the certification have a vested interest in perpetuating their own status. Perhaps we should heed Socrates' proclamation that "An education obtained with money is worse than no education at all".[515]

Not only is the need to pay for higher education becoming undermined, but the very existence of the university as an institution is being questioned by some. Clark Aldrich writes, "With the presence of online universities, growing virtual communities, high-value open-source content, and emerging portfolio and other 'credit for real world experience' programs, the illusion of inevitability of a conventional undergraduate education is finally shattered and the value-proposition is challenged".[516] Many of the top tech company founders haven't finished high school or university, while Peter Thiel, the co-founder of Paypal, felt so strongly about the weaknesses of traditional schooling that he set up the Thiel Fellowship, a two-year program sponsoring young people who choose "to skip or stop out of college to receive a $100,000 grant and support from the Thiel Foundation's network of founders, investors, and scientists".[517] As financial experts Brady and Woodward write, "Many top leaders are increasingly seeing college as a waste of time".[518]

The educational landscape of the future is so different to that of today that many cannot see it looming in front of their eyes. When it is upon us, there is no doubt that the unschoolers will be not only prepared, but already living it.

The Cutting Edge

As for the future, your task is not to see it, but to
enable it.

—ANTOINE DE SAINT-EXUPÉRY [519]

THE VERY STRUCTURE OF the online world is a template
for many progressive movements, and the unschooling community is not least of these. Activist groups such as Anonymous, Idle No More, and the Occupy movement are the an-
tithesis to our pervasive and oppressive celebrity culture, and
the cult of the individual. The focus is on is actions not ac-
tors. It can be about working together or alone, long term or
short term; what matters are your motivations and the outcome. The ethos is humanitarian, not individualistic. People
contribute what they can to a given project that attracts
them, according to their abilities and the needs of the project.
Information and support flows both ways, with experience
and knowledge being picked up through the process of working on a project – much like an apprentice, but on a more

fluid and adaptive basis. This is also a good description of the way unschoolers have structured their family and community lives for decades, though to the end of learning rather than political change (not that unschoolers are strangers to having to work together to protect their rights under law). A core member of Bitcoin's development team, Amir Taaki, says "the rich and fruitful history of the true hackers is... a thriving intellectual culture focused on problem solving, self-directed learning and the free exchange of knowledge".[520] This could easily describe the unschooler's ideal too.

Hacking as a cultural phenomenon is probably as old as our species – anyone who takes something to pieces in any sense of the word, in order to reassemble it in a more efficient or useful manner, is hacking. But in relation to technology, its use can be traced back to at least 1955, in the minutes of an an MIT meeting, becoming part of general computing lexicon by the sixties.[521] Today it is used both as a term for criminal acts (e.g. financial databases being hacked) and for general lifestyle choices (e.g. 'hacking your health' à la The Bullet-proof Diet). There are many strong parallels between hacker culture and unschooling: a belief in the need for information to be free and accessible; the rejection of illegitimate authori-ty; horizontal or peer-to-peer relationships rather than verti-cal or hierarchical; valuing creativity; transcending borders; the autonomy to choose one's work; an enthusiasm for prob-lem-solving that equates to play; mutual education; a respect for peer-review; expertise as the basis of meritocracy (find-ing mentors and using the expertise of the extended commu-nity wherever it is found); networks of free citizens; and a drive for self-determination.[522] Compare these lessons to the competitive school culture, where only one person will rise to the top out of the hundreds competing for every place.

How much wasted energy does that involve? How does that further anyone's cause other than your own? What real legacy is there in working to better yourself alone? Working together we are adaptive and vital; competing, we make each other feel inadequate and resentful.

Both unschoolers and hackers create their own agenda rather than listening to someone else's. We have the freedom to choose what to think, what we study, where we roam. Why do studies keep finding more political engagement amongst home educators? Perhaps because children are used to having a say in decisions that affect them, and are used to seeing that their opinions make a difference. It is natural for them to assume that this scales up to the communal and national sphere. School is a hierarchy with no real democracy, and children are not regularly given to experiencing their opinions making any difference to their lives. It is no wonder we are drawn to escape into social media, which when used well, is a tool for building networks - the opposite in structure and character to hierarchies. The less formalised and commercialised the media platform, the more of a meritocracy it is. Unlike hierarchical structures with formalised rules and procedures, democratic networks aren't controlled by a single central authority. Decisions are made through consensus, and the ties that bind people to the group are loose, meaning that when they are no longer invested in the issue, they no longer participate and influence decisions.

Unschoolers are not so much like groups such as Anonymous though, as they are like us. While the recent way of organising mass actions is hailed as democratic, horizontal, anarchistic and modern, unschoolers have been organised in this way for years (the free universities which are springing from recent political movements are also a microcosm of the unschooling movement). John Holt, one of the fathers of the homeschooling movement, wrote:

> *Leaders are not what many people think – people with huge crowds following them. Leaders are people who go their own way without caring, or even looking to see whether anyone is following them. 'Leadership qualities' are not the qualities that enable people to attract followers, but those that enable them to do without them... True leaders... do not make people into followers, but into new leaders. The homeschooling movement is full of such people, 'ordinary' people doing things that they never would have thought they could do...This is why it may be a little misleading to speak of the homeschooling 'movement'. Most people think of a movement as something like an army, a few generals and a great many buck privates. In the movement for homeschooling, everyone is a general.*[523]

Gatto wrote of "The quiet revolution of the homeschoolers taking place under our noses right now which may be the most exciting social movement since the pioneers, not least because it is leaderless".[524]

It can require a mature, responsible and self-aware consciousness to home educate: issues that threaten our freedom arise regularly, and need to be negotiated within a group which by its very nature distrusts those who try to speak for the entire community. We learn to work together when need be, whilst retaining our independence, following projects we wish to implement on a localised basis, all the time considering the ramifications of our actions on the wider community. This does spill over into arguments at times; 99% of these are via chat boards, amongst people who may have never met in real life, but who share a common interest in preserving their right to live as they choose, whilst ensuring the best outcome for the community as a whole. This is not an easy task. In groups such as Anonymous, offshoots arise, implode, fall out dramatically online and go their own way whether it is in keeping with an overall aim or not. Unschoolers don't have that luxury without jeopardising their existence altogether. Perhaps the very fact that this anarchic, self regulating, and mature group of people have been managing their affairs this way seemingly unnoticed, for so long, is a testament to the fact that when all is said and done, issues are settled and harmony maintained within the community itself through democratic and self-managed means. Maybe this structure works so well as it is the way we are wired to be. "Hunter-gatherers were fiercely egalitarian," writes Gray;

> *They eschewed any attempts by one person to control the behavior of others... they made all decisions within the band through debate until consensus was reached. Such egalitarianism was necessarily coupled with extraordinary personal autonomy... Remarkably, these principles of equality and autonomy were applied as much to children as to adults. Adults did not tell children what to do any more than they told other adults what to do; they believed that children's own wills should be their guides... It can be argued that hunter-gatherer societies were the original democracies.[525]*

For all the time that has passed since the Agrarian Revolution, we have not had time in evolutionary terms for our brains to adapt to the new social structures and interpersonal relationships that a control-heavy system such as farming requires. We are the same people as our hunter-gatherer ancestors: our brains are fundamentally the same, and our innate ways of relating and learning have not had time to adapt. So it is no wonder that when given the freedom to create our own structures, whether in person or online, we tend to structures that reflect those of our ancestors, and those of indigenous communities today. The success of this way of organising is demonstrated by its adoption on many fronts. Graeber writes, "traditional anarchist principles - autonomy, voluntary association, self-organization, mutual aid, direct democracy - have gone from the basis for organizing within the globalization movement, to playing the same role in radical movements of all kinds everywhere".[526] It is not only a successful way of structuring communities, but an extremely effective way of learning. The way in which hackers work on a project mirrors the world of unschooling perfectly: "People can work on anything they like, they are not required to submit resumes, acquire accreditation, seniority, or approval from an individual authority. If their work is good enough it will be accepted by the user group. Everyone can work on the system that interests them, doing the jobs at the level they are capable of, with as much or as little involvement as they choose". This also produces the three motivators which provide the greatest job satisfaction: autonomy, mastery and purpose.[527] Given the parallels between the most effective ways to learn, and the way we can organise ourselves online, the use of technology should be crucial to any future models of education.

Information Overload

The amount of information freely available on the internet is not only a gift for unschoolers, but is increasing the ability of us all to contribute to advancing knowledge. We can fact check, compare reviews, opinions, advance our own ideas, and ask for advice, from a far greater pool of amateurs and professionals at our fingertips than our immediate community could ever provide. British author Neil Gaiman writes,

> *Information has value, and the right information has enormous value. For all of human history, we have lived in a time of information scarcity, and having the needed information was always important, and always worth something: when to plant crops, where to find things, maps and histories and stories – they were always good for a meal and company. Information was a valuable thing, and those who had it or could obtain it could charge for that service. In the last few years, we've moved from an information-scarce economy to one driven by an information glut. According to Eric Schmidt of Google, every two days now the human race creates as much information as we did from the dawn of civilisation until 2003. That's about five exobytes of data a day, for those of you keeping score. The challenge becomes, not finding that scarce plant growing in the desert, but finding a specific plant growing in a jungle. We are going to need help navigating that information to find the thing we actually need.*[528]

Others see the volume of information as a problem in itself. Pedagogue Neil Postman argues that our society relies too heavily on information to fix our problems, especially the fundamental problems of human philosophy and survival, and that information, ever since the printing press, has become a burden and garbage instead of a rare blessing. According to Postman, "Information is now a commodity that can be bought and sold, or used as a form of entertainment, or worn like a garment to enhance one's status. It comes indiscriminately, directed at no one in particular, disconnected from usefulness; we are glutted with information, drowning in information, have no control over it, don't know what to do with it... the tie between information and action has been severed".[529]

The move from scarcity of information to abundance is so marked, that it has spawned new scientific disciplines, including Agnotology, the study of culturally induced ignorance or doubt, particularly the publication of inaccurate or misleading scientific data. The *Encyclopedia of World Problems and Human Potential* records that "There are many causes of culturally induced ignorance. These include the influence of the media, either through neglect or as a result of deliberate misrepresentation and manipulation. Corporations and governmental agencies can contribute to the subject matter studied by agnotology through secrecy and suppression of information, document destruction, and myriad forms of inherent or avoidable culturopolitical selectivity, inattention, and forgetfulness".[530] To try and counteract this, the discipline of Cognitronics aims to explicate these distortions in our perception of the world, and look for ways to improve cognitive mechanisms of processing information.[531] It is clear that such a wealth of information requires a new way of learning: no more can we trust that a teacher or news broadcaster is telling us The One And Only Truth. We are all aware now that every piece of information has another to counteract it, and we must become both technically and politically literate in order to navigate the flow.

Studies suggest that being taught to doubt at a young age could make people better lifelong learners. Learning that science for example, is an ongoing process, that the most seemingly obvious facts can change in the face of new evidence, and that even authority figures can get things wrong or be biased, is a valuable lesson to learn, and prevents us from being closed to new ideas or conflicting evidence. That, in turn, means that doubters - people who base their views on evidence, rather than faith - are likely to be better citizens.[532] Scientist Lawrence M. Krauss writes, "One conclusion we might draw is that we ought to resist ideology in the first place. If we want to raise citizens who are better at making evidence-based judgments, we need to start early, making skepticism and doubt part of the experience that shapes their identities from a young age".533 This is naturally hard in a school setting where debate about answers undermines the entire edifice of rewarding 'correct' answers and penalising 'wrong' ones.

More and more people are researching for themselves and sharing information - whether medical, political, scientific or artistic. Experts are becoming independent. But this all requires the ability to sift through vast amounts of information, evaluate the legitimacy of a source, read with a critical eye, and come to a conclusion which may select some aspects and reject others. It is frequently argued that we use this wealth of varying opinions to simply cherry pick those views which reinforce our existing beliefs, but do not actually change our minds about anything at all.534 There is not surprising when we think of the variety of news sources available, for example. Do we spend hours every day reading a variety of opposing views on any given event, in order to reach our own conclusions, or do we find a source who views the world as we do, and simplify matters by trusting their version? Never before have we had to learn to negotiate these matters in such a pressing way, and at an increasingly young age. In the face of this influx of information, we need to learn how to negotiate it, we need critical thinking, and we need to know who we are and what we want. To avoid getting lost or swamped needs a strong moral foundation against which to judge, and high standards as a filter. Professor Joe Kinchelo suggests a democratic curriculum, which includes "exploring where knowledge comes from, the rules of its production, and the ways we can assess its quality and the purposes of its production".[535]

Many people try to protect their children from the excesses of technology, some to the point of rejecting it altogether. All that we wish to protect our children from in the physical world can be found online, and the internet is subject to the controls and agendas of huge multi-nationals, just as the physical world is. Neil Postman, who saw parenting itself as an act of 'cultural resistance', believed that the most rebellious act of all as a parent today,

> *is the attempt to control the media's access to one's children. There are, in fact, two ways to do this. The first is to limit the amount of exposure children have to media. The second is to monitor carefully what they are exposed to, and to provide them with a continuously running critique of the themes and values of the media's content. Both are very difficult to do and require a level of attention that most parents are not prepared to give to child-rearing. Nonetheless, there are parents who are committed to doing all of these things, who are in effect defying the directives of their culture. Such parents are not only helping their children to have a childhood but are, at the same time, creating a sort of intellectual elite.*[536]

Of course our children are often well aware of the nature of media. Dr. Peter Gray recounts an experience that shows children can be far more critical and creative than we give them credit for:

> *Every kid is different, just as every adult is, and we can't get into their heads and find out just what they are getting out of something that we don't understand. I know well a kid who, for years, spent hours per day watching television shows that I thought were really disgustingly dumb; but, over time, I discovered that she was getting a lot out of them. They were making her think in new ways. She under-*

stood all the ways in which the shows were dumb, at least as well as I did; but she also saw ways in which they were smart, and she analyzed them and learned from them. They contributed greatly to her abilities as an actress (she eventually had major parts in high-school plays), because she acted out the parts vicariously, in her mind, as she watched. They also contributed to her fascination with certain aspects of human psychology. She now wants to go into clinical psychology as a career.[537]

The Gaze

What we should not be doing with technology is to use it constrain and demean our children ever further. The current generation are being accustomed to constant surveillance. From security cameras in classrooms, to microchipped ID cards tracking students' every movement during school hours, hierarchy and control is emphasised, and children learn that their every move is watched by someone higher up the chain. It also reduces our children ever further to a list of numbers. When we are trained to accept such intrusion into our lives from the start, it becomes more likely that we will accept it throughout our adult lives (and the fear of being surveilled, of course, makes a population easier to control). And just as surveillance damages society, so it damages children. The feeling of being watched – whether we actually are or not – is referred to in Lacanian psychoanalytic theory as The Gaze. "It is the anxious state that comes with the awareness that one can be viewed. The psychological effect, Lacan argues, is that the subject loses a degree of autonomy upon realizing that he or she is a visible object... The gaze is integral to systems of power and ideas about knowledge".[538] People self-regulate and modify their behaviour when they believe that they are constantly being watched, even if they cannot directly see who or what is watching them.[539] The level of surveillance we allow into our lives is a fundamental issue for home education, with a constant rumble of proposed new measures to constrain and regulate our freedom. Yet Slavoj Zizek argues that in a society where everything is permitted - increasingly the opposite of our current society - we in fact increase our self-regulation, not due to fear, but self awareness.[540] In this light, it is no wonder unschooled children often seem so mature and responsible, with a strong sense of self agency. They are the least intrusively surveilled and constrained children of all.

The future is always signposted by those who refuse to submit to the Gaze, those who will not be constrained by fear of the state, of what others think, or who is watching. They are pushed to the margins of society for questioning the dominant ideology. In this generation, it is the unschoolers, the hackers, and the 'conspiracy' theorists. What these groups have in common is that they create their own ways of routing around the mainstream, denying the manufacturing of consent (something insidious to the control of information, from media to government to schools). It used to be that those who controlled language controlled information. Now it is those who control the internet, the link between language and internet being, of course, that they are both the transmitters of knowledge.

The future is shaped by those who feel the Gaze of society in its most controlling, shaming, conformist aspect - and who turn that Gaze back upon society to show up its faults and foibles, and eventually force change. But the Gaze of society, in the form of the state, wants to keep the masses in a state of dependency, ignorance and immaturity, to ensure its own survival. As long as people believe they must be led, believe they need to be told what to do by sanctioned experts, are prohibited from seeing the truth of a situation, they will let others lead. Schools do this job in tandem with a fake democracy. When a government does not allow us to see the results of our decisions, by never following through with a course of action or by lying about the results, we are not able to learn from experience, and never able to decide the best course of action for ourselves. We are infantilised by a system which wants to act in an eternal loco parentis, and is increasingly using technology to maintain an ever-present parental Gaze.

Automation

Whatever our attitude to technology - and even some Amish have been spotted texting, sending emails, using Amazon and Facebook[541] - we will soon not be able to avoid it in day to day life, even if we can, by some feat, do so now. It is predicted that by the early 2030s, up to 47% of jobs in the US will be at risk of automation, 35% in Britain, and 49% in Japan.[542] (A survey by Pricewaterhouse Coopers predicts rates of 38% for the US; 30% in the UK, 35% in Germany and 21% in Japan).[543] It is the level of routine operations in a given job that dictates how vulnerable it will be to automation. Frey and Osborne, who wrote the most widely quoted study on the topic, list the most at-risk jobs as transport and logistics (such as taxi and delivery drivers), office support (such as receptionists and security guards), and sales and services (such as cashiers, counter and rental clerks, telemarketers and accountants).[544] We are already seeing software which can perform legal tasks or even journalism, such as news bots creating sports and market reports.

A potential benefit of job losses due to automation is the introduction of much shorter working hours for all. David Spencer, a professor of economics and political economy, advocates sharing out work to overcome the anomaly of overwork for some and unemployment for others. The "Profound question is whether we should be asking society to tolerate long work hours for some and zero work hours for others. Surely society can achieve a more equitable allocation of work that offers everyone enough time to work and enough time to do what they want?" Spencer cites arguments for shorter working hours from J.S. Mill (who advocated a 'gospel of leisure', arguing that technology should be used to curtail work time as far as possible), to Marx (who saw a reduction in working time as an essential ingredient of a future communist society, with work curtailed by the use of technology, expanding the 'realm of freedom' in which people could realise their creative capacities in activities of their own choosing), to Bertrand Russell (who wrote an essay 'In Praise of Idleness', with a stress on technology as a means to shorten work time), to Keynes (who in 1945 suggested that less work represented the 'ultimate solution' to unemployment, and looked forward to 2030 when people would be required to work only 15 hours a week).[545]

Not everyone agrees that automation will be all-pervasive, nor that it will present a major change to the way we work, given the number of new jobs that have yet to be invented. Those jobs that rely on more personal interaction, creativity, and high unpredictability, are less likely to disappear. *The Economist* confidently predicts that "AI will not cause mass unemployment, but it will speed up the existing trend of computer-related automation, disrupting labour markets just as technological change has done before, and requiring workers to learn new skills more quickly than in the past... companies and governments will need to make it easier for workers to acquire new skills and switch jobs as needed".[546] This does rather sound like code for workers needing to be accustomed to insecure and unpredictable employment conditions. It also reflects the calls from futurists and business for a new way of learning that is more about adaptability, problem solving and creative thinking. The idea that we all need to achieve proficiency in certain set areas of knowledge is crumbling rapidly. Perhaps ironically, given the usual calls by techies to make all knowledge free, some are seeing the opportunity to market education in ever more flexible packages: entrepreneur and computer scientist Sebastian Thrun for example, states that "People will have to continuously learn new skills to stay current," and as such has launched 'nanodegrees' which can be completed in a few months alongside a job. A nanodegree in data science or website programming costs $200 a month, with a 50% refund for completing the course within a year.[547]

The advent of automation, and even artificial intelligence, brings another issue to the forefront: how will we distribute wealth in the event of mass job losses? Many have proposed a Universal Basic Income, whereby all citizens receive a fixed amount to live on, topping it up with work if they choose. Thomas Paine and John Stuart Mill suggested the idea during the Industrial Revolution, and its proponents say that it will give people more freedom to decide how many hours to work, encourage people to take on temporary jobs, and might even encourage them to retrain by providing a guaranteed income while they do so.[548] Just as many people have grave misgivings about such an idea, predicting that many people would happily do no work at all. We could argue that this is utopia – the freedom to work as and when we choose, if at all, while our lifestyle is maintained by automated drones. But is there any motivation in this situation to stretch ourselves, to maintain and improve our knowledge, to try to achieve something better? If we are no longer providers of essential financial support for our household, from where will we derive our sense of purpose and self worth? To some extent this is a problem women have faced since the devaluation of motherhood - once you no longer bring in a wage, your value as a person rests on how valuable a mother you are. But with someone else raising our children for us in school, how long can our labour-free, child-free days continue to fulfil us? One thing is certain: mass automation would undermine the need for round the clock childcare. With our children no longer occupational orphans, how long will childcare, crèche, and eventually school itself last?

A situation where many jobs are lost to automation, but the profits used to support the populace, harks back to our hunter-gatherer days, with hours of freedom and non-atomised communities. The great difference however is in our relationship to our children. In hunter-gatherer groups even today, the education of the children is a shared responsibility, and the driving, enlivening force for day to day life. The constant presence of children in the community means we must always be role models, always be ready to help or teach, always be aware of why we do what we do. In the event of the majority of families being economically free to educate their own children, it may be the best way to ensure that we still feel motivated, still feel we are contributing to something worthwhile, and still educate ourselves to benefit our children. In the event of a less utopian future, Dr Brian Ray, in the Homeschool Population Report 2010, writes, "If fewer jobs are available nationwide then it might be more likely that one parent would be at home to conduct home-based education. Further, if the economy is down in general, families have less monetary resources available after taxes, including those they pay for state schools, and therefore less to put toward tuition in private schools. Thus, homeschooling might increase as a percentage of private-education choice".[549]

Many writers clearly explain what we are doing wrong in the world. Too often we can all see the problems, but struggle to know what we can do, whether as an individual or as a society. Everything seems so inextricably bound up. Johann Hari came to the conclusion that one of the best things we can do to counter the epidemic of depression and anxiety is to democratise work places to make them cooperative structures[550] - SUMA or the original Co-operative Bank spring to mind. To combine this with a Universal Basic Income, to allow automation to take over many repetitive, menial tasks, and free us up to work less hours, in a democratic workplace, with a guarantee of having enough money to feed and house our families; to be motivated to make something of ourselves because our unschooled children are truly our responsibility to raise and inspire... These are potential solutions which are very much within our grasp now.

A future society with far more free time would change the entire structure of our communities and landscape. We would not need to buy so much of our food, having the time to grow our own; more wasteland could be used for allotments, community orchards etc; we would become more aware of those areas in our community which need attention; we could have healthier people generally due to homegrown food and time to exercise. Our community structures could be strengthened, with elderly and disabled people able to be cared for in the home by family or neighbours. Businesses would see more local trade during the week. There would be less pressure on services at peak times, but a more even spread throughout the day and week. There would be far less pressure to fit in holidays at set times of year (schools forbearing). Communities would have time to prepare for celebrations locally and rekindle traditions that have been abandoned due to lack of time and interest, e.g. local Bonfire Nights. People would have more time to be involved in civic affairs, making more decisions at the community level. More people would be available to set up local sports teams and compete between communities, as well as having more time for voluntary community service. We could even have e-sports teams, with all the benefits of team work, critical thinking, and responsibility.

If we project from the home education community as it is now, the rise of small-scale home-based businesses is likely; clubs and classes open to all ages and abilities would be more widely available; college classes would open their doors to people of all ages with more demand for a variety of educational and sporting activities; and if we have the willpower, libraries could re-open as community hubs with a variety of resources available, along with much more affordable public transport enabling travel for all sorts of educational and social reasons. We can even dream of educational and quality programmes broadcast on tv during the day time, not relegated to the small hours or obscure channels. We should encourage everyone to offer their skills in some form. Children generally do not want to hang around the streets particularly, but with nothing else to do and no adults to interest them in any alternative, it is inevitable. The return of adults to the community, being seen to work on various things, whether on cars or in gardens or having decent conversations at their leisure, makes it far less likely that our children will wander around bored or unnoticed. Children like to join in with projects, help adults, feel noticed and welcomed.

What cannot not be automated is our creativity, invention, and lateral thinking. There is still much science to be understood, and until we have discovered the principles and data required, we cannot automate our predictions or experiments. Nor can we replace the more personalised aspects of life (e.g. designing for, or fixing, localised specific problems); small scale decision making (where statistics and data cannot predict the best outcome for a specific situation); things we enjoy participating in such as sports, traditions and celebrations; and the genuine care of and interaction with others, including our children. These are the things that form our culture, that give us a sense of who we are in the grand scheme of history, that create memories, and directly affect those around us. In this respect, a considered level of automation may free us to be more fully human.

CHAPTER 14

Conclusion

Let everyone sweep in front of his own door, and the
whole world will be clean.

—JOHANN WOLFGANG VON GOETHE [551]

INEQUALITY IS UNSTABLE. IT is also to some extent necessary* and inevitable; the disparity, however, obviously
needs to be kept as small as possible. When it becomes too
distorted, it is a severe problem. So any means which can
help reduce the disparity deserve investigation and attention.
One of the root causes of our inequality at the moment is
education. Without it, or with a poor one, we are likely to be
in the group that suffers disproportionately. We can predict a
child's likely outcome in life on the day they start school,
based on the race, sex, family structure, social class, income,
and education level of their parents. We tend to assume this

* See Kurt Vonnegut's 1961 short story *Harrison Bergeron* for an
example of enforced equality taken to its (il)logical conclusion.

is nothing to do with school per se, but a problem that is integral to, and experienced throughout, society. But when we look at the empirical evidence, this is simply not true of home educated children:. One *cannot* predict their outcome or test scores based on the race, sex, income, education level or class of their parents. This can only mean one thing: that school itself nurtures and exaggerates those factors that affect our success in life.

In the scheme of history, school as we know it today is the aberration. It was instituted at a certain point in history, but what is necessary at one point is not necessarily best for the long term. For some time now, home educated students have been outperforming school students by all measures. School itself is nurturing and entrenching a system of inequality, and however well you are doing out of the deal right now, what causes problems in one area of society will one day catch up with everyone. Those who object to home education believe it harms children to be kept at home. Home educators believe it harms children to be sent to school. Which causes more harm? In a healthy, stable and motivated family, I believe it does far more harm to send a child to school than to raise them ourselves. Harm both to the child, and to society as a whole, now and in the future. I am not claiming this method is perfect, nor that everyone is suited to doing it. But in comparison to the problems that school presents, unschooling is, I believe, far superior. And insofar as it reduces the inequality of access to further education and career potential, it deserves close examination.

So what do we see as the final point of education? Do we want education to be integral to life, or separate to the rest of life? Do we want to leave future generations with a system that works for a while, but leaves us backed into a corner in the face of change? Or do we want to create a structure that is strong enough and flexible enough to adapt as needed, whilst giving the highest number of people the best chance of a fulfilling life? Holt believed that "Since we can't know what knowledge will be most needed in the future, it is senseless to try to teach it in advance. Instead, we should try to turn out people who love learning so much and learn so well that they will be able to learn whatever needs to be learned".[552] This is, by some suggestions, the definition of intelligence itself - the speed and ability with which we adapt to new information. And we must remember the difference between real learning, and formulaic teaching. The freedom to explore our imaginations, to experiment, to fail without shame, to follow tangents and invent something new has been significantly damaged through schooling. Those who are at the leading edge of innovation often work outside of formal structures and reward systems. It is often those who do not fit into the system of being told how one 'should' do something, that discover a completely new way of doing things.

Everyone feels they are being taken advantage of by those at the other end of the spectrum. Many of us feel hindered by our education, due to its failings and lack of opportunities. No matter how well we do on paper, many simply do not have the necessary connections; others are constrained by the pressure of having so much money invested in their education and the weight of expectation that comes along with it, that they never get a chance to know what would truly make them happy. Schools have come so far from their supposed intentions that very few actually benefit from the system. Time and again, we tweak or overhaul or redesign, but we never stray from the idea of schooling itself. Something has to significantly change. The whole structure needs to be dismantled. This would not be a wanton destruction of a valid and venerable institution, woven in to the fabric of society over time. In the span of history, school is more akin to a social experiment that lasted some generations, before the problems outweighed the benefits. In an unschooled world, teachers and mentors would still exist, tuition and classes and group learning and courses of study, exams to prove competency - but only where requested. Not imposed regardless of the student's will or readiness.

Changing the Dominant Order

When people become accustomed to others controlling their behaviour, controlling their options, limiting them in some way, and dictating their choices and reactions, they can no longer do it for themselves. When given freedom, they are lost. It is no wonder many children are so angry and wild. Restrictions are placed upon them by people who can't fully justify those rules, and that are inconsistent with the way they see the rest of society behaving. They have never been given the freedom to find who they are and what they believe, and why certain behaviours are necessary. Everything has been held in a state of tension.

Johann Hari, on his quest to understand the plague of depression in our society, came across the work of Australian scientist Michael Marmot. After several years of study, Marmot found that contrary to expectations, those in higher status positions, e.g. civil servants at the top of Whitehall, were less likely to suffer stress and related diseases than those far lower down the ladder. His conclusion was that the less control you have over your work, the more likely you are to suffer stress and depression. "Humans have an innate need to feel that what we are doing, day-to-day, is meaningful. When you are controlled, you can't create meaning out of your work".[553] But why do we think this applies to children any less than to adults? Would it even be such a pervasive problem for adults if the problem hadn't originally been created in school? If we had not been raised to believe someone else has the right to fill our daily life with personally meaningless tasks, would we so easily accept it as adults? Would we accept that such increasingly authoritarian structures are the only way to have a comfortable standard of living - even the only way to survive? We seem to have reached a saturation point of the level of control that is needed to maintain order in such a complex agrarian society; we simply do not have enough freedom to make us feel that the compromises we make with our time and freedom is worth the pay-off of a comfortable and secure life. Because for very many of us, we are submitting to the control and increasing curtailments of freedom, but not even seeing the return of our most basic needs being met. Why would we submit to a system that promises rewards for some level of submission, when we are can't guarantee we can afford our next meal? Hari's conclusion is that "The only real way out of our epidemic of despair is for all of us, together, to begin to meet those human needs – for deep connection, to the things that really matter in life".[554]

More and more of us can see that those human needs we so desperately need met, are not ever going to be met if we carry on as we are. No amount of political action which substitutes a new order for an old order is going to change anything. "The State" said the German anarchist Gustav Landauer, "is not something which can be destroyed by a revolution, but is a condition, a certain relationship between human beings, a mode of human behaviour; we destroy it by contracting other relationships, by behaving differently".[555] Or as David Graeber puts it, "The theory of exodus proposes that the most effective way of opposing capitalism and the liberal state is not through direct confrontation but by means of what Paolo Virno has called 'engaged withdrawal,' mass defection by those wishing to create new forms of community".[556] Arguments against the idea that society can be successfully transformed simply by behaving as if it were so are valid; but until the mass of humanity start to think differently, no real structural change can take place. The root of our conceptions about how society should function, how we should behave, and how we relate to our daily lives, are imposed from our earliest years through schooling. If we wish to free future generations from a slave mentality, we should not make them beholden to it in the first place. This is the power of unschooling.

The Duty to Act

There are many books out there which profoundly challenge the way we currently structure the lives of children. I refer to some of them; of course there are many, many more. If the importance of these works were really appreciated and acted upon, the world would be transformed. But while we wait for a top-down approach that never comes, we can institute these changes ourselves from the bottom up. Those of us who understand that there is a better way have a duty to put it into practice where we can, and to influence others by our own example.

The intention of this book is not to undermine those parents who send their children to school. Many parents have no choice for economic or family reasons, and may never have had reason to question the current system. What I do hope to have done is question why we accept such a damaging model, not just for children, but for the society they are inheriting. Only by understanding the full implications of schooling can we become indignant enough to demand change, especially for those children who do not have the luxury of being taught in a different way. Once we understand the implications, however, it is incumbent upon us to do something.

Just because something is not possible for all, does not mean it should be banned. Not everyone can afford to eat organic food, go on holiday to the Bahamas or attend university. We don't ban it for everyone. If no one goes ahead and tests the waters, how do we know if a system works? Those who do unschool pave the way for others, find the best methods, set up networks, collect resources, and open up opportunities for those who come after. If enough of us who can do it, do so, there is ever more chance that resources and ways will be made available for all those who wish to home educate to do so. Canada and Russia, for example, provide both money and resources to registered home educators, and in many paces in the United States it is common for home educated children to join after school sports clubs and orchestras along with the schooled pupils. There are a myriad of ways that everyone can benefit from the diversity of options made viable by swelling numbers of home educators. The last stand is usually that this is all well and good, but we can't all afford to home educate. But why can't we? Because we are strikingly unequal in terms of income. And as I have tried to show, this will not change as long as so many of us uncritically support the school system. I am almost tempted to argue that those of us who can afford to home educate have a duty to do so. It is the poorest who have the most to gain from unschooling.

The Shell of the Old

When 'ordinary' people, who don't see themselves as religiously motivated or politically radical, choose in large numbers to home educate, it is becoming mainstream, and it is having an impact. As Joseph Todd writes in *Anarchist Pedagogies*, "Judging by the reception of homeschooling by the State, teachers' unions, the public, the media, etc, deschoolers are on the right track because the institution is threatened and actively trying to subvert deschooling projects and silence the movement".[557] And this raises an important issue in relation to home education, certainly in the UK: we are not obliged to tell anyone we are home educating, unless we have withdrawn our children from school. Those of us who have never sent our children to school in the first place can fairly easily never have any contact with local government agencies. This is no doubt why unschooling has worked so well for so many - the absence of interference and restrictions has allowed a natural evolution of networks and co-ops to evolve, allowed unschoolers to freely   find what works and what doesn't, allowed our children to explore the world without arbitrary measures of their achievements to get in the way. It is the epitome of an anarchist space springing up within the shell of the existing structure, and we have utilised that to the best of our abilities without drawing a level of attention to ourselves which could undermine the whole project. Graeber writes, "There are times when the stupidest thing one could possibly do is raise a red or black flag and issue defiant declarations. Sometimes the sensible thing is just to pretend nothing has changed, allow official state representatives to keep their dignity, even show up at their offices and fill out a form now and then, but otherwise, ignore them".[558] And this has, for the most part, worked well for the home education community. Some of us have contact with the local authorities, some meet with representatives, some send in reports of their children's work. Some only make themselves known when there is new legislation being considered that threatens to disrupt the system that is working very well for us all. Others may never have contact with anyone official at all.

But the landscape is changing. Graeber writes, "The contemporary world is riddled with such anarchic spaces, and the more successful they are, the less likely we are to hear about them. It's only if such a space breaks down into violence that there's any chance outsiders will even find out that it exists". Home education has not broken out into violence by any means, but elements of the media are doing their best to suggest that it is a threat both to children and to the rest of society. High profile cases of children being neglected and abused, however erroneously reported or associated with home education, has understandably caused concern about the number of children who could potentially be suffering. I have tried to address this issue, but it is not the only problem. Under the freedom to home educate is also bound the ability to set up a small, private school, and teach whatever you choose. The UK government is currently concerned that extremists are using the banner of home education to set up ideologically driven schools. As such, they would like to register all home educators in order to protect those children that are perceived to be being brainwashed. I understand the sentiment, but this sounds, to all intents, like an attempt to register perceived extremists - Muslim extremists to be specific - by the backdoor. We need to be very clear about the reasons for any changes to the law.

These issues aside, with growing numbers of unschoolers, and much more attention being paid to how it works, why it works, and whether it could work better, unschooling is reaching a new point in its evolution. And that will require a change of mindset for many of us. We cannot demand utter privacy and invisibility on the one hand, but resent accusations of creating a parallel society on the other. We cannot use the resources of the community and expect to have a say in decisions, but refuse to acknowledge our existence to the local councils who allocate funding to those very services we wish them to maintain. By keeping our heads down we are doing the larger project no favours at all. I completely understand why so many of us try to keep a low profile, and just want to be allowed to get on with our lives, but that is looking increasingly unlikely to happen, and it is not fair on the few to stand up for the rest. We have increasing numbers, but we need visibility, and we need to generate understanding amongst the wider public. We cannot complain that we are misunderstood if we act defensively, refuse to engage, and don't take every opportunity to counter the all-too-easy attacks on us by the media. Has any minority group won their battle by keeping their heads down and hoping it all goes away? They win when people start acting as a community, raising their visibility amongst the public, and showing that they are not a threat to the majority way of life. As Holt points out, "Private action, however radical and satisfying, only becomes political when it is made known".[559]

This book at times no doubt reads as a catalogue of faults that our society has accumulated since we adopted settled agriculture, such a list that it almost seems insuperable. But with the advent of technology and automation, we have a chance to redress the situation, and return to a more traditional - and equitable - set up. Along with automation, campaigns such as the 4 Day Week campaign, and calls for a Universal Basic Income, seem like good ways to address many of the problems. Critics such as Jordan B. Peterson very fairly ask what will motivate many of us to do anything at all with our lives once our basic needs are reliably and easily met. I believe that in unschooling we have the answer. A world where our basic needs are fulfilled, and we spend less time in obligatory work, also begs the question of whether our children need to spend so much of their lives being raised by others at all. In taking on the responsibility of teaching our children ourselves, we have the most natural and motivating reason to try to better ourselves, constantly.

Unschooling is not just one small part of the movement to reestablish control over our own lives; it is fundamental. Gatto believed that to free children from the school system "would provoke a genuine age of enlightenment in human history".[560] Governments are doing everything in their power, it seems, to prevent this. Let's do it anyway.

Acknowledgements

Thank you to my mother for proof reading this book.

Thank you to friends across the world who encouraged me, supported me, read drafts, commented, and thought this book was worth writing.

References

Chapter 1

1 Paula Rothermel, 'Home-Education: Comparison of Home- and School-Educated Children on PIPS Baseline Assessments', *Journal of Early Childhood Research*, Vol. 2, p.294

2 Paula-Jane Rothermel, *Home-Education: Rationales, Practices and Outcomes*, 2002, PhD Dissertation, University of Durham School of Education.

3 Dr. Brian Ray, *Homeschool Progress Report 2009: Academic Achievement and Demographics*, 2009, National Home Education Research Institute, http://bit.ly/2HdBTro (Accessed: 12 May 2018)

4 Lawrence M. Rudner, *Scholastic Achievement and Demographic Characteristics of Home School Students in 1998*, Educational Policy Analysis Archives 7(8),1999

5 Dick M. Carpenter II, 'Mom Likes You Best: Do Homeschool Parents Discriminate Against Their Daughters', *University of St. Thomas Journal of Law and Public Policy*, Volume 7 Issue 1 Fall 2012, http://bit.ly/2Jo0Gy4 (Accessed: 12 May 2018)

6 Brian D. Ray, 'A Review of Research on Homeschooling and What Might Educators Learn?', *Pro-Posições*, vol.28 no. 2 Campinas May/Aug. 2017, http://bit.ly/2sqsTu7 (Accessed: 12 May 2018)

7 Frank Field, *The Foundation Years: Preventing Poor Children Becoming Poor Adults* (*The Report of the Independent Review on Poverty and Life Chances*), 2010, The Stationary Office, Great Britain Cabinet Office

8 Richard Garner, Social class 'determines child's success', *The Independent*, 17 September 2008, https://ind.pn/2JiLKBl (Accessed April 29 2018)

9 John Taylor Gatto, Presentation remarks on *The Fourth Purpose Film Series*, Project Introduction, May 15th 2003

10 Erik H. Erikson, *Insight and Responsibility*, 1972, W. W. Norton & Company

11 Ivan Illich, *Deschooling Society*, 1971, Harper and Row

12 Jonathan Kozol, *The Night is Dark and I am Far from Home*, 1990, Pocket Books

13 Ivan Illich, *Deschooling Society*, Op. Cit.

14 George Monbiot, 'The Lairds of Learning', *George Monbiot*, 29 August 2011, http://bit.ly/2LfxW7L (Accessed: 19 February 2018)

Chapter 2

15 Ivan Illich, *Deschooling Society*, Op. Cit.

16 George Monbiot, 'Moral decay? Family life's the best it's been for 1,000 years', *The Guardian*, 14 May 2012, http://bit.ly/2JboT7i (Accessed: 20 February 2018)

17 Alvin Toffler, *The Third Wave*, 1980, Bantam Books

18 John Holt, *How Children Fail*, 1964, Pitman Publishing Company

19 Raymond Moore and Dorothy Moore, *Better Late than Early*, 1975, Reader's Digest Press

20 Ibid.

21 Graeme Paton, 'Bright Children Should Start School at Six, Says Academic', *The Telegraph*, 16 May 2012, http://bit.ly/2LTyFfX (Accessed: 20 February 2018)

22 Catherine Gaunt, 'Re-discovered Research Says Early School Starting Age 'Harms Children', *Nursery World*, 15 May 2012, http://bit.ly/2HbL5MF (Accessed: 7 May 2018)

23 John Taylor Gatto, *The Underground History of American Education*, 2000, The Oxford Village Press

24 Jonas Himmelstrand, 'Universal Daycare Leaves Sweden's Children Less Educated', *National Post*, 26 April 2011

25 Michael Baker, Jonathan Gruber, and Kevin Milligan, 'Universal Child Care, Maternal Labor Supply, and Family Well-Being', *Journal of Political Economy* 116, no. 4 (August 2008): 709-745.

26 Kyung Hee Kim, 'The Creativity Crisis: The Decrease in Creative Thinking Scores on the Torrance Tests of Creative Thinking', *Creativity Research Journal*, Vol. 23 , Issue 4, 2011

27 John Taylor Gatto, *The Underground History of American Education*, Op. cit.

28 Ibid.

29 Christine Marie Solari, *"It's Tensious Work": A Case Study of Anti-Racist Educators*, Doctoral Thesis, San Francisco State University, California, January 2016 http://bit.ly/2xxlzAS (Accessed: 11 May 2018)

30 Malcom Gladwell, *Outliers: The Story of Success*, 2008, Penguin

31 Ivan Illich, *Deschooling Society*, Op. Cit.

32 John Taylor Gatto, *Weapons of Mass Instruction: A Schoolteacher's Journey Through the Dark World of Compulsory Schooling*, 2010, New Society Publishers

33 John Taylor Gatto, *The Underground History of American Education*, 2000, The Oxford Village Press

34 Ibid.

35 Dorothy Sayers, *The Lost Tools of Learning*, 1947, http://bit.ly/2sChuqF (Accessed: 27 March 2018)

36 Keith Thomas and Martin Rees, 'Fidei defensores', *Times higher Education*, 8 November 2012, http://bit.ly/2kK80Go (Accessed: 19 February 2018)

37 Ivan Illich, *Deschooling Society*, Op. Cit.

38 Paulo Freire, *Pedagogy of the Oppressed*, 1970, New York : Herder and Herder, p. 77

39 Walter Karp, quoted in David Colfax and Micki Colfax, *Homeschooling for Excellence*, 2009, Grand Central Publishing

40 Ann Hendon, 'H.L. Mencken on Governments and Politicians', *The American Mercury*, 22 April 2010, http://bit.ly/2J7AsjS (Accessed: 7 May 2018)

41 Eric Robinson, Rethinking what we mean by 'education', The Caroline Benn Memorial Lecture 2009, http://bit.ly/2s-robfM (Accessed: 27 March 2018)

42 Peter Gray Ph,D., 'The Evolutionary Biology of Education: How Our Hunter-Gatherer Educative Instincts Could Form the Basis for Education Today', *Evolution: Education and Outreach*, March 2011, Volume 4, Issue 1

43 David Colfax and Micki Colfax, *Homeschooling for Excellence*, 2009, Grand Central Publishing

44 Ivan Illich, *Deschooling Society*, Op. Cit.

45 John Holt, *How Children Learn*, 1967, New York: Pitman Publishing Corporation

Chapter 3

[46] John Dewey, Logic: Theory of Inquiry, 1938, New York Henry Holt and Company

[47] Eleanor Busby, 'Number of children being homeschooled in UK rises by 41% over three years', *Independent*, 26 April 2018, https://ind.pn/2HThtnN (Accessed: 16 June 2018)

[48] Brian D. Ray, Ph.D., Research Facts on Homeschooling, *National Home Education Research Institute*, 13 January 2018, http://bit.ly/2LiBuGq (Accessed: 28 March 2018)

[49] Mike Fortune-Wood, *A Short History of Home Education: A community memory of home education in the UK*, 2005, http://bit.ly/2Jcxmau (Accessed: 20 February 2018)

[50] David V. Hicks, *Norms and Nobility: A Treatise on Education*, 1999, University Press of America

[51] Eric Robinson, 'Rethinking what we mean by 'education', *The Caroline Benn Memorial Lecture 2009*, http://bit.ly/2s-robfM (Accessed: 19 February 2018)

[52] William Ayers, Michael Klonsky and Gabrielle Lyon Eds., *A Simple Justice: The Challenge of Small Schools*, 2000, Teachers College Press

[53] Peter Gray Ph,D., 'The Evolutionary Biology of Education: How Our Hunter-Gatherer Educative Instincts Could Form the Basis for Education Today', *Evolution: Education and Outreach*, March 2011, Volume 4, Issue 1

[54] Paulo Freire, *Pedagogy of the Oppressed*, 1970, New York: Herder and Herder

[55] John Holt, *How Children Learn*, 1967, Pitman Publishing

[56] N.H.S. Grundtvig, Wikipedia, http://bit.ly/2J8y3oY (Accessed: 20 February 2018)

[57] John Holt, *How Children Learn*, 1967, Pitman Publishing

[58] Charlotte Mason, *Formation of Character*, 2010, Bottom of the Hill Publishing

59 Mary Beard et al, 'Back to school, Mr Gove: authors choose their GCSE set texts', *The Guardian*, 6 June 2014, http://bit.ly/2xABaRe (Accessed: 19 February 2018)

60 Jean Bendell, *School's Out: Educating Your Child at Home*, 1987, Ashgrove Publishing Ltd

61 John Taylor Gatto, *Weapons of Mass Instruction*, 2010, New Society Publishers

62 Anu Partanen, 'What Americans keep ignoring about Finland's school success', *The Atlantic*, 29 December 2011, https://theatln.tc/2sCihHT (Accessed: 19 February 2018)

63 John Taylor Gatto, 'I Quit, I Think', *Wall Street Journal*, 25 July 1991

64 Dorothy L. Sayers, *The Lost Tools of Learning*, Op. cit.

65 Rothermel, 'Home-Education: Comparison of Home- and School-Educated Children on PIPS Baseline Assessments', *Journal of Early Childhood Research*, Vol. 2, p.294

66 Brian D. Ray, Ph.D., Research Facts on Homeschooling, *National Home Education Research Institute*, 13 January 2018, http://bit.ly/2LiBuGq (Accessed: 28 March 2018)

67 Brian D. Ray, 'Academic Achievement and Demographic Traits of Homeschool Students: A Nationwide Study', *Academic Leadership*, Volume 8 Issue 1 Winter 2010, 3 February 2010, http://bit.ly/2LTw1XN (Accessed: 12 May 2018)

68 Dorothy L. Sayers, *The Lost Tools of Learning*, Op. cit.

69 Kirsten Asmussen, Judy Corlyon, Hanan Hauari and Vincent La Placa, 'Supporting Parents of Teenagers', Policy Research Bureau, *Department for Education and Skills*, Research Report RR830, 2007 http://bit.ly/2sqNEpl (Accessed: 30 April 2018)

70 Ibid.

71 USA International Business Publications, *Denmark Company Laws and Regulations Handbook*, 2008

72 Paulo Freire, *Pedagogy of the Oppressed*, 1970, Herder and Herder

73 'Daily Life at the folk high schools', http://bit.ly/2J5Xqlm (Accessed: 19 February 2018)

74 Paulo Freire, *Pedagogy of the Oppressed*, 1970, Herder and Herder

75 Eric Robinson, 'Rethinking what we mean by 'education', Op. cit.

76 Ivan Illich, *Deschooling Society*, Op. Cit.

77 Herbert Gerjuoy, quoted in Alvin Toffler, *Future Shock*, 1970, Random House

Chapter 4

78 Jack Donovan et al (Eds.), *The Poems of Shelley: Volume Three: 1819 - 1820*, 2011, Routledge

79 Henry A. Giroux, *Neoliberalism's War on Higher Education*, Haymarket Books, 2014

80 Adolf Hitler, 1 May 1937, quoted in William L. Shirer, *The Rise and Fall of the Third Reich*, 2011, Simon and Schuster Export

81 David Quinn, 'Nazis were the first to ban home-schooling for kids', *Irish Independent*, 5 September 2014, http://bit.ly/2LVgbvV (Accessed: 19 February 2018)

[82] Michaéla C Schippers, Ad W A Scheepers and Jordan B Peterson, *A Scalable Goal-Setting Intervention Closes Both the Gender and Ethnic Minority Achievement Gap*, 9 June 2015, Palgrave Communications, https://go.nature.com/2Lj-LOOx (Accessed: 11 May 2018)

[83] Brian D. Ray, *Home Education: Reason and Research*, 2009, NHERI Publications, http://bit.ly/2J8rLG8 (Accessed: 11 May 2018)

[84] Dick M. Carpenter II, 'Mom Likes You Best: Do Homeschool Parents Discriminate Against Their Daughters', Op. cit.

[85] Dr. Brian Ray, *Homeschool Progress Report 2009: Academic Achievement and Demographics*, Op. cit.

[86] Brian D. Ray, 'A Review of research on Homeschooling and What Might Educators Learn?', Op. cit.

[87] John Taylor Gatto, *The Underground History of American Education*, 2000, The Oxford Village Press

[88] Jonathan Kozol, *The Night Is Dark And I Am Far From Home*, 1990, Touchstone Books

[89] Written evidence submitted by the British Chambers of Commerce to the UK Commons Select Committee on Education, November 2011

[90] John Fowles, *The Aristos*, 2001, Vintage Classics

[91] Clark Aldrich, *Unschooling Rules: 55 Ways to Unlearn What We Know about Schools and Rediscover Education*, 2011, Greenleaf Book Group

[92] Ibid.

[93] *Schooling The World: The White Man's Last Burden*, 2010, directed by Carol Black

[94] Doris Lessing, *The Golden Notebook*, 1962, Michael Joseph

95 John Taylor Gatto, 'Why Schools Don't Educate', New York City Teacher of the Year Award
acceptance speech, 31 January 1990

96 Jonathan Kozol, *The Night Is Dark And I Am Far From Home*, 1990, Touchstone Books

97 20 September 2014, Accessed via wayback machine, http://bit.ly/2HeUnru (Accessed: 21 February 2018)

98 Howard Gardner, *Multiple Intelligences: New Horizons in Theory and Practice*, 2006, Basic Books

99 Daniel Pink, *A Whole New Mind: Why Right-Brainers Will Rule the Future*, 2008, Marshall Cavendish

100 Tony Wagner, *Creating Innovators: The Making of Young People Who Will Change the World*, 2014, Simon & Schuster Children's Publishing

101 John Dewey, *Experience And Education*, 2008, Free Press

102 Michael W. Apple, 'The Politics of Official Knowledge: Does a National Curriculum Make Sense?', *Teachers College Record*, Volume 95, Number 2, Winter 1993, Columbia University, http://bit.ly/2J84MLp (Accessed: 7 may 2018)

103 R. Connolly, 'Freire, Praxis and Education', in *Literacy and Revolution: The Pedagogy of Paulo Freire*, 1980, Pluto Press

104 Ira Shor, *Empowering Education*, 1992, University of Chicago Press

105 Jonathan Kozol, *The Night Is Dark And I Am Far From Home*, 1990, Touchstone Books

106 Christian W. Beck, 'Home Education – Globalisation Otherwise?', Presented at the BERA conference in Manchester 15 – 18 September 2004, http://bit.ly/2srEPMb (Accessed: 6 may 2108)

[107] Jonathan Kozol, *The Night Is Dark And I Am Far From Home*, 1990, Touchstone Books

[108] Ibid.

[109] Henry A. Giroux, 'Doing Cultural Studies: Youth and the Challenge of Pedagogy', *Harvard Educational Review*, 64:3 Fall 1994, http://bit.ly/2JlCvjN (Accessed: 7 may 2018)

[110] John Taylor Gatto, 'Why Schools Don't Educate', *New York City Teacher of the Year Award acceptance speech*, 31 January 1990

[111] William Ronald Johnson, 'A Multiple Case Study Investigating the Influence of Homeschool Parents' Perception of Success on the Learning Environment', *Liberty University*, Lynchburg, VA, 2014, http://bit.ly/2sz9o1X (accessed: 12 May 2018)

[112] Brian D. Ray, Ph.D., Research Facts on Homeschooling, *National Home Education Research Institute*, Op. Cit.

[113] Michael W. Apple, 'Away With All The Teachers: The Cultural Politics of Home Schooling', *International Studies in Sociology of Education*, 10:1, 61-80, 2011

[114] Christian W. Beck, 'Home Education – Globalisation Otherwise?', Op. cit.

[115] Alfred North Whitehead, *The Aims of Education and Other Essays*, 1929, Macmillan Company

[116] John Taylor Gatto, 'Why Schools Don't Educate', New York City Teacher of the Year Award acceptance speech, 31 January 1990

[117] European Convention on Human Rights, Protocol 1, Article 2, Signed 4 November 1950

[118] John Taylor Gatto, *Dumbing Us Down: The Hidden Curriculum of Compulsory Schooling*, 2017, New Society Publishers

119 Clark Aldrich, *Unschooling Rules*, 2011, Greenleaf Book Group LLC

120 Martin Rees, 'Fidei Defensores', *Times Higher Education*, 8 November 2012, http://bit.ly/2LTlJa5 (Accessed: 21 February 2018)

121 John Taylor Gatto, 'Why Schools Don't Educate', *New York City Teacher of the Year Award acceptance speech*, 31 January 1990

122 Clark Aldrich, *Unschooling Rules*, 2011, Greenleaf Book Group LLC

Chapter 5

123 George Dennison, *The Lives of Children*, 1969, Random House

124 Paula Rothermel, 'Home-Education: Comparison of Home- and School-Educated Children on PIPS Baseline Assessments', *Journal of Early Childhood Research*, Vol. 2, p. 294

125 *The Impact of Parental Involvement on Children's Education*, Department for Education and Skills, http://bit.ly/2JR0R1J (Accessed: 16 June 2018)

126 Frank Field, *The Foundation Years: Preventing Poor Children Becoming Poor Adults (The Report of the Independent Review on Poverty and Life Chances)*, 2010, The Stationary Office, Great Britain Cabinet Office

127 Paula-Jane Rothermel, *Home-Education: Rationales, Practices and Outcomes*, 2002, PhD Dissertation, University of Durham School of Education.

128 Paula Rothermel, 'Home-Education: Comparison of Home- and School-Educated Children on PIPS Baseline Assessments', *Journal of Early Childhood Research*, Vol. 2, p. 294

129 Adam Lopez, 'How Finnish Schools Shine', *The Guardian*, 9 April 2012, http://bit.ly/2Ja8BLL (Accessed: 14 March 2018)

130 Paula-Jane Rothermel, *Home-education : Rationales, Practices and Outcomes*, 2002 Durham Theses, Durham University, http://bit.ly/2sDyyfX (Accessed: 4 May 2018)

131 Ibid.

132 Paula Rothermel, 'Home-Education: Comparison of Home- and School-Educated Children on PIPS Baseline Assessments', *Journal of Early Childhood Research*, Vol 2(3) 273–299, 2004, Sage Publications

133 Alan Thomas, *Educating Children at Home*, 1998, Cassell Education

134 Barbara Tizard and Martin Hughes, *Young Children Learning*, 1984, Fontana

135 OECD, *Equity and Quality in Education: Supporting Disadvantaged Students and Schools*, 2012, OECD Publishing, http://bit.ly/2HPcRyQ (Accessed: 14 June 2018)

136 Jessica Shepherd, 'Dividing Younger Pupils by Ability Can Entrench Disadvantage, Study Finds', *The Guardian*, 9 February 2012, http://bit.ly/2LjZCZp (Accessed: 14 March 2018)

137 Adam Lopez, 'How Finnish Schools Shine', Op. cit.

138 Robert T. Carter (Ed.), *Addressing Cultural Issues in Organizations: Beyond the Corporate Context*, 2000, Sage Publications, Inc.

139 Lauren Schiller and Christina Hinton, It's True: Happier Students Get Higher Grades, The Conversation, 30 July 2015, http://bit.ly/2JqzBKk (Accessed: 7 May 2018)

[140] Adam Lopez, 'How Finnish Schools Shine', Op. cit.

[141] Ibid.

[142] OECD, *Equity and Quality in Education: Supporting Disadvantaged Students and Schools*, Op. cit.

[143] J.A. Banks, 'Multicultural Education: Historical Development, Dimensions and Practice', *Review of Research in Education*, 19 1993, p.3

[144] Linda Darling-Hammond, Kim Austin, Ira Lit and Na'ilah Nasir, *The Classroom Mosaic: Culture and Learning*, Stanford University School of Education, http://bit.ly/2LSPRT7 (Accessed: 6 May 2018)

[145] Ibid.

[146] Ibid.

[147] Anu Partenan, 'What Americans Keep Ignoring About Finland's School Success', *The Atlantic*, 29 December 2011 https://theatln.tc/2J6W9RI (Accessed: 14 March 2018)

[148] Ibid.

[149] Lloyd Khan, *Shelter (Shelter Library of Building Books)*, 2000, Shelter Publications

[150] Rhodri Davies, 'Venezuela's Indigenous University', *Al Jazeera*, 19 May 2012, http://bit.ly/2JrAfYf (Accessed: 20 March 2018)

[151] Stephen Corry, *Tribal peoples for tomorrow's world*, 2011, Survival International

[152] Ibid.

[153] Ibid.

[154] United Nations Housing Rights Programme, Report No. 8, *Urban Indigenous Peoples and Migration; A Review of Policies, Programmes and Practices*, 2010, UN-Habitat

155 'Social justice for Indigenous peoples', Speech by Michael Dodson, Aboriginal and Torres Strait Islander Social Justice Commissioner at the Third David Unaipon Lecture, October 1993, Australian Human Rights Commission

156 Finding Our Talk, Mushkeg Media, 2009

157 Kate Hodal, 'Moken Nomads Leave Behind Their 'Sea Gypsy' Life for a Modern Existence', *The Guardian*, 13 September 2012, http://bit.ly/2xE2M87 (Accessed: 2 May 2018)

158 Stephen Corry, *Tribal peoples for tomorrow's world*, 2011, Survival International

159 Ibid.

160 Noam Chomsky, 'Destroying the Commons: How the Magna Carta Became a Minor Carta', *TomDispatch*, 22 July 2012, http://bit.ly/2Ja7egb (Accessed: 20 March 2018)

161 Ibid.

162 William Shutkin, '*The Land That Could Be: Environmentalism and Democracy in the Twenty-First Century*', The MIT Press, 2000

163 George Monbiot, 'The Promised Land', *monbiot.com*, 16 July 2012, http://bit.ly/2JdX52i (Accessed: 20 March 2012)

164 Indian Land Tenure Foundation, '*Land Tenure Issues*', http://bit.ly/2sAbBdy (Accessed: 20 March 2012)

165 Noam Chomsky, 'How the Magna Carta became a Minor Carta, part 1', *The Guardian*, 24 July 2012, http://bit.ly/2srxyw4 (Accessed: 26 March 2018)

166 Elinor Ostrom, *Governing the Commons*, 1991, Cambridge University Press

167 Colin Donoghue, 'Native Americans and OM: Potential Power Partnership', *Media Roots*, 23 December 2011, http://bit.ly/2xCMtZc (Accessed: 26 March 2018)

168 Ahmed Djoghlaf, Felix Dodds (Eds), *Biodiversity and Ecosystem Insecurity: A Planet in Peril*, 2011, Routledge

169 Anthony J. Parel (Ed), *Gandhi, Freedom and Self-rule (Global Encounters: Studies in Comparative Political Theory)*, 2000, Lexington Books

170 Joel Spring, *Horace's School*, 1997 Boston: Houghton Mifflin

171 Linda Darling-Hammond, Kim Austin, Ira Lit and Na'ilah Nasir, *The Classroom Mosaic: Culture and Learning*, Op. cit.

172 *Urban Indigenous Peoples and Migration: Challenges and Opportunities*, Sixth Session of the UN Permanent Forum on Indigenous Issues, 21 May 2007, http://bit.ly/2xDPHeZ (Accessed: 5 May 2018)

173 Roque Roldán Ortega, *Models for Recognizing Indigenous Land Rights in Latin America*, Environment Department working papers; no. 99, Biodiversity Series, 2004, World Bank, Washington, DC. http://bit.ly/2kLld1y (Accessed: 3 June 2018)

174 Peter Linebaugh, *The Magna Carta Manifesto: Liberties and Commons for All*, 2009, University of California Press

175 Indigenous Land Rights, Wikipedia, http://bit.ly/2LUSjsf (Accessed: 30 April 2018)

176 Urban Indigenous Peoples and Migration: Challenges and Opportunities, UN Permanent Forum on Indigenous Issues

177 Ibid.

Chapter 6

178 Finding Our Talk, Mushkeg Media, 2009

179 Ibid.

180 Paroma Basu, 'What Happens When a Language Dies?', *National Geographic News*, 26 February 2009, http://bit.ly/2Jpl2Xt (Accessed: 30 April 2018)

181 Leroy Little Bear, *Reclaiming indigenous Voice and Vision*, Marie Batistte (Ed), 2011, University of British Columbia Press

182 Urszula Clark, *Language and Identity in Englishes*, 2013, Routledge

183 Louis-Jean Calvet, *Language Wars and Linguistic Politics*, 1999, Oxford University Press

184 The Mother-Tongue Dilemma, *Education Today*, No. 6 July - September 2003, UNESCO (Accessed: 5 May 2018)

185 Sheriff judges aye-aye a contemptible no-no, 11 December 1993, The Herald, http://bit.ly/2Hg1gsk (Accessed: 26 March 2018)

186 Stephen Corry, *Tribal peoples for tomorrow's world*, 2011, Survival International

187 Lera Boroditsky, 'How Does Our Language Shape The Way We Think?', 6 November 2009, *Edge*, http://bit.ly/2Liigkb (Accessed: 26 March 2009)

188 Language: At threat of extinction, 17 July 2014, *Al Jazeera*, http://bit.ly/2xAtrD2 (Accessed: 26 March 2009)

189 Lera Boroditsky, 'How Does Our Language Shape The Way We Think?', 6 November 2009, *Edge*, http://bit.ly/2Liigkb (Accessed: 26 March 2009)

190 Ibid.

191 Ibid.

192 Ibid.

193 The Mother-Tongue Dilemma, *Education Today*, No. 6 July - September 2003, UNESCO http://bit.ly/2J3hlYa (Accessed: 5 May 2018)

194 Dr. Muhammad Tariq Khan, 'Education in Mother Tongue - A Children's Right', *International Journal of Humanities and Management Sciences* Volume 2, Issue 4 (2014) ISSN 2320–4044, http://bit.ly/2xzP9XH (Accessed: 30 April 2018)

195 Ibid.

196 Ibid.

197 Penelope Bender, Nadine Dutcher, David Klaus, Jane Shore and Charlie Tesar, 'In Their Own Language: Education for All', *Education Notes*, 2005, The World Bank, http://bit.ly/2JrpgOy (Accessed: 5 May 2018)

198 Paul Mashegoane, 'Fallacy of Teaching Maths and Science in Mother Tongue', *Huffington Post*, 6 September 2017, http://bit.ly/2LilJy6 (Accessed: 30 April 02018)

199 The Mother-Tongue Dilemma, *Education Today*, Op. cit.

200 *Urban Indigenous Peoples and Migration: Challenges and Opportunities*, Op. cit.

201 Monica Mark, 'Nigeria's Love of Pidgin Dey Scatter My Brain Yet Ginger My Swagger', *The Guardian*, 24 September 2012, http://bit.ly/2HhGlVR (Accessed: 26 March 2018)

202 Linda King and Sabine Schielmann, *The Challenge of indigenous Education: Practice and Perspectives*, 2004, UNESCO

203 'Stronger Futures Intervention, Not So Strong Locals Say', *Treaty Republic*, 5 March 2012, http://bit.ly/2Hgs6k8 (Accessed: 5 May 2018)

204 Felicia R. Lee, 'Lingering Conflict in the Schools: Black Dialect vs. Standard Speech', *NY Times*, 1994, https://nyti.ms/2JrBKFR (Accessed: 26 March 2018)

205 Raphiq Ibrahim, Zohar Eviatar and Mark Leikin, 'Speaking Hebrew With an Accent: Empathic Capacity or Other Non-personal Factors', *International Journal of Bilingualism*, 2008, http://bit.ly/2LftCpi (Accessed: 5 May 2018)

206 Multilingual Education, Wikipedia, https://en.wikipedia.org/wiki/Multilingual_Education (Accessed: 26 March 2018)

207 UNESCO, 'The Mother-Tongue Dilemma', *Education Today Newsletter*, July - September 2013, http://bit.ly/2l7WViu (Accessed: 14 June 2018)

208 Jessica Huseman, 'The Rise of Homeschooling Among Black Families', *The Atlantic*, 17 February 2015, https://theatln.tc/2JfKqfj (Accessed: 14 March 2018)

209 Ephrat Livini, 'Muslim Home Schooling on the Rise', *ABC News*, 23 August (year not given), https://abcn.ws/2xJMw5Q (Accessed: 5 May 2018)

210 Preethi Nallu and Zack Embree, The Amazon's Keepers Reach Out to The World, Al Jazeera, 16 July 2012, http://bit.ly/2J9OYDO (Accessed: 5 May 2018)

211 *Report of the Royal Commission on Aboriginal Peoples*, October 1996, Government of Canada, http://bit.ly/2J9chxC (Accessed: 5 May 2018)

212 *Native American Children And Home School*, http://bit.ly/2so4m9h (Accessed: 5 May 2018)

213 Celia Haig-Brown, *Making the Spirit Dance Within*, 1997, James Lorimer & Company Ltd

214 Stephen Corry, *Tribal peoples for tomorrow's world*, 2011, Survival International

215 Jean-Paul Restoule, Aboriginal Worldviews and Education, Coursera, 2013

216 Bill Fogarty, 'Learning for The Western World? The Indigenous Education Dilemma', *The Conversation*, 13 December 2012, http://bit.ly/2xMxk83 (Accessed: 26 March 2018)

217 Jean-Paul Restoule, Aboriginal Worldviews and Education, Coursera, 2013

218 Linda King and Sabine Schielmann, *The Challenge of indigenous Education: Practice and Perspectives*, 2004, UNESCO

219 Christian W. Beck, 'Home Education – Globalisation Otherwise?', Op. cit.

220 Stephen Corry, *Tribal peoples for tomorrow's world*, 2011, Survival International

221 Linda King and Sabine Schielmann, *The Challenge of indigenous Education: Practice and Perspectives*, 2004, UNESCO

222 *Urban Indigenous Peoples and Migration: Challenges and Opportunities*, Op. cit.

223 Patrick Barkham, 'The Power of Speech', 10 November 2008, *The Guardian*, http://bit.ly/2kKZarE (Accessed: 26 March 2018)

224 The Hadza, Survival International, http://bit.ly/2LT8jde (Accessed: 15 June 2018)

225 Linda King and Sabine Schielmann, *The Challenge of indigenous Education: Practice and Perspectives*, 2004, UNESCO

226 Angayuqaq Oscar Kawagley and Ray Barnhardt, in *Ecological Education in Action*, Smith & Williams (Eds), 1998, SUNY Press

Chapter 7

227 Lisa Delpit, *Other People's Children: Cultural Conflict in the Classroom*, 2013, The New Press

228 Sophie von Stumm and Robert Plomin, 'Socioeconomic Status and the Growth of Intelligence From Infancy Through Adolescence', *Intelligence*, 48, Jan-Feb 2015, http://bit.ly/2k-MEM9I (Accessed: 11 May 2018)

229 Frank Field, 'Focus On The Under-fives To Give All Children An Equal Chance', *The Guardian*, 24 September 2012 http://bit.ly/2JcDKyh (Accessed: 26 March 2018)

230 Richard Garner, Social class 'determines child's success', Op. cit.

231 Frank Field, 'Focus On The Under-fives To Give All Children An Equal Chance', *Op. cit.*

232 Robert Erikson and John H. Goldthorpe, *The Constant Flux: Study of Class Mobility in Industrial Societies*, 1992, Clarendon Press

233 Cristina Iannelli and Lindsay Paterson, *Does Education Promote Social Mobility?*, Centre for Educational Sociology Briefing No. 35, University of Edinburgh, June 2005, http://bit.ly/2sqB2Py (Accessed: 5 May 2018)

234 Cristina Iannelli and Lindsay Paterson, 'ESRC Research Project Education and Social Mobility in Scotland in the Twentieth Century', Working Paper 5 Education and Social Mobility in Scotland, http://bit.ly/2Jo1Vxg (Accessed: 3 June 2018)

235 Ibid.

236 W.W. Charters, *Handbook of Research on Teaching*, N.L. Gage (Ed.), 1963, American Educational Research Association

237 Bill Gabrenya, *Research Skills for Psychology Majors: Everything You Need to Know to Get Started*, Op. cit.

238 Ibid.

239 Melvin L. Kohn, 'Social Class and Parent-Child Relationships: An Interpretation', *American Journal of Sociology*, Vol. 68, No. 4 January 1963, pp. 471-480

240 Clark Aldrich, *Unschooling Rules: 55 Ways to Unlearn What We Know about Schools and Rediscover Education*, 2011, Greenleaf Book Group

241 Ivan Illich, *Deschooling Society*, 1971, Harper and Row

242 Paulo Freire, *Pedagogy of the Oppressed*, 1970, New York : Herder and Herder

243 Noam Chomsky, 'Education is Ignorance', Excerpted from *Class Warfare*, 1995, http://bit.ly/2sCshRr (Accessed: 28 March 2018)

244 Robert M. Hauser, 'Educational Stratification in the United States', *Sociological Enquiry*, Volume 40, Issue 2, April 1970 Pages 102-129

245 Ivan Illich, *Deschooling Society*, 1971, Harper and Row

246 Kraus, Piff, Keltner, 'Social Class as Culture: The Convergence of Resources and Rank in the Social Realm', August 8, 2011, *Current Directions in Psychological Science*, Volume: 20 issue: 4, page(s): 246-250

247 Dacher Keltner, 'Social Class as Culture', Op. cit.

248 Tom Lamont, 'Alan Moore: Why I Turned my Back on Hollywood', The Guardian, 15 December 2012, http://bit.ly/2J5pCeh (Accessed: 5 May 2018)

249 Paul Piff, 'Upper Class People More Likely to Behave Un-ethically', *National Science Foundation*, 7 March 2012, http://bit.ly/2JraMhs (Accessed: 26 March 2018)

250 Empathy and Pro-Social Behavior in Rats, Inbal Ben-Ami Bartal, Jean Decety, Peggy Mason Science 09 Dec 2011: Vol. 334, Issue 6061, pp. 1427-1430, http://bit.ly/2xFgIyO (Accessed: 26 March 2018)

251 Ibid.

252 Kraus, Piff, Keltner, 'Social Class as Culture: The Convergence of Resources and Rank in the Social Realm', August 8, 2011, *Current Directions in Psychological Science*, Volume: 20 issue: 4, page(s): 246-250

253 Authoritarian Schooling: A Catalogue of Damage compiled by David Gribble, http://bit.ly/2LfDYVY (Accessed: 5 May 2018)

254 Ibid.

255 David Graeber, 'Caring Too Much, That's The Curse of The Working Classes', *The Guardian*, 26 March 2014, http://bit.ly/2ssSTVX (Accessed: 19 February 2018)

256 Rachel Hosie, 'Powerful People Act as if They've Sustained a Traumatic Brain Injury, Find Scientists', *Independent*, 26 June 2017, https://ind.pn/2Lk7Mkv (Accessed: 19 February 2018)

257 Melvin L. Kohn, 'Social Class and Parent-Child Relationships: An Interpretation', *Op. cit.*

258 Ibid.

259 Gillian Evans, *Educational Failure and Working Class White Children in Britain*, 2006, Palgrave Macmillan

260 Department for Education, *The Impact of Parental Involvement on Children's Education*, 2008, http://bit.ly/2ssXsQ6 (Accessed: 27 March 2018)

261 Ibid.

262 Leslie Gutman and Rodie Akerman, *Determinants of Aspirations: Wider Benefits of Learning Research Report No. 27*, 2008, Centre for Research on the Wider Benefits of Learning, Institute of Education, University of London: London.

263 'Urban Indigenous Peoples and Migration; A Review of Policies, Programmes and Practices', 2 June 2010, *International Expert Group Meeting on Urban Indigenous Peoples and Migration* held in Santiago, Chile, March 27-29, 2007

264 Mark Bracher, *Radical Pedagogy: Identity, Generativity, and Social Transformation*, 2006, Palgrave Macmillan

265 Ibid.

266 From a review by Anon, of Gillian Evans, *Educational Failure and Working Class White Children in Britain*, 2006, AIAA, https://amzn.to/2HfqU0B (Accessed: 10 May 2018)

267 John Taylor Gatto, *The Underground History of American Education*, 2000, The Oxford Village Press

268 Brian Wheeler, 'Home Schooling: Why More Black US Families Are Trying It', BBC News, 15 March 2012, https://bbc.in/2t9l0ch (Accessed: 15 June 2018)

269 Noam Chomsky, 'Education is Ignorance', Op. cit.

270 Native American Children And Home School, Op. ci.

271 George Dei interviewed by Scott Anderson, 'Africentric Schools', *UofT Magazine*, Autumn 2009, http://bit.ly/2sxRI6E (Accessed: 28 March 2018)

272 Octaviana V. Trujillo, 'A Tribal Approach to Language and Literacy Development in a Trilingual Setting', in *Teaching Indigenous Languages* Jon Reyhner (Ed), 1997, Flagstaff, AZ: Northern Arizona University

273 Eva Swidler, Learning About Culture & Community: Unschooling in the Real World, *Life Learning Magazine*, http://bit.ly/2ssAGYJ (Accessed: 28 March 2018)

274 Bill Gabrenya, *Research Skills for Psychology Majors: Everything You Need to Know to Get Started*, http://bit.ly/2JbLu3L (Accessed: 14 March 2018)

275 Paul Beaumont, 'The Houla Massacre Shows How Killing Can Become Normal', *The Guardian*, 29 May 2012, http://bit.ly/2so1qcL (Accessed: 14 March 2018)

276 Ibid.

277 Ibid.

278 Dacher Keltner, 'Social Class as Culture', *Association for Psychological Science*, 8 August 2011, http://bit.ly/2HgOtpH (Accessed: 14 March 2018)

279 Charles Q. Choi, 'Rich People More Likely to Lie, Cheat, Study Suggests', *Live Science*, 27 February 2012, http://bit.-ly/2HgaFQT (Accessed: 14 March 2018)

280 Colin Ward, *Education Without Schools*, 1973, Ed. Peter Buckmann Condor

281 Brian D. Ray, Ph.D., Research Facts on Homeschooling, Op. cit.

282 Paula Rothermel, Home-Education: Comparison of Home- and School-Educated Children on PIPS Baseline Assessments, *Journal of Early Childhood Research*, Vol. 2, pp. 273-99.

283 Ibid.

284 Ibid.

Chapter 8

285 Russell Brand, 'Big Brother Isn't Watching You', *The Guardian*, 11 August 2011, http://bit.ly/2kLTXQx (Accessed: 19 February 2018)

286 *Schooling The World: The White Man's Last Burden*, 2010, directed by Carol Black

287 Linda Blair, 'Why Do We Find Failure So Difficult to Bear?', *The Guardian*, 10 February 2015, http://bit.ly/2J5d-R7u (Accessed: 4 May 2018)

288 Jerry Muller, Against metrics: how measuring performance by numbers backfires, *Aeon*, 24 April 2018, http://bit.ly/2Ju-OwmO (Accessed: 29 April 2018)

289 Waziyatawin and Michael Yellow Bird (Eds.), *For Indigenous Minds Only: A Decolonization Handbook*, 2012, SAR Press

290 David Brooks, *The Road to Character*, 2015, Allen Lane

291 The Children's Commissioner for England, *Life in 'Likes': Children's Commissioner report into social media use among 8-12 year olds*, 4 January 2018, http://bit.ly/2Leeus7 (Accessed: 4 May 2018)

292 'Dr. Gabor Maté on ADHD, Bullying and the Destruction of American Childhood', *Democracy Now*, 24 November 2010, http://bit.ly/2ssT9UZ (Accessed: 4 May 2018)

293 'Research Shows Child Rearing Practices of Distant Ancestors Foster Morality, Compassion in Kids', *Notre Dame News*, University of Notre Dame, 17 September 2010, https://ntrda.me/2JnFHLL (Accessed: 4 May 2018)

294 'Dr. Gabor Maté on ADHD, Bullying and the Destruction of American Childhood', Op. cit.

295 St. Petersburg-USA Orphanage Research Team, *The Effects of Early Social-Emotional and Relationship Experience on the Development of Young Orphanage Children*, http://bit.ly/2LktpRM (Accessed: 4 May 2018)

296 Jonathan Kozol, *The Night Is Dark and I Am Far From Home*, 1975, Houghton Mifflin

297 Ibid.

298 Ibid.

299 Ibid.

300 Dan Hind, 'Greek lessons', *Al Jazeera*, 27 Aug 2012, http://bit.ly/2Hfxy6R (Accessed: 4 May 2018)

301 Jonathan Kozol, *The Night Is Dark and I Am Far From Home*, 1975, Houghton Mifflin

302 Ibid.

303 Sean Coughlan, 'UK schools "most socially segregated"', 11 September 2012, *BBC News*, https://bbc.in/2kLZQgG (Accessed: 19 February 2018)

304 Martin V. Covington, *Making the Grade: A Self-Worth Perspective on Motivation and School Reform*, 1998, Cambridge University Press

305 'Why we should stop grading students on a curve', *New York Times*, 11 September 2016, https://nyti.ms/2LhgnnL (Accessed: 3 June 2018)

306 A College Lecturer, 'Market failure: the profiteers behind Gove's exam fiasco', *Counterfire*, 4 September 2012, http://bit.ly/2kL2xii (Accessed: 19 February 2018)

307 Bruce E. Levine, '8 Reasons Young Americans Don't Fight Back: How the US Crushed Youth Resistance', *Alternet*, 31 July 2011, http://bit.ly/2LV7RMl (Accessed: 19 February 2018)

308 Alfie Kohn, 'The case against grades', *Educational Leadership*, November 2011, http://bit.ly/2kHSqLk (Accessed: 19 February 2018)

309 Jerry Muller, 'Against Metrics: How Measuring Performance by Numbers Backfires', Op. cit.

310 Michael Horn, 'Disrupting the classroom', *Foundation for Economic Education*, 7 February 2013, http://bit.ly/2HeRebf (Accessed: 19 February 2018)

311 Peter Gray Ph.D., 'The Evolutionary Biology of Education: How Our Hunter-Gatherer Educative Instincts Could Form the Basis for Education Today', *Evolution: Education and Outreach*, March 2011, Volume 4, Issue 1, pp 28–40

312 Charlie Rose, *A Conversation With Anarchist David Graeber*, 2006, http://bit.ly/2kKtcMn (Accessed: 4 May 2018)

313 Noam Chomsky interviewed by Bernie Dwyer, 'Corporate Journalism', *Radio Havana*, 28 October 2003, http://bit.ly/2kLr1s0 (Accessed: 4 May 2018)

314 Homa Khaleeli, 'Why prison uniforms are a bad idea', *The Guardian*, 30 April 2013, http://bit.ly/2xzSGFr (Accessed: 19 February 2018)

315 Clark Aldrich, *Unschooling Rules*, 2011, Greenleaf Book Group LLC

316 David Graeber, *Fragments of an Anarchist Anthropology*, 2004, Prickly Paradigm Press

317 Linda Blair, 'Why do we find failure so difficult to bear?', *The Guardian*, 10 February 2015, http://bit.ly/2J740yj (Accessed: 19 February 2018)

318 Kathryn S. Plaisance and Thomas A.C. Reydon (Eds.), *Philosophy of Behavioral Biology*, Springer, 2012

319 Sarah Crown, 'A life in writing: David Almond', *The Guardian*, 21 August 2010, http://bit.ly/2JpBvuU (Accessed: 19 February 2018)

320 Rachel Cooke, 'The art of Judy Chicago', *The Guardian*, 4 November 2012, http://bit.ly/2xDFpLZ (Accessed: 19 February 2018)

321 Grant Cardone, *The 10X Rule: The Only Difference Between Success and Failure*, 2011, Wiley

322 Mark Brake and Emma Weitkamp Eds., *Introducing Science Communication: A Practical Guide*, 2009, Palgrave

323 Linda Blair, 'Why do we find failure so difficult to bear?', Op. cit.

324 Peter Van Greenaway, *The Man Who Held the Queen to Ransom and Sent Parliament Packing*, 1972, Penguin

325 Allan Bloom, *The Closing of the American Mind*, 1998, Simon and Schuster

326 Julian Assange, *Statement after Six Months in Ecuadorian Embassy*, 20 December 2012, http://bit.ly/2HgEAIz (Accessed: 4 May 2018)

Chapter 9

327 *Monty Python's Life of Brian*, 1979, UK, Dir. Terry Jones

328 Paula-Jane Rothermel, *Home-education : Rationales, Practices and Outcomes*, Op. cit.

329 Chris Klicka, 'Socialization: Homeschoolers Are in the Real World', *Homeschool Legal Defense Association*, March 2007, http://bit.ly/2HftCmN (Accessed: 4 May 2018)

330 Ibid.

331 Ibid.

332 Julia Lawrence, 'Number of Homeschoolers Growing Nationwide', *Education News*, 21 May 2012, http://bit.ly/2HetZht (Accessed: 30 May 2018)

333 Gordon Neufeld and Gabor Maté, *Hold onto Your Kids: Why Parents Need to Matter More Than Peers*, 2006, Ballantine Books

334 Ibid.

335 Ibid.

336 Andrea Mrozek, 'Nurturing children: Why "early learning" doesn't help', *The Institute of Marriage and Family Canada*, 30 August 2012, http://bit.ly/2JcHWy1 (Accessed: 18 February 2018)

337 Clark Aldrich, *Unschooling Rules*, 2011, Greenleaf Book Group LLC

338 Susan Cain, *Quiet: The Power of Introverts in a World That Can't Stop Talking*, 2013, Penguin

339 Anthony Storr, *Solitude*, 1988, Flamingo

340 Ibid.

341 Susan Cain, *Quiet: The Power of Introverts in a World That Can't Stop Talking*, 2013, Penguin

342 Bryan Walsh, 'The Upside Of Being An Introvert (And Why Extroverts Are Overrated)', *Time*, 6 February 2012, https://ti.me/2LjnVX4 (Accessed: 18 February 2018)

343 Zosia Bielski, 'Giving introverts permission to be themselves', *The Globe and Mail*, 26 March 2017, https://tgam.ca/2kIn2w3 (Accessed: 18 February 2018)

344 Sir Joshua Reynolds, *The Works of Sir Joshua Reynolds*, Volume 1 of 2, Discourse XII, 1797, T. Cadell and W. Davies, The Strand, London

345 Anthony Storr, *Solitude*, 1988, Flamingo

346 Paula-Jane Rothermel, *Home-education : Rationales, Practices and Outcomes*, Op. cit.

³⁴⁷ Gordon Neufeld and Gabor Maté, *Hold onto Your Kids: Why Parents Need to Matter More Than Peers*, 2006, Ballantine Books

³⁴⁸ Sarah Boseley, 'Children bullied by peers "at greater mental health risk"', *The Guardian*, 28 February, 2015, http://bit.ly/2J5h1rS (Accessed: 18 February 2018)

³⁴⁹ Homeschooling, Wikipedia, Accessed via the WaybackMachine, http://bit.ly/2LTBKwJ (Accessed: 3 June 2018)

³⁵⁰ Brian D. Ray, 'Research Facts on Homeschooling', Op. cit.

³⁵¹ John Stuart Mill, *On Liberty*, 2006, Penguin Classics

³⁵² Paula Rothermel, *Home-Education: Aims, Practices and Outcomes*, Paper presented at the Annual Conference of the British Educational Research Association, University of Exeter, England, 12-14 September 2002

³⁵³ David Guterson, *Family Matters: Why Homeschooling Makes Sense*, 1993, Harvest Books

³⁵⁴ Ibid.

³⁵⁵ Wendy Charles-Warner, *Home Education and the Safeguarding Myth: Analysing the Facts Behind the Rhetoric*, February 2015, http://bit.ly/2sCSoYr (Accessed: 2 May 2018)

³⁵⁶ Ibid.

³⁵⁷ Brian D. Ray, 'Homeschooling and Child Abuse, Child Neglect, and Child Fatalities', *National Home Education Research Institute*, 2 February 2017, http://bit.ly/2JcQ7un (Accessed: 12 May 2018)

³⁵⁸ Petition, *NSPCC: Withdraw your report "Children Not Educated In School: Learning from case reviews*, http://bit.ly/2JoQUvv (Accessed: 3 June 2018)

359 Wendy Charles-Warner, 'Safeguarding', *New Foundations Home Education*, 2012, http://bit.ly/2tarnN7 (Accessed: 19 June 2018)

360 Wendy Charles-Warner, *Home Education and the Safeguarding Myth: Analysing the Facts Behind the Rhetoric,* Op. cit.

361 Action For Home Education, *Lies, Damned Lies and Statistics*, July 2009, http://bit.ly/2MDmapq (Accessed: 19 June 2018)

362 Erik H. Erikson, *Insight and Responsibility*, 1972, W. W. Norton & Company

363 KR, 'A Home Educating Mum Writes to Her MP', 17 January 2018, http://bit.ly/2K1NUCu (Accessed: 19 June 2018)

364 Petition, *NSPCC: Withdraw your report "Children Not Educated In School: Learning from case reviews,* http://bit.ly/2JoQUvv (Accessed: 3 June 2018)

365 David Guterson, *Family Matters: Why Homeschooling Makes Sense*, 1993, Harvest Books

366 Homeschooling, Wikipedia, http://bit.ly/2HftUtN (Accessed: 20 February 2018)

367 David Guterson, *Family Matters: Why Homeschooling Makes Sense*, 1993, Harvest Books

368 missdisco, 'Regulating Home Education', *Liberal Conspiracy*, 18 June 2009, http://bit.ly/2Hfuckn (Accessed: 18 February 2018)

Chapter 10

369 Erik H. Erikson, in Robert Coles (Ed.), The Erik Erikson Reader, 2001, W.W. Norton & Co.

370 Ibid.

371 Jane McGonigal, *Reality Is Broken*, 2012, Vintage

372 David Graeber, 'On The Phenomenon of Bullshit Jobs', *libcom.org*, 20 August 2013, http://bit.ly/2kOdgsB (Accessed: 4 May 2018)

373 L.M. Calkins, *The Art of Teaching Writing*, 1986, Heinemann Educational Books

374 Mark Bracher, *Radical Pedagogy: Identity, Generativity and Social Transformation*, 2009, Palgrave Macmillan

375 Peter Gray Ph.D., 'The Evolutionary Biology of Education: How Our Hunter-Gatherer Educative Instincts Could Form the Basis for Education Today', *Evolution: Education and Outreach*, March 2011, Volume 4, Issue 1, pp 28–40

376 Robert B. Zajonc and Patricia R. Mullally, 'Birth order: Reconciling conflicting effects', *American Psychologist*, 52(7), 685-699.

377 'What Are the Benefits of Mentoring?', Durham University, http://bit.ly/2srRsam (Accessed: 4 May 2018)

378 Erik H. Erikson, *Inisght and Responsibility*, 1964, W.W. Norton & Company

379 Jane McGonigal, *Reality Is Broken*, 2012, Vintage

380 Paul Ekman, *Emotions Revealed: Understanding Faces and Feelings*, 2004, W&N

381 Jane McGonigal, *Reality Is Broken*, 2012, Vintage

382 Erik H. Erikson, *Inisght and Responsibility*, 1964, W.W. Norton & Company

383 Christopher Alexander et al, *A Pattern Language: Towns, Buildings, Construction*, 1978, OUP USA

384 Erik H. Erikson, *Inisght and Responsibility*, 1964, W.W. Norton & Company

385 Ivan Illich, *Deschooling Society*, 1971, Harper and Row

386 Christopher Alexander et al, *A Pattern Language: Towns, Buildings, Construction*, 1978, OUP USA

387 Ibid.

388 Gregory A. Smith and Dilafruz R. Williams (Eds.), *Ecological Education in Action: On Weaving Education, Culture, and the Environment*, 1998, State University of New York Press

389 Christopher Alexander et al, *A Pattern Language: Towns, Buildings, Construction*, 1978, OUP USA

390 Stephen Moss, 'Ray Mears: "I will never trust 24-hour news again"', *The Guardian*, 4 September 2013, http://bit.ly/2so99Yj (Accessed: 18 February 2018)

391 Eric Robinson, 'Rethinking what we mean by 'education', Op. cit.

392 Paula-Jane Rothermel, *Home-education : Rationales, Practices and Outcomes*, Op. cit.

393 Grace Llewellyn, *The Teenage Liberation Handbook: How to Quit School and Get a Real Life and Education*, 1997, Thorsons

394 Paula Rothermel, University of Hong Kong Education Conference 2014, http://bit.ly/2J3nvYi (Accessed: 18 March 2018)

395 Oliver and Rachel DeMille, 'The Seven Keys of Great Teaching', http://bit.ly/2kJyZBG (Accessed: 4 May 2018)

396 Christopher Alexander et al, *A Pattern Language: Towns, Buildings, Construction*, 1978, OUP USA

397 George Dennison, *The Lives of Children: The Story of the First Street School*, 1969, Random House, p.13

398 Brain D. Ray, *Homeschooling Grows Up*, 2003, National Home Education Research Institute, http://bit.ly/2syPIBJ (Accessed: 12 May 2018)

399 William Heard Kilpatrick, Wikipedia, http://bit.ly/2JcESC6 (Accessed: 4 May 2018)

400 'Flipping the Classroom', *The Economist*, 17 September 2011, https://econ.st/2JjXV0L (Accessed: 4 May 2018)

401 Peter Gray, 'The Evolutionary Biology of Education: How Our Hunter-Gatherer Educative Instincts Could Form the Basis for Education Today', *Evolution: Education and Outreach*, March 2011, Volume 4, Issue 1, pp 28–40

402 Christopher Alexander et al, *A Pattern Language: Towns, Buildings, Construction*, 1978, OUP USA

403 Marie Batiste, *Reclaiming Indigenous Voice and Vision*, 2000, UBC Press

404 Polly Curtis and Allegra Stratton, 'Revealed: Secret Government Plans to Win Back Women', *The Guardian*, 13 September 2011, http://bit.ly/2Jn6VC1 (Accessed: 4 May 2018)

405 Angayuqaq Oscar Kawagley and Ray Barnhardt, 'Education Indigenous to Place: Western Science Meets Native Reality', *Alaska Native Knowledge Network*, http://bit.ly/2kM4b3s (Accessed: 19 February 2018)

406 Raymond Neckowaya, Keith Brownleea, and Bruno Castellana, 'Is Attachment Theory Consistent with Aboriginal Parenting Realities?', *First Peoples Child and Family Review*, Volume 3, Number 2, 2007 Special Edition, pp.65-74

407 Alan Thomas, *Educating Children at Home*, 1998, Cassell Education

408 Ibid.

409 William Jon Watkins, *The Tracker: The True Story of Tom Brown, Jr.*, 1996, Berkley Books

410 Karl Groos, *The Play of Animals*, 1898, transl. Elizabeth L. Baldwin, New York: Appleton

411 Ibid

412 Leslie Thatcher, ' "If You Can Think Differently, You Can Act Differently" ', *Truthout*, 3 February 2010, http://bit.ly/2JamwS1 (Accessed: 4 May 2018)

413 Clark Aldrich, *Unschooling Rules*, 2011, Greenleaf Book Group LLC

414 Ibid.

415 Colin Ward, *Anarchism as a Theory of Organization*, 1966, http://bit.ly/2xCVGRp (Accessed: 4 May 2018)

416 Melissa Benn, 'Michael Gove's GCSE reforms are tame, backward and not even new', *The Guardian*, 17 September 2012, http://bit.ly/2JpDP56 (Accessed: 18 February 2018)

417 Thom Hartmann, *The Last Hours of Ancient Sunlight*, 2004, Crown Publications

418 Stephen Corry, *Tribal peoples for tomorrow's world*, 2011, Survival International

419 Melati Kaye and Brian Orland, 'Indonesia's Last Nomadic Sea Gypsies', *Al Jazeera*, 6 October 2012, http://bit.ly/2J9UiXO (Accessed: 4 May 2018)

Chapter 11

420 Camille Paglia, 'Motherhood Gets A Raw Deal From Feminists', *The Globe and Mail*, 6 October 2012, https://tgam.ca/2JsekQD (Accessed: 4 May 2018)

421 Wendy McElroy, 'Can a Feminist Homeschool Her Child?', *Foundation for Economic Freedom*, 1 February 2002, http://bit.ly/2ssWX8J (Accessed: 20 February 2018)

422 Ibid.

423 Deborah Orr, 'If full-time parenting was that fulfilling, more men would have been doing it', *The Guardian*, 29 March 2013, http://bit.ly/2sC8hhR (Accessed: 4 May 2018)

424 Naomi Stadlen, *How Mothers Love: And How Relationships are Born*, 2015, Piaktus

425 Susan Maushart, *Wifework: What Marriage Really Means For Women*, 2003, Bloomsbury Publishing

426 Slavoj Zizek, 'Tolerance as an Ideological Category', *Critical Enquiry*, Autumn 2007

427 Denise Cummins Ph.D., 'The truth about children of working mothers', *Psychology Today*, 19 May 2015, http://bit.ly/2LhOmMT (Accessed: 18 February 2018)

428 Claire Paye, 'The Toughest Media Questions - Answered', *Mothers At Home Matter Newsletter*, Autumn 2017

429 Ibid.

430 Weaning, Wikipedia, http://bit.ly/2xEco2H (Accessed: 29 May 2018)

431 Breastfeeding Prevalence at 6-8 Weeks After Birth (Experimental Statistics), Quarter 3 2017/18 Statistical Commentary (April 2018 release), Public Health England, http://bit.ly/2HiBbca (Accessed: 29 May 2018)

432 Paula-Jane Rothermel, *Home-education : Rationales, Practices and Outcomes*, Op. cit.

433 'Child development and early learning', *Facts for Life*, Fourth Edition, http://bit.ly/2JbvpuC (Accessed: 18 February 2018)

434 Dr Jane Williams, 'Why the first year is so important to future learning', *Pregnancy Babies & Children's Expo*, http://bit.ly/2sDrtvE (Accessed: 18 February 2018)

⁴³⁵ Ibid.

⁴³⁶ Kristen Finello, 'Learning Milestones', *Parents Magazine*, http://bit.ly/2xJTNTc (Accessed: 18 February 2018)

⁴³⁷ Gordon Neufeld and Gabor Maté, *Hold onto Your Kids: Why Parents Need to Matter More Than Peers*, 2006, Ballantine Books

⁴³⁸ Ibid.

⁴³⁹ David Williamson, 'Kinnocks' daughter-in-law and Denmark's PM Helle Thorning-Schmidt speaks out for working women', 28 February 2012, *Wales Online*, http://bit.ly/2kIptPd (Accessed: 4 May 2018)

⁴⁴⁰ David Graeber, 'On the Phenomenon of Bullshit Jobs', *Strike! Magazine*, Summer (2013) pp. 10-11.

⁴⁴¹ The Kremlin, Moscow, *Presenting the Order of Parental Glory*, 31 May 2017, http://bit.ly/2LW2f4G (Accessed: 2 April 2018)

⁴⁴² Kirsten Asmussen, Judy Corlyon, Hanan Hauari and Vincent La Placa, 'Supporting Parents of Teenagers', Op. cit.

⁴⁴³ 'ONS: Record numbers working from home', *BBC News*, 4 June 2014, https://bbc.in/2sIQBS3 (Accessed: 18 February 2018)

⁴⁴⁴ Mark Ellis, 'Working from home soars with 1.5million people shunning the office for a more flexible life', *Mirror Online*, 20 May 2016, http://bit.ly/2J8kl5N (Accessed: 18 February 2018)

⁴⁴⁵ Estella Shardlow, 'Free wifi and comfy seats: London's best cafés to work in', *The Telegraph*, 5 May 2016, http://bit.-ly/2JtQCUl (Accessed: 18 February 2018)

⁴⁴⁶ Alexander Brown, '10 Great cafes in Bath where you can work remotely', *Bath Chronicle*, 1 July 2016, http://bit.ly/2sr-RnmL (Accessed: 18 February 2018)

447 Paula-Jane Rothermel, *Home-education : Rationales, Practices and Outcomes*, Op. cit.

448 Patrick Collinson, 'Cost of raising children in UK higher than ever', *The Guardian*, 16 February 2016, http://bit.ly/2xJCL7k (Accessed: 18 February 2018)

449 Dr. Brian Ray, 'Homeschool Progress Report 2009: Academic Achievement and Demographics', Op. cit.

450 Christopher Alexander et al, *A Pattern Language: Towns, Buildings, Construction*, 1978, OUP USA

451 'ONS: Record numbers working from home', Op. cit.

452 Christopher Alexander et al, *A Pattern Language: Towns, Buildings, Construction*, 1978, OUP USA

453 Ibid.

454 Modern Times: Camille Paglia & Jordan B Peterson, Published on Oct 2, 2017, http://bit.ly/2JjYF63 (Accessed: 4 May 2018)

455 Joe Rogan Experience #724 Christina Sommers, Streamed Live on Nov 18 2015, http://bit.ly/2Ldzxul (Accessed: 2 May 2018)

456 Angayuqaq Oscar Kawagley and Ray Barnhardt, 'Education Indigenous to Place: Western Science Meets Native Reality', Op. cit.

457 Leonard Shlain, *The Alphabet Versus the Goddess: Male Words and Female Images*, 1998, Allen Lane, London

458 Leonard Shlain, 'Writing on the wall for goddesses', *Times Higher Education*, 7 May 1999, http://bit.ly/2HgdiSw (Accessed: 18 February 2018)

459 Peter Gray Ph.D., 'The Evolutionary Biology of Education: How Our Hunter-Gatherer Educative Instincts Could Form the Basis for Education Today', *Evolution: Education and Outreach*, March 2011, Volume 4, Issue 1, pp 28–40

460 Neil Postman, *The Disappearance of Childhood*, 1994, New York: Vintage

461 David Graeber, *Fragments of an Anarchist Anthropology*, 2004, Prickly Paradigm Press

462 *Schooling the World*, 2010, Dir. Carol Black

463 United Nations Housing Rights Programme, Report No. 8, *Urban Indigenous Peoples and Migration; A Review of Policies, Programmes and Practices*, 2010, UN-Habitat

464 Paula-Jane Rothermel, *Home-education : Rationales, Practices and Outcomes*, Op. cit.

465 Sugata Mitra, Hole in the Wall, Wikipedia, http://bit.ly/2sAm3BO (Accessed: 2 April 2018)

466 Georgia Hanias, African grannies go solar, *New Internationalist*, 1 June 2012, http://bit.ly/2LRfnI9 (Accessed: 2 April 2018)

467 *Schooling the World*, 2010, Dir. Carol Black

468 Eduardo Avila, 'Students Connect With Their Community Roots at Bolivia's Aymara Indigenous University', *Rising Voices*, 9 July 2015, http://bit.ly/2JrvNc2 (Accessed: 2 April 2018)

469 United Nations Housing Rights Programme, Report No. 8, *Urban Indigenous Peoples and Migration; A Review of Policies, Programmes and Practices*, 2010, UN-Habitat

470 Ibid.

471 Rachel DeMille, 'Steel to Gold: Feminism vs. Stateswomanship', *TJEd*, 15 March 2011, http://bit.ly/2LfJAzE (Accessed: 18 February 2018)

Chapter 12

472 Peter Gray Ph.D., 'The many benefits, for kids, of playing video games', *Psychology Today*, 7 January 2012, http://bit.-ly/2Hf1gZy (Accessed: 18 February 2018)

473 Alvin Toffler, *Powershift*, 1990, Bantam Books

474 Howard Gardner, *Five Minds for the Future*, 2006, Harvard Business School Press

475 Tony Wagner, *The Global Achievement Gap*, 2009, Basic Books

476 Daniel Pink, *A Whole New Mind*, 2008, Marshall Cavendish

477 John Taylor Gatto, 'The Curriculum of Necessity or What Must an Educated Person Know?', *Information Liberation*, 10 September 2009, http://bit.ly/2HgJwgz (Accessed: 10 February 2018)

478 Ibid.

479 Special Report, 'Re-educating Rita', *The Economist*, 25 June 2016, https://econ.st/2LdzRtq (Accessed: 19 February 2018)

480 John Taylor Gatto, 'The Curriculum of Necessity or What Must an Educated Person Know?', *Information Liberation*, 10 September 2009, http://bit.ly/2LV1PeX (Accessed: 18 February 2018)

481 Ivan Illich, *Deschooling Society*, 1971, Harper and Row

482 Christopher Alexander et al, *A Pattern Language: Towns, Buildings, Construction*, 1978, OUP USA

483 Carole Cadwalladr, 'Do Online Courses Spell the End forr the Traditional University?', *The Guardian*, 11 November 2012, http://bit.ly/2ssEN77 (Accessed: 19 February 2018)

484 Ibid.

485 Jason Tanz, 'The Techies Who Are Hacking Education by Homeschooling Their Kids', *Wired*, 2 April 2015, http://bit.ly/2LW2QmW (Accessed: 18 February 2018)

486 Sean Coughlan, 'University offers science degree online for £5,650 per year', *BBC Online*, 6 March 2018, https://bbc.in/2ssHNQT (Accessed: 18 March 2018)

487 Edutopia, 'PBL Research Summary: Studies Validate Project-Based Learning', *Edutopia*, 1 November 2001, https://edut.to/2LT68rb (Accessed: 18 February 2018)

488 Ibid.

489 Ibid.

490 Ibid.

491 Ibid.

492 Bloom's Digital Taxonomy, Andrew Churches, 2008, http://bit.ly/2xDb1RN (Accessed: 30 April 2018)

493 Clive Thompson, 'Teenagers and social networking – it might actually be good for them', *The Guardian*, 5 October 2013, http://bit.ly/2sDFbyy (Accessed: 18 February 2018)

494 Peter Gray Ph.D., 'The many benefits, for kids, of playing video games', Op. cit.

495 Neil Postman, *Amusing Ourselves to Death*, 1985, Methuen Publishing Ltd, quoted in http://bit.ly/2kIsDm0 (Accessed: 19 February 2018)

496 Peter Gray Ph.D., 'The many benefits, for kids, of playing video games', Op cit.

497 Ibid.

498 James Paul Gee, 'High Score Education', *Wired*, 5 January 2003, http://bit.ly/2kKVvu9 (Accessed: 18 February 2018)

[499] James Paul Gee, *Learning by Design: Good Video Games as Learning Machines*, Available at http://bit.ly/2L-gu46w (Accessed: 4 May 2018)

[500] Peter Gray Ph.D., 'Cognitive benefits of playing video games', *Psychology Today*, 20 February 2015, http://bit.ly/2LW9MQP (Accessed: 18 February 2018)

[501] Ibid.

[502] Peter Gray Ph.D., 'The many benefits, for kids, of playing video games', Op. cit.

[503] H.P. Loveboat, 'What Video Games Can Teach Us about Alternative Education', 14 January 2014, Accessed: 19 February 2018 via http://bit.ly/2sDPd2Z

[504] Robert Twigger, 'Master of Many Trades', *Aeon*, 4 November 2013, http://bit.ly/2JcOzQV (Accessed: 18 February 2018)

[505] Jane McGonigal, *Reality Is Broken*, 2012, Vintage

[506] John Seabrook, 'Game Master', *The New Yorker*, 6 November 2006, http://bit.ly/2sCCai1 (Accessed: 19 February 2018)

[507] Hara Estroff Marano, 'Class Dismissed', *Psychology Today*, 1 May 2006, http://bit.ly/2xCJekN (Accessed: 19 February 2018)

[508] Jason Tanz, 'The Techies Who Are Hacking Education by Homeschooling Their Kids', Op. cit.

[509] Penelope Trunk, 'Finally, Silicon Valley funds homeschooling: Elon Musk leads with Ad Astra', *Penelope Trunk*, 1 June 2015, http://bit.ly/2kHK1r0 (Accessed: 19 February 2018)

[510] Jason Tanz, 'The Techies Who Are Hacking Education by Homeschooling Their Kids', Op. cit.

511 Anne-Marie Tupuola, 'Pasifika Edgewalkers: Urban Migration, Resilience and Indigenous Transcultural Identities', *Expert Group Meeting on Urban Indigenous Peoples and Migration,* Santiago de Chile, Chile, 27-29 March 2007

512 Anne-Marie Tupuola, 'Pasifika Edgewalkers: Complicating the Achieved Identity Status in Youth Research', *Journal of Intercultural Studies*, Vol. 25, Issue 1, 2004, p.90

513 Angayuqaq Oscar Kawagley and Ray Barnhardt, 'Education Indigenous to Place: Western Science Meets Native Reality', Op. cit.

514 Gregory A. Smith and Dilafruz R. Williams (Ed.s), *Ecological Education in Action: On Weaving Education, Culture, and the Environment*, 1999, SUNY Press

515 Widely attributed to Socrates

516 Clark Aldrich, *Unschooling Rules*, 2011, Greenleaf Book Group LLC

517 The Thiel Foundation, *About the* Fellowship, http://bit.ly/2LhQt3h (Accessed: 19 February 2018)

518 Chris Brady and Orrin Woodward, *Financial Fitness: The Offense, Defense, and Playing Field of Personal Finance*, 2013, Obstacles Press

Chapter 13

519 Antoine de Saint-Exupéry, *The Wisdom of the Sands (Citadelle)*, 1948, University of Chicago Press

520 Joss Winn and Mike Neary, 'Hackers are vital to the university culture of openness and innovation', *The Guardian*, 18 October 2011, http://bit.ly/2xCiiBv (Accessed: 18 February 2018).

521 Ben Yagoda, 'A Short History of "Hack"', *The New Yorker*, 6 March 2014, http://bit.ly/2HhV7fh (Accessed: 18 February 2018)

522 Winn, J. and Neary, M. (2011) 'Hackers are vital to the university culture of openness and innovation', Op. cit.

523 John Holt and Pat Farenga, *Teach Your Own: The John Holt Book Of Homeschooling*, Da Capo Press, 2003

524 John Taylor Gatto, The Curriculum of Necessity or What Must an Educated Person Know?, Information Liberation, September 2009, http://bit.ly/2Jah8yn (Accessed: 2 May 2018)

525 Peter Gray Ph.D., 'The Evolutionary Biology of Education: How Our Hunter-Gatherer Educative Instincts Could Form the Basis for Education Today', *Evolution: Education and Outreach*, March 2011, Volume 4, Issue 1, 28–40.

526 David Graeber, *Fragments of an Anarchist Anthropology*, 1994, Chicago: Prickly Paradigm Press

527 Anonymous, 'A proposal for governance in the post 2011 world', *WL Central*, 24 December 2011, http://bit.ly/2LVEgCP (Accessed: 18 February 2018)

528 Neil Gaiman, 'Why our future depends on libraries, reading and daydreaming', *The Guardian*, 15 October 2013, http://bit.ly/2LiQpAi (Accessed: 18 February 2018)

529 Neil Postman, 'Informing Ourselves to Death', *Speech at meeting of the German Informatics Society*, 11October 1990, Stuttgart, http://bit.ly/2st15FL (Accessed: 19 February 2018)

530 Agnatology, *The Encyclopedia of World Problems and Human Potential*, 5 July 2015, http://bit.ly/2LhQJiL (Accessed: 19 February 2018)

531 'Agnotology: the cultural production of ignorance', Workshop, Stanford University, 7-8 October 2005, https://stanford.io/2LenEov (Accessed: 19 February 2018)

[532] Lawrence M. Krauss, 'Teaching Doubt', *The New Yorker*, 15 March 2015, http://bit.ly/2xzs3jQ (Accessed: 18 February 2018)

[533] Ibid.

[534] Thakkar R.R., Garrison M.M., Christakis D.A., 'A Systematic Review for the Effects of Television Viewing by Infants and Preschoolers', *Pediatrics*, 5 November 2006

[535] Joe Kincheloe, *Knowledge and Critical Pedagogy: An Introduction*, 2008, Springe

[536] Neil Postman, *The Disappearance of Childhood*, 1994, New York: Vintage

[537] Peter Gray Ph.D., 'The many benefits, for kids, of playing video games', Op. cit.

[538] Gaze, Wikipedia, http://bit.ly/2szMibu (Accessed: 19 February 2018)

[539] Ibid.

[540] Christopher Kul-Want, *Introducing Slavoj Zizek: A Graphic Guide*, 2011, Icon Books

[541] Kevin Williams, 'Amish.biz', *Aeon*, 20 November 2015, http://bit.ly/2J5efTr (Accessed: 18 February 2018)

[542] Carl Benedikt Frey and Michael A. Osborne, 'The future of employment: How susceptible are jobs to computerization?', *Machines and Employment Workshop* hosted by the Oxford University Engineering Sciences Department and the Oxford Martin Programme on the Impacts of Future Technology, 17 September 2013, http://bit.ly/2HgngDF (Accessed: 19 February 2018)

543 Richard Berriman and John Hawksworth, 'Will robots steal our jobs? The potential impact of automation on the UK and other major economies', *UK Economic Outlook*, March 2017, pp. 30-47, https://pwc.to/2sCbsWP (Accessed: 19 February 2018)

544 Carl Benedikt Frey and Michael A. Osborne, 'The future of employment: How susceptible are jobs to computerization?', Op. cit.

545 David Spencer, 'Why work more? We should be working less for a better quality of life', *The Guardian*, 4 February 2014, http://bit.ly/2LWRzmq (Accessed: 18 February 2018)

546 Special Report, 'Automation and Anxiety', *The Economist*, 25 June 2016, https://econ.st/2LhXOjD (Accessed: 18 February 2018)

547 Special Report, 'Re-educating Rita', Op. cit.

548 Special Report, 'Automation and Anxiety', Op. cit.

549 Brian D. Ray Ph.D., '2.04 million homeschool students in the United States in 2010', *National Home Education Research Institute*, 3 January 2011, http://bit.ly/2st1qs1 (Accessed: 19 February 2018

550 Johann Hari, 'Is everything you think you know about depression wrong?', *The Guardian*, 7 January 2018, http://bit.ly/2JqRSao (Accessed: 28 March 2018)

Chapter 14

551 Johan von Goethe, source unknown

552 John Holt, *How Children Fail*, 1964, Pitman Publishing Company

553 Johann Hari, 'Is everything you think you know about depression wrong?', Op. cit.

[554] Ibid.

[555] Colin Ward, *Influences: Voices of Creative Dissent*, 1991, Green Books

[556] David Graeber, *Fragments of an Anarchist Anthropology*, 1994, Chicago: Prickly Paradigm Press

[557] Robert H. Haworth, *Anarchist Pedagogies*, 2012, PM Press

[558] David Graeber, *Fragments of an Anarchist Anthropology*, 1994, Chicago: Prickly Paradigm Press

[559] John Holt and Pat Farenga, *Teach Your Own: The John Holt Book Of Homeschooling*, 2003, Da Capo Press

[560] John Taylor Gatto, 'The Curriculum of Necessity or What Must an Educated Person Know?', Op. cit.